To MJ —
a contemporary "daughter"!
XXOO

Wallis

PRAISE FOR
DAUGHTERS *of the* DECLARATION

"Claire and David have written a remarkable book that brings to life the unsung early heroes in American philanthropy who happen to be women. Each story brings to life a fearless, entrepreneurial woman whose creativity, focus and perseverance benefitted the American social sector in immeasurable ways. Without a doubt, these women laid the cornerstones for American fundraising, public, private and government partnerships, and even micro credit."—Eileen R. Heisman. President/CEO, National Philanthropic Trust

"We all stand on the shoulders of those who have come before us. Claire and David's book honors our sisters who have preceded us. Their examples, their spirit and their history still inspire modern day women to be this generation's daughters of the declaration. It is a timely and powerful living legacy. A must-read!" —Colleen S. Willoughby, Founder, Washington Women's Foundation, Seattle

"This engaging book establishes the prominent role that women have long played in the great breakthroughs that have shaped American history. It offers a broad definition of social change that reminds all of us that the daughters of the declaration are still alive in their work today. That's a very good thing."—Paul C. Light, Professor of public service at NYU's Robert F. Wagner School of Public Service and author of *Driving Social Change*

"Daughters of the Declaration is a gift to this nation and the world about the role of women in American civil society. The untold stories of countless social entrepreneurs are now available to inspire future generations of female leaders from all walks of life. Claire and David provide such an intimate and compelling historical account—anyone who reads this book will feel personally connected to the women behind important social movements. What a beautiful—and needed—book!"—Susan Taylor Batten, President & CEO Association of Black Foundation Executives (ABFE)

1,24
Bus.
$5

DAUGHTERS *of the* DECLARATION

DAUGHTERS *of the* DECLARATION

How Women Social Entrepreneurs
Built the American Dream

CLAIRE GAUDIANI &
DAVID GRAHAM BURNETT

PublicAffairs
New York

Copyright © 2011 by Claire Gaudiani and David Graham Burnett.

Published in the United States by PublicAffairs™,
a Member of the Perseus Books Group

All rights reserved.
Printed in the United States of America.

No part of this book may be reproduced in any manner whatsoever without written permission except in the case of brief quotations embodied in critical articles and reviews. For information, address PublicAffairs, 250 West 57th Street, Suite 1321, New York, NY 10107.

PublicAffairs books are available at special discounts for bulk purchases in the U.S. by corporations, institutions, and other organizations. For more information, please contact the Special Markets Department at the Perseus Books Group, 2300 Chestnut Street, Suite 200, Philadelphia, PA 19103, call (800) 810-4145, ext. 5000, or e-mail special.markets@perseusbooks.com.

Book Design by Pauline Brown
Typeset in 12 point Goudy Old Style Std by the Perseus Books Group

The Library of Congress has cataloged the printed edition as follows:
Gaudiani, Claire.
  Daughters of the declaration : how women social entrepreneurs built the American dream / Claire Gaudiani and David Graham Burnett.
      p. cm.
  Includes bibliographical references and index.
  ISBN 978-1-61039-031-6 (alk. paper)
  ISBN 978-1-61039-032-3 (EB)
  1. Women philanthropists—United States—History. 2. Social entrepreneurship—United States—History. 3. Endowments—Economic aspects—United States.
  4. Social change—United States—History. I. Burnett, D. Graham. II. Title.
  HV541.G38 2011
  361.7'60820973—dc23
                                              2011021700

First Edition

10 9 8 7 6 5 4 3 2 1

With great love and admiration
To our mothers,
Olive Burnett and Vera Gaudiani,
and our mothers' mothers,
Annie Wagner Graham and Rosa Cosenza Rossano,
Who were each benevolent and even sometimes entrepreneurial
republican mothers,
in gratitude, especially for the virtues they taught.

*If opinion and manners did not forbid us to march to glory
by the same paths as the Men, we should at least equal
and sometimes surpass them in our love of the public good.*

—*Esther Reed,* The Sentiments of an American Woman, *1780*

CONTENTS

INTRODUCTION

This is a book about how America became successful. Our nation is built on three interdependent sectors: the governmental sector, the private or for-profit sector, and the voluntary or not-for-profit sector. None of these existed when the Declaration of Independence was written. All three sectors have been created by the work of American citizens. This three-part system is a unique American asset. We believe that the synergy of these sectors is responsible for our record of social, scientific, economic, and political success over our nation's 350-year history.

Daughters of the Declaration focuses on the development of the not-for-profit sector and on the citizens who created it. There are many democratic governments and market-driven economies around the world, but Americans have invented a unique third sector that mobilizes citizen idealism and responsibility. It provides a marketplace where buyers and sellers of ideas to improve the nation (and the world) can meet and do business. Millions of organizations offer their ideas for making the world a better place in which to live. Some of these organizations are quite large—universities, mega-churches, and medical research institutes—but most are small and local, for example, soup kitchens, county museums, animal welfare groups, park conservancies, and health clinics, to name but a few.[1] They are all sellers of ideas, competing for investments of money and time by volunteer donors.

All investors in this marketplace, in turn, hope for a return on their investments. Their returns are not measured in personal financial gains, but in what we call "social profit," that is, improvements in the collective well-being of our communities and our nation.[2] Some cases of social profit are obvious. We all benefit when researchers supported by voluntary contributions discover a cure for a debilitating disease or a way to improve our food supply. All members of a community benefit when they raise enough money to build a community center that everyone can use. But "we, the people" also profit from educating all children of all citizens to their highest potential. Who knows which one may produce the next great job-creating business idea or medical breakthrough? We profit collectively when any citizen in need is helped to regain his or her self-reliance and optimism about the future. Cynicism is democracy's greatest enemy, and any loss of hope for the future is a loss to our collective well-being. *Daughters of the Declaration* recounts the stories of some of America's greatest ideas for the generation of social profit and the entrepreneurs who delivered their value for all of us.

Many Americans (and most foreigners) believe that famous capitalists created the tradition of citizen investment to improve the nation—Andrew Carnegie and John D. Rockefeller in the late nineteenth century, or Andrew Mellon and Henry Ford in the early twentieth—all of whom created private foundations devoted to the betterment of society. These great entrepreneurs certainly made important contributions to our nation, both through their business leadership and their personal philanthropy. As the nation prospered after the Civil War and great fortunes accumulated, these men set an important example for wealthy citizens.

But the notion that the great industrialists created America's social profit sector is simply wrong. It suggests that citizen responsibility for building a just society was led by very wealthy, politically connected men, and that the effort began in the second half of the nineteenth century: In fact, the social profit sector was developed not by the great men of industry, but by women. Idealistic and determined women embraced the production of social profit in the new nation long before the "robber barons" created foundations and universities bearing their names. Women did so before elected officials defined a meaningful role for government in such matters as public health, education, workplace safety, or the ownership of slaves. Women began this work at a time when they were not even entitled to own property or inherit wealth.

We call these women "social entrepreneurs" because they display the same drive, imagination, and resourcefulness as their capitalist counterparts. The Founders established an idealistic framework for America's national experiment in democratic governance. They asserted that the new nation would be built on the belief that all men are created equal, and are endowed with the right to life, liberty, and the pursuit of happiness. Over the subsequent decades, a set of energetic women took up the challenge to make these great ideals into a lived reality for their fellow citizens. In addition to their domestic duties, these women defined engaged citizenship and a system of governance "by the people." They led the hard work of turning good intentions expressed in the Declaration of Independence and the Constitution into improvements in the lives of citizens. They turned a general "spirit" of mutual support into a working civil society by formulating plans, selling their ideas to investors, and delivering on their promises to their fellow citizens. These women embody the American spirit of enterprise, and American optimism, energy, and persistence. They are social entrepreneurs as surely as Rockefeller, Vanderbilt, and Frick were business entrepreneurs.

The great issues of our nation were debated among citizens throughout the nineteenth century because of the efforts of social entrepreneurs. These women were students of their times, whether they enjoyed the benefits of formal education or not. They insisted that the gaps they perceived in the social fabric of the nation be addressed, and they made certain to engage a variety of voices in the debates, perhaps more effectively than their elected representatives. Their organizational and listening skills, as well as their genuine interest in the well-being of others, produced the kind of democratic discourse that would have made the Founders proud.

As they debated the Declaration of Independence, the Founders recognized that their ideal republic would hinge on a critical balance between "competing goods." The nation would require individual enterprise and personal freedom to prosper, but it would also require a spirit of generosity and mutual support among citizens. One could not prosper individually at the expense of a fellow citizen. We will say more about this tension in Chapter 1, but it seems clear to us that the social profit sector, as invented by women entrepreneurs, kept this tension in balance over the first 150 years of our nation's history. The resulting balance produced unprecedented economic and social progress.

Daughters of the Declaration traces the work of social entrepreneurs from the Revolutionary War through the passage of the Fair Labor Standards Act in 1938. During this period, women aimed to abolish slavery, limit child labor, integrate immigrants, bathe the poor, educate blacks, beautify their cities, and, of course, obtain the right for all citizens to vote, regardless of race or gender, to name but a few of their social enterprises. During this same period, women's role in the affairs of the nation expanded from "republican motherhood" carried out in their own homes to the cabinet of the president of the United States. This evolution is certainly in part the story of women's gender-based fight for recognition and equality. But that story is not our focus. We wish to recount the nation's progress in building a fairer, more just society, one in which citizens have managed to balance the competing goods of personal enterprise and concern for fellow citizens, and to maintain a commitment to "self-interest, rightly understood."[3] To achieve this delicate balance, women built new institutions, challenged elected officials to redefine the role of government in light of changing social conditions, and demonstrated to all concerned that little platoons of citizens are the best source of energy and imaginative problem-solving for the greater good.[4]

Women social entrepreneurs did what we are all supposed to do as citizens of the Republic, according to Thomas Jefferson. He affirmed that "for the support of this Declaration . . . with a firm reliance on the protection of divine Providence . . . we mutually pledge to each other our Lives, our Fortunes and our sacred Honor." The pledge to support the document was a pledge to make "the self-evident truths" into a reality for all fellow citizens. It is impossible to know whether Jefferson envisioned the kind of work these women would undertake when he penned those words, but many women social entrepreneurs quote the Declaration as a reason for their work and as a way to inspire and involve others in it.

The ideals proposed in our founding documents can only be pursued. They will never be achieved. It is that pursuit that defines American culture. Our social entrepreneurs have enabled America to live in the dynamic present. America lives in its own "present becoming future," always calling itself out of less and worse and into more and better. Living in the present progressive is an act of idealism, optimism, and confidence. The origins of this attitude are found and sustained in the myriad of social enterprises over the past 230 years. These efforts are a source of inspiration and wisdom for all who care about ensuring the continuing pursuit of the Constitution's ideals.

The creativity and energy of an engaged citizenry is our most valuable asset. As the nation struggles with the effects of economic destabilization and embarks on the second decade of the new millennium, we believe it is relevant to study the history of social entrepreneurship and to recognize what our foremothers accomplished in much more challenging times. Many students now pursue the study of entrepreneurship and philanthropy; some will enter the business world having taken a course in social enterprise or venture philanthropy and will do a better job of recognizing the interdependence of social and financial profit as a result. Others will bring their business school or public policy training to the social profit sector and enhance the sector's efficiency and accountability practices. This is all to the good. But social entrepreneurship is a function of the hearts and minds of citizens who believe that the future of the Republic depends on their individual capacity to deliver access to the rights to life, liberty, and the pursuit of happiness to their fellow citizens. The stories in *Daughters of the Declaration* will, we hope, both inspire and instruct succeeding generations of concerned citizens as they have inspired us.

ONE

The American Creed

America is the only nation in the world founded on a creed.
That creed is set forth with dogmatic and even theological lucidity in
the Declaration of Independence. . . .
—G. K. Chesterton, *What I Saw in America*, 1923

The American colonies had established a 140-year history by 1776. It had taken plenty of optimism, idealism, and personal enterprise for the colonists to survive and prosper. Such "virtues in the people" encouraged the men drafting a declaration of independence from England to think boldly. After months of debate, they produced a creed that commits all Americans to personal responsibility for defending the rights of their fellow citizens. This belief also forms the basis for our social profit sector.

All men are created equal; that they are endowed by their Creator with certain unalienable rights; that among these are life, liberty, and the pursuit of happiness; that, to secure these rights, governments are instituted among men, deriving their just powers from the consent of the governed. . . .

This creed established a new set of relationships among individual citizens and between citizens and their government. In

Europe, monarchs had ruled by "divine right" and the people were subjects. Laws and moral authority flowed down from the seat of governmental power. In America, the government would be of, by, and for the citizens themselves. Each citizen would therefore be responsible for contributing judgment, energy, and personal virtue to building the just society that the Declaration announced. In return for the personal freedom that a successful democracy could offer, everyone would have to accept at least some responsibility for the well-being of fellow citizens.

Of course, the Declaration of Independence did not simply drop from the sky in 1776. It was produced by a group of men whose thinking was shaped by the debates of their time. One such debate had to do with "human nature." Were free individuals predisposed to constructive, virtuous behavior to support the common good? Or did self-interested, shortsighted, even destructive behavior follow when man was left to his own devices? Although such questions seem rather theoretical to us today, they had great relevance for the group of men considering a form of government that would turn over "power to the people."

The questions were difficult to answer empirically. Nevertheless, the Founders focused on matters of virtue and self-discipline, and whether these qualities, with proper education, would dominate the behavior of the majority. The issue of whether men could be counted on to behave in responsible ways lay at the heart of the democratic proposition. Without at least a general tendency toward virtuous behavior on the part of the citizenry, a government by the people would surely deteriorate into competing subgroups intent upon exploiting each other. The Founders' concern for virtue is very important to the origins of our social profit sector.

The Founders' vision of an ideal government was shaped by the thinkers they knew best. Most were classically educated men who had studied the political writings of Aristotle. Declaration signer John Witherspoon, the president of Princeton University, affirmed the centrality of Aristotle: the "political rather than the metaphysical Aristotle [continued] his impressive influence as an analyst of 'mixed government.'"[1] One track of Princeton's curriculum prepared young men for government leadership through extensive readings and a thesis that "became a training ground for the application of Aristotle, Cicero, Polybius and other classical masters to the debates on the Declaration and the Constitution."[2]

Aristotle taught that human beings desire only one thing as an end in itself and that is the good life. Achieving this goal creates our happiness and is necessarily linked to the relationships we have with others. The good life depends on the practice of virtue.[3] Thus, our governmental institutions should call on us to practice these behaviors because we are naturally predisposed to act virtuously in the pursuit of the good life. Aristotle envisions displays of courage, self-restraint, generosity, magnanimity, sociability, justice, prudence, and wisdom in the activities and relationships of citizens in a republic. In *The Politics*, free men are identified through their virtues. These virtues are not to be practiced for the sake of ensuring wealth. Wealth building is defined by what is necessary to support a virtuous life. Aristotle contends that one must stick to the path of virtue in the reasonable hope that the strong connection between doing good and living joyfully will eventually assert itself and give way to the improvement of one's fortunes. Clearly, this was an encouraging perspective for those contemplating a government of and by the people.

The Founders were also familiar with contemporary thinking about the relationship between governments and individuals. It was a popular topic across Europe. These eighteenth-century writers argued that human beings, rather than focusing on their imperfections and shortcomings and begging God for mercy, should perhaps see their capacity to reason as a great and powerful gift from a less judgmental God. They argued that human reason was to be celebrated and cultivated rather than condemned as a dangerous source of human pride. All humans, endowed with this great gift, were by definition worthy of respect and had a claim to equality. All were responsible for their own salvation, rather than predestined to Heaven or Hell. Taken to the extreme, this view suggested that citizens possessed the capacity to govern themselves, provided they could manage their "free will" through the practice of self-discipline.

Foremost among such thinkers in the minds of the Founders was Charles Secondat, better known as (baron de) Montesquieu, the man who is credited with proposing a three-part system of representative government. Historian Peter Gay has written: "Montesquieu was the most influential writer of the eighteenth century and the . . . Founding Fathers used the writings of 'that great man'—the epithet that Hamilton used in *The Federalist Papers*, No. 9—probably more than anyone else."[4]

In the preface of *The Spirit of the Laws*, Montaigne discusses moral virtue, Christian virtue, and political virtue.[5] Each is distinct, but the last "entailed a devotion to equality before the laws of a republic. . . ." Today, we generally refer to this idea as the "rule of law." Political virtue pursues justice for each citizen and thus the collective "greater good" of all citizens.

Montesquieu calls political virtue the "life force of democracy." It is synonymous with love of country, love of equality, and with the self-sacrificing patriotism that defines an energetic public-spiritedness devoted to building the greater good. For the virtuous citizen, there is never a conflict between private interests and the democratic government the citizen loves.

When citizen virtue does not provide the basis of governance, as is the case in a monarchy, Montesquieu points out that things can go very badly. "When virtue is banished, ambition invades the hearts of those who are capable of receiving it, and avarice possesses the whole community. Desires then change their objects; what they were fond of before becomes now indifferent; they were free with laws, and they want to be free without them. . . ."[6]

Montesquieu illustrates his point with some unflattering examples from European court life. He had clearly witnessed plenty of the self-serving intrigue that dominated the royal courts. He has this to say about the failings of royalty:

> Ambition with idleness, the thirst for riches without labour; flattery, treason, perfidy, violation of engagements, contempt of civil duties, fear of the prince's virtue, hope for his weakness, but above all, the perpetual ridicule of virtue; are, I think, the characteristics by which the courtiers of all ages and countries have been constantly distinguished.[7]

Presumably, Jefferson and the Founders feared a similar fate might befall their republic in several decades, should self-discipline break down among the male citizenry.

Montesquieu defines virtue differently from earlier European court writers such as Machiavelli (1469–1527). The system of monarchy had its own ideals of virtuous behavior. According to the author of The Prince, "virtu" meant a soldier's code of honor, a willingness to sacrifice the self for those to whom one had pledged loyalty. Montesquieu advances a less martial notion; virtue in a working republic is a love of country felt by citizens at all levels, rich and poor, educated and illiterate. Virtue causes citizens to act out their love of their democracy through their work toward equality and frugality, and when acquisitions or wealth make citizens unequal, they should be eager to share their bounty generously.[8] The Founders embraced this ideal throughout the crafting of the Declaration and the Constitution. It became a cornerstone of American exceptionalism and an opportunity for women to play a particularly vital role in the development of the new nation.

The Founders had more than theory to go on as they developed a vision for the new nation. They knew that their fellow colonists, for all their differences and competing interests, shared some important commitments and habits of mind that would be essential to making democracy work. Foremost among these were a tradition of mutual assistance and a commitment to a spirit of enterprise. Interdependence among citizens became a key building block in the Founders' vision for a new, independent nation. So, too, did individual economic enterprise.

John Winthrop had laid out the need for both enterprise and collaboration with fellow citizens in a speech he delivered on the *Arabella*, the ship that brought him and 400 others to the shores of Massachusetts in 1630:

> In this newe lande, we must work as one man and abridge ourselves of our superfluities for the supply of each other's necessities. . . .[9]

Winthrop imagined in his community of 400 souls a new kind of society, "a city on a hill." Everyone, in the "newe lande," was expected to share. At a practical level, this strategy promised the only hope of survival. Gradually, a tradition of barn raisings, cornhuskings, potluck meals, and quilting bees flourished in the villages of New England. Neighborly generosity was supplemented by frugality and diligence, and the Massachusetts Bay Colony survived. The citizens even agreed to provide education for the sons of colonial families. The first public school, the Boston Latin School, opened in 1635. Sons of farmers, candle makers, and blacksmiths received "scholarships" to Harvard College, beginning in the 1640s. In the following decade, colonists whose sons had gotten such tuition subsidies began sending gifts of grain and other supplies to the college to express their gratitude.

Winthrop, the devout and idealistic Puritan minister, was also the chair of the board of the Massachusetts Bay Company, a fur and lumber trading enterprise chartered by the king of England. The sale of shares in the company had financed the initial trip across the Atlantic. All community members were shareholders in Winthrop's company. They all (men, that is) had a vote on issues of importance, and all stood to profit from the success of their mutual enterprise. Of course, they all remained subjects of the British king, but Winthrop had cleverly edited the Massachusetts Bay Company charter, leaving out the section about returning to England for the "annual meeting" of the board. Winthrop planned to stay put in the "newe lande." He also understood that financial enterprise was essential to the success of the colonists.

Historians have noted the mindset of immigrants to America before the Revolutionary War: "Almost all, searching rationally for personal betterment or greater security, were, or hoped to be, family-scale entrepreneurs."[10] There was ample evidence that this spirit translated into action in the New World as well. Road builders linked the New England towns and villages together, and increases in land values followed rapidly.[11] Developers built meetinghouses, negotiated with Native Americans, and recruited ministers and other settlers for their towns. They profited only if settlements were successful. Most of the colonists were not content with simple maintenance of existing levels of productivity and well-being. Edwin J. Perkins estimates that "half of all farm households met the basic qualifications . . . for inclusion in the entrepreneurial category. Few of them may have actually achieved great wealth, but they nonetheless aimed at steadily accumulating productive assets."[12]

Prosperity was greatly to be desired and there seems to have been great admiration for men who could provide for their families and actually achieve a measure of comfort. In the years immediately before the disastrous conflicts with King George III over tax and trade policies, there was a growing interest in what at the time would have been considered luxury goods imported from England and France. Even small farmers and their wives might consider the purchase of a clock or some cutlery for their modest homes.[13] So the Founders' debates were certainly influenced by the need for a government that would advance private enterprise.

Self-interest proved to be a powerful force in motivating colonial entrepreneurs and building the first cycles of prosperity. But by 1776, the challenge was to devise a form of government that honored this powerful individualism while preserving the tradition of mutuality. The accumulation of wealth, as positive as it might be, always harbored the danger of greed, even given the remarkable examples of selfless behavior among the colonists from the earliest days up to the time of the Revolution. The Founders were well aware of human tendencies to deviate from the path of virtue. Self-discipline was the only force that could enable citizens to assure their own self-control.[14] John Adams shared the concern that sufficient wealth could lead to weakened male self-control:

> The generation of the American Revolution believed that the success of their experiment in republican government required male self-control. Jefferson and Benjamin Rush joined Adams' concern and wrote about the dependence of the republican society on male self-control.[15]

Thus, deliberations turned to the delicate issue of what role, if any, the government could or should play in the area of "self-management." The Founders did benefit from their knowledge of a recent case study in nation building, that of Scotland. Thomas Jefferson, Alexander Hamilton, Henry Knox (first secretary of war), Edmund Randolph (first attorney general), and George Washington were all of Scottish ancestry. Nine of the thirteen governors of the original colonies shared Scottish roots, including Patrick Henry of Virginia. Jefferson's tutors were Scottish. Franklin had traveled extensively through Scotland in 1759 and maintained an active correspondence with the scholars in Edinburgh before and after his second visit in 1771. Benjamin Rush, another signer of the Declaration, studied medicine at the University of Edinburgh, graduating in 1768. In that same year, he succeeded in convincing the Reverend John Witherspoon to leave Scotland and accept the presidency of Princeton University, where both Rush and James Madison had been educated.

Scotland in the early eighteenth century was a nation at the margins of civilized Europe, and very much under English control. By the second half of the century, the Scots had managed to escape both famine and financial collapse, and they were enjoying remarkable economic and social gains. How had this been achieved? Perhaps there were some lessons to be learned from these achievements.[16]

The Scottish case did seem to involve groups of influential men debating those same Enlightenment concerns that preoccupied the American revolutionaries.

> The Scottish Enlightenment, then, consisted of a self-conscious band of programmatic intellectuals . . . seeking to enlist private wealth on the side of their country's public good.[17]

The Scottish leaders were persuaded that "human reason could indeed integrate the productive values, the civic virtues, and personal liberty through a dedication to human flourishing."[18]

One of the most influential, Francis Hutcheson, believed firmly that personal liberty was essential to the pursuit of happiness. But, he argued, the *source* of happiness for human beings is helping others to achieve happiness. Hutcheson held that man's ability to reflect on his own actions provided a powerful tool for self-control. His most famous pupil, Adam Smith, had embraced this view in his *The Theory of Moral Sentiments*, written well before his more famous treatise, *The Wealth of Nations*. Smith, the first modern economist and champion of free enterprise, wrote both *The Theory of Moral Sentiments* and *The Wealth of Nations* in response to the problem of freedom and self-control. In *The Wealth of Nations*, Smith wrote:

> The natural effort of every individual to better his own condition . . . is so powerful a principle that it is alone, not only capable of carrying on the society to wealth and prosperity, but of surmounting a hundred impertinent obstructions with which the folly of human laws too often incumbers [*sic*] its operations.[19]

No wonder Smith has earned the admiration of free marketers worldwide. But years earlier, following his mentor Hutcheson, Smith had carefully defined the virtuous, principled men who could be entrusted with the freedom to pursue their self-interest. He argued that self-awareness enabled men to discern the reactions of others to their actions and to be shaped by those reactions. Thus, any action that reduces the happiness of the other (greed, avarice, selfishness) reduces our own happiness when reflected back to us. Echoing Aristotle, Smith puts it as follows: "Virtue is the surest and readiest means of obtaining both safety and advantage [i.e., prosperity]." The achievement of prosperity (through the pursuit of self-interest) depended on the energetic pursuit of the good life, a life in which our actions are positively

10

viewed by, and create happiness for, our fellow citizens. This piece of synthetic reasoning—the interdependence of prosperity and virtue—is perhaps the most important "theoretical" idea that the Founders learned from the Scottish case study. It should remind us that Smith's famous "invisible hand" in the marketplace was a product of virtuous behavior by the human beings creating the marketplace.

There were additional practical lessons from the Scottish experience. England and Scotland had had a fraught relationship for centuries. The desperate state of the Scottish economy at the turn of the eighteenth century induced the leaders to petition England to drop the heavy taxes imposed on Scottish trade. Long resistant to these entreaties, English officials finally struck a compromise. In 1707, the Act of Union was signed, permitting Scottish ships open access to English ports and free trade, but the price of this economic opportunity was high indeed. The Scots were forced to agree to surrender a significant element of their hard-won political autonomy. They would give up their own Assembly of elected representatives and instead send representatives to the English Parliament.

Faced with the loss of their own representative body, the Scots had to forge new structures to support Scottish society. To their credit, they developed a system of extragovernmental societies that drew citizens together to advance both commercial interests and social well-being. In 1723, the Honorable Society of Improvers began as a group of citizens dedicated to sharing ideas for progress in agriculture. Just two years later, the Society for the Improvement in Medical Knowledge was launched. Next began the Edinburgh Society for Encouraging Arts, Sciences, Manufactures, and Agriculture, followed by the Society for Improving Philosophy and Natural Knowledge (science). This latter group became the Royal Society of Edinburgh in 1783. Societies acted as venture investors and as social service providers. They sponsored the work of young inventors such as James Watt, who developed the steam engine in 1769. They provided a form of life insurance for the widows and children of fellow members.

These private associations were not entities of government or any business. They were designed and run by private citizens for the betterment of their own interests and those of their country. The scheme proved remarkably powerful. Production grew; trade grew; and the population of the nation increased. By the end of the century, Scotland was cited as a beacon of economic and social progress.

Benjamin Franklin created an improvement club in the colonies long before the Revolution. In 1727, he brought his personal and professional acquaintances together for weekly meetings governed by a set of strict rules.

> I should have mentioned before, that, in the autumn of the preceding year [1727], I had form'd most of my ingenious acquaintance into a club of mutual improvement, which we called the JUNTO; we met on Friday evenings. The rules that I drew up required that every member, in his turn, should produce one or more queries on any point of Morals, Politics, or Natural Philosophy [physics], to be discuss'd by the company; and once in three months produce and read an essay of his own writing, on any subject he pleased. Our debates were to be under the direction of a president, and to be conducted in the sincere spirit of inquiry after truth, . . .[20]

In 1743, Franklin and his colleague John Bartram launched the American Philosophical Society. Franklin drafted "A Proposal for Promoting Useful Knowledge among the British Plantations in America," announcing that progress in the colonies now enabled the inauguration of a formal Improvement Society. Here was perhaps the first of many imports from Scotland of the idea that voluntary, extragovernmental associations of citizens could, and should, strive for the improvement of society.

> The first Drudgery of Settling new Colonies, which confines the Attention of People to mere Necessaries, is now pretty well over; and there are many in every Province in Circumstances that set them at Ease, and afford Leisure to cultivate the finer Arts, and improve the common Stock of Knowledge. To such of these who are Men of Speculation, any Hints must from time to time arise, may Observations occur, which if well-examined, pursued and improved, might produce Discoveries to the Advantage of some or all of the British Plantations, or to the Benefit of Mankind in general.[21]

Franklin went on to point out that the American colonies were so large and diverse that many great ideas were simply being lost, and he proposed centrally located Philadelphia as the seat for the society. The society's focus became the study of the "useful" sciences. Its members sought to improve animal husbandry and crop production, with a particular interest in grains useful in the production of beer. They also took an interest in mining, geology, and ways of assaying ore. Their interest in land development led to investigations of improved mapmaking and surveying techniques.

Above and beyond the specific accomplishments of the Philosophical Society, Franklin demonstrated the power of citizens to organize effectively to address social and commercial needs outside a governmental framework, just as the Scots had done so successfully.

There was a second important lesson in the Scottish case that caught the attention of the colonial thinkers, and it had to do with the role of women in society. As early as 1725, Francis Hutcheson had written that women were both the means and the beneficiaries of social progress. His contemporary, Henry Home (Lord Kames), echoed this idea: "The gentle and insinuating manners of the female sex," Kames wrote, "tend to soften the roughness of the other sex; and where-ever women are indulged with any degree of freedom, they polish sooner than men."[22]

Here was a quite provocative idea—that women, so often associated with the sensual, the emotional, and the self-indulgent, could have a beneficial effect on the male of the species. Eventually, the idea of women's civilizing power was extended among Scottish thinkers to the realm of marriage. John Witherspoon wrote extensively on the primacy of marriage over single life. He advanced the notion that love in the context of marriage illustrates the human capacity for selflessness, for living beyond self-interest. He saw this experience as a powerful learning opportunity for men, one that could readily be extended to the civic sphere. He wrote:

> while other passions concentrate man on himself, love makes him live in another. It subdues selfishness, and reveals to him the pleasure of ministering to the object of his love. . . . The lover becomes a husband, a parent, a citizen.[23]

Here was a line of reasoning that confirmed the optimism expressed by Hutcheson and the other Scots earlier in the century. A loving marriage illustrates the life well lived, in which happiness for oneself comes through the creation of happiness for someone else. Fifty years after Kames wrote these words, the touring Frenchman Alexis de Tocqueville identified Americans' embrace of what he called "self-interest, rightly understood." This idea, that by helping others one advances one's own happiness, became a cornerstone of the American experiment with democracy.[24]

The Scots provided the Founders with a rich legacy. They had built a theoretical bridge between the freedom to pursue self-interest and the responsibilities of democratic citizenship. They offered practical guidance in the establishment of citizen-based improvement organizations that could serve the interests of both economic and social progress. And, most important for our purposes, the Scots offered new ways of thinking about the role of women in a democratic society.

TWO

The Women of
the New Nation

A woman of virtue and prudence is a
public good—a public benefactor.
—Gentlemen's and Ladies Magazine, 1789

At the time of the American Revolution, women in America were in much the same shape as the men in Scotland after their deal with England in 1707. Both groups were excluded from the formal political sphere. In fact, American women had little formal standing at all. The American Founders retained most of the traditional English civil laws concerning marriage and sought to apply them consistently across all the states.[1] These included the notion that women's legal standing was defined by their marriage status, an idea called *couverture*, derived from the French word for "covering or covered." A woman's relationship to the state was firmly subordinated to her relationship to her spouse. She and her physical property became her husband's property at the time of marriage. Married women were prohibited from entering into legal contracts, according to legal writer Tapping Reeve of Connecticut, not because they had no property to serve as collateral as one might expect, but because they were not at liberty to act as independent agents.

Reeve provided a helpful example of his reasoning. "What if a married woman were found to have breached a contractual obligation and were sentenced to a prison term?" he hypothesized. Then the husband would be deprived of access to his conjugal rights and this would be unacceptable before the law.[2]

Married women's lives were confined, rather severely, to the domestic sphere. Life revolved around home responsibilities: child rearing, provisioning and cooking, cleaning, and sewing, and very often, helping a spouse with his trade or business through record keeping and the like. It was considered "unwomanly," or unacceptable, for women to venture beyond these zones except for church attendance and inappropriate for a woman to "earn" money or even speak in public. Her physical and intellectual efforts were dedicated to the maintenance and morality of her family and community.

These limitations, however, did not eliminate the potential of the "weaker sex" to contribute to the creation of the new Union. Because the success of a democratic republic relied on the character of citizens, women's potential to influence the character of their spouses *and* to raise virtuous children took on great importance to the political success of the emerging nation.

The idea that a loving family provided a model of loyal citizenship in a democracy—the idea originally advanced by John Witherspoon—was embraced by the popular press of the new nation.[3] The family should be based on the love of the couple and their commitment to lives as virtuous helpmates. This design would make future citizens fit for democratic citizenship. The family was the critical transmitter of customs, morals, and manners. Although no writer identified a direct political role for women akin to that of man—for example, voting or holding elective office—women brought husbands the joy of a true partner and companion, and were recognized as influential polishers of men's more brutish proclivities. Mothers were essential educators of children whose virtues would ensure the progress each generation should seek to achieve. In short, a functioning family would serve as a microcosm of a successful society.

> (Woman) has the power to make public decency . . . a fashion— and public virtue the only example. And how is woman to accomplish that great end? By her influence on the manners of men.[4]

Such appreciation of women's power in matters of manners and virtue represents a rather remarkable shift in thinking in revolutionary America. The virtues normally associated with women—temperance, prudence, faith, and charity—were not typically seen as the building blocks for male leaders of society. The virtues of strength, courage, loyalty, and sacrifice had traditionally been taught to young men by older male leaders. So it was "revolutionary" in its own way that women would be entrusted with shaping the virtue of men and boys.

Additionally, it is fair to say that women had not always been associated with virtuous behavior in the Judeo-Christian tradition, in fact, quite the contrary. Given the pervasive power of biblical literalism among regular folks in the late eighteenth and early nineteenth centuries,[5] most would have more likely identified women as a source of evil than of virtue. Puritan leaders of the "new England" colonies such as Massachusetts and Connecticut had interpreted the story of Adam and Eve as an illustration of woman's waywardness and her responsibility for evil in the world. As daughters of Eve, women had been derogated as co-destroyers (with the Devil) of men's purity and joy in Eden. They were more frequently portrayed as sentimental, fickle temptresses absorbed with useless finery and idle chatter than as essential contributors to the success of a nation. Women (and some men) had been accused of witchcraft throughout the seventeenth century, culminating in the infamous Salem witch trials of the 1690s. Of the twenty persons ultimately put to death, fifteen were women. It is difficult to generalize about these various persecutions, but they surely suggest a certain nervousness on the part of powerful men about women's potential to destabilize God's order in the world as they saw it.[6]

Fortunately, several contemporary colonial women provided the Founders with clear evidence that women deserved consideration in the plans for a new nation. There were, for instance, the many stories of "Molly Pitcher," a composite characterization of brave women who fought the British alongside their husbands at Valley Forge, Monmouth, and elsewhere. Although the name seemingly refers to their assigned task of carrying water to the front lines to cool the cannons, many accounts suggest that more than one of these women kept the cannons firing when their husbands were felled by enemy fire.[7]

Female leadership was also found far from the front lines. Such is the lesson to be drawn from the life of Esther DeBerdt Reed, whose patriotism and organizational skill influenced a generation of political leaders concerning the value of women to the future of the Republic.

Esther Reed's life was much too brief. She died in 1780, at the age of thirty-three. But what a precedent she established. In 1778, when the Republic was more an idea than a reality, she developed a remarkable national goal: All American women should contribute to the Revolutionary War effort. Women's self-sacrifice and self-discipline would equal that of the men leading the political and military efforts. So she devised a system for collective action and went to work to make it happen. Given what we know about the status of women at the time, this was a genuinely ambitious goal. Reed did not live to see her grand vision fully implemented, but all builders of national service organizations can trace their roots to her audacious thinking.

Reed had lived in America for less than a decade in 1778, having been raised in England by prosperous Huguenot parents. She met an American student, Joseph Reed, when he boarded with her family in London while studying law. They married in 1770 and arrived in Philadelphia on the eve of the Revolutionary War. Joseph joined the American army, rising rapidly to the rank of general, while Esther gave birth to five children in rapid succession. Philadelphia was a war zone at the time, and Reed was obliged to live life on the run. As a general's wife, she became a "high-profile target" for both rampaging British troops and for the equally rabid local royalists who opposed the Revolutionary War effort. Over a period of three years, she relocated her family and household four times in the Philadelphia–South Jersey region.

In 1778, Joseph was elected "president" (governor) of Pennsylvania, and Esther was expecting their sixth child. Nevertheless, she penned a document in that year that is still admired today, entitled "Sentiments of an American Woman."[8] Published as a broadsheet (a handbill to be passed out in public), "Sentiments" is a masterpiece of social entrepreneurship. In two pages, Reed laid out a bold vision, a creative strategy, and a detailed plan to put the strategy into action.

Her vision was simple and compelling: American women must contribute to the "deliverance of their country" with the same courage and energy as the soldiers fighting in the field. She invoked Esther, Judith, and Joan of Arc, "heroines of antiquity, who have rendered their sex illustrious, and have proved to the universe, that, if the weakness of our Constitution, if opinion and manners did not forbid us to march to glory by the same paths as the Men, we should at least equal, and sometimes surpass them in our love for the public good." Then she called for sacrifice by women. Sacrifice entailed denying themselves fine things and contributing the savings to the war effort:

> If the house in which we dwell, if our barns, our orchards are safe at the present time from the hands of those incendiaries, it is to you (our men) that we owe it. And shall we hesitate to evidence to you our gratitude? Shall we hesitate to wear clothing more simple; hair dressed less elegant, while at the price of this small privation, we shall deserve your benedictions? Who, amongst us, will not renounce with the highest pleasure, those vain ornaments, when she shall consider that the valiant defenders of America will be able to draw some advantage from the money which she may have laid out and these presents will perhaps be valued by them [the soldiers] at a greater price, when they will have it in their power to say: *This is the offering of the Ladies*.

She then set out (on the reverse side of her broadsheet) an eleven-point "strategic plan" for the collection of funds and the delivery of same to General Washington, the commander of the revolutionary troops. She called for women to solicit contributions door-to-door. She specified fund-raising targets in paper money and in specie (gold and silver coins, the preferred form). She gave detailed "bundling" strategies to ensure that donations forwarded from the local level would reach a minimum size. She outlined whether and how donors should be recognized, and to whom collected funds should be sent (always to a local [female] treasurer and then on to the wife of the governor of the state or directly to Martha Washington).

Reed proposed that the funds collected should be used to boost the soldiers' morale, not to replace basic supplies such as ammunition and rations that the government should provide. She lost this argument with General Washington, who believed that it was all too likely that a gift of cash to "boost a soldier's morale" would inevitably encourage the purchase of strong local spirits. He wanted the funds to go toward better uniforms for his men. At his urging, many groups of women used their collected funds to buy cloth and sew uniform shirts, often embroidering their own names under the collars.

Esther's tract spawned its first female "association" in her hometown of Philadelphia. Women went door-to-door in pairs to collect from every woman in town. The call of patriotic duty made the work an honor to perform, even for the wives of wealthy men. The Philadelphia group raised some $7,000. As reports came in that the soldiers took great pride in the solidarity, sacrifice, and gratitude of the Philadelphia women, Reed used the feedback to leverage her vision. She wrote personal letters to ladies of high standing in other cities to seek their engagement in the work of the women of the Republic. Always enclosing a copy of her "Sentiments," she requested that the recipients each send their own personal letters to notable women in their circles. Her idea reached women all over the colonies through what might well be the first direct-mail campaign.

Sadly, Esther, or Hettie, as she was known to all, died as her efforts were taking root in additional states—Maryland, New Jersey, and Virginia were launching their own women's fund-raising organizations following her model. It would fall to Sarah Bache, Benjamin Franklin's daughter, to carry on Reed's work to support the soldiers in the Revolutionary Army. An estimated $300,000 was raised nationally by the campaign, equal to tens of millions of dollars today.

Reed had demonstrated a woman's capacity to envision, design, and implement an ambitious social profit enterprise that mobilized the talents and resources of her sisters for the good of the nation. John Adams famously got a reminder from home from his own "partner" while he labored on the Declaration, when on March 31, 1776, his wife, Abigail, reminded him in no uncertain terms about the importance of women to the success of the new Republic:

> I long to hear that you have declared an independency, and by the way in the new Code of Laws which I suppose it will be necessary to make I desire that you would Remember the Ladies, and be more generous and favorable to them than your ancestors. Do not put such unlimited power into the hands of the Husbands. Remember all Men would be tyrants if they could. If particular care and attention is not paid to the Ladies we are determined to ferment a Rebellion, and will not hold ourselves bound by any Laws in which we have no voice, or Representation.[9]

Although the stirring example of Esther Reed and the sharp encouragement of Abigail Adams were not sufficient to persuade the already divided delegates to propose the direct enfranchisement of women, they did accept the notion that women were uniquely suited to exert their moral authority in domestic settings, and that such authority was important to the future of the Union. They believed that the earlier children were taught self-discipline and virtuous behavior, the more likely these teachings would shape their character as adults. Declaration signer Benjamin Rush wrote simply that "the first impressions upon the minds of children are generally derived from women."[10]

Linda Kerber calls the role "republican motherhood."[11] Women would be expected to perform a critical task for the nation: imbuing their offspring with the virtues that would sustain self-control, thus avoiding the dreaded tyranny alluded to by Abigail Adams. In the new nation, a woman's most important role was to train her sons for citizenship by instilling in them self-reliance and self-control.[12] Republican women could "perpetuate the republic by their refusal to countenance lovers who were not devoted to the service of the state, and by commitment to raise sons who were educated for civic virtue and for responsible citizenship. They would also raise self-reliant daughters who, in their turn, would raise republican sons."[13]

These responsibilities for virtue on the part of women were ultimately enshrined, somewhat amusingly for the modern reader, in the same law books that had elaborated the workings of *couverture*. Under this system, given that women were virtually invisible as legal agents, husbands were responsible for crimes committed by their wives in their presence or with their approval. There were, however, two exceptions to this rule: the first being treasonous behavior by the wife (too serious a crime to allow a substitute party to shoulder blame) and the second being the keeping of a brothel, even with the knowledge of her husband. In this case, the keeping of a brothel is "an offense of which the wife is supposed to have the principal management." In other words, this domain of moral turpitude was women's responsibility before the law, and could not, in fact, be shared with, or pushed off onto, her husband.[14]

Whatever the merits of such legal reasoning, women benefited from their role as transmitters of virtue in a variety of ways. The confluence of private family life and public life encouraged the expectations that good women shaping good families would create good citizens leading good lives in a good community nested in a good nation. These responsibilities, in turn, raised the issue of education for women. Education became the key to making our women virtuous and respectable; our men brave, honest, and honorable—and the *American* People in general *an* EXAMPLE *of* HONOUR *and* VIRTUE to the rest of the world.[15]

To their credit, several of the Founders identified the issue of women's education. Benjamin Rush[16] laid out the Founders' thinking, carefully working around the issue of direct enfranchisement:

> The equal share that every citizen has in the liberty and the possible share he may have in the government of the country make it necessary that our ladies should be qualified to a certain degree by a peculiar and suitable education, to concur in instructing their sons in the principles of liberty and government.[17]

Secondly, the institution of marriage became, at least for some, a quasi-patriotic act. The press and literary productions ridiculed parents who tried to force their daughters to marry self-indulged fops for their money instead of republican gentlemen for their character. The contemporary writer Judith Sargent Murray and her husband were models of an egalitarian marriage just as that ideal began to emerge in the new nation.

"I expect to see our young women forming a new era in female history," wrote Murray in 1798.[18] Her optimism was matched by a Miss Jackson. Upon graduation from a girls' academy, she waxed even more eloquent:

> A woman who is skilled in every useful art, who practices every domestic virtue, may by her example inspire her brothers, her husband, or her son with such a love of virtue, such just ideas of the true value of civil liberty, that future heroes and statesmen, who arrive at the summit of military or political fame shall exultingly declare, it is to my mother I owe this elevation.[19]

This perspective reflects a core principle of the Founders' intent for the nation. Virtue was not an element of government or its institutions, but of individuals. The government's job was to protect the individual liberties essential to the development of personal integrity. The aspirations of the Founders created great expectations that women could, in fact, become reliable guarantors of the virtues that the Republic would need from its male citizens. In this way, it was hoped, individual citizens would retain a personal sense of responsibility for the well-being of their fellow citizens. They would retain the motivation and the capacity to make the promises of the Declaration a reality for all citizens.

A skeptic might argue that such reasoning conveniently left those in charge of virtue, that is, women, firmly outside the government. Many of the Founders would have been surprised by how women responded to the challenge presented to them. Most presumed that women's work in building virtue in the citizenry would occur within their private domestic spheres. After all, women were already fully occupied keeping hearth and home together. Mothers know, however, that children (and some men) learn good behaviors only when they see them being practiced. How could a mother teach her children to "love your neighbor" if she marched them past a poor widow and her little ones looking for food in the town square? Inevitably, the town square became that mother's classroom.

THREE

Enterprise:
Commercial and Social

Mothers do hold the reins of government and
sway the ensigns of national prosperity and glory.
—A nineteenth-century minister

The image of a patriotic mother on her way to church through a New England town square, accompanied by her children, is not difficult to envision. Nor is her possible confrontation with a mother widowed by the Revolutionary War who had been reduced to begging. The importance of this imaginary encounter lies in the response of the woman whose family was intact. Would Christian charity suffice in such circumstances, or did the new nation expect more of its citizens? We believe that a certain number of women interpreted their responsibilities more broadly. They recognized the importance of the entrepreneurial spirit of the colonists to the future of the new nation, and they were prepared to apply these principles to their civic duties in the same way that men had sought to advance their commercial enterprises.

The Founders counted on virtuous citizens to make the rights to life, liberty, and the pursuit of happiness a reality for all citizens. The success of the republic would be measured by the number of citizens who could exercise such rights on a daily basis. This required initiative on the part of each and every citizen. There would be little use waiting for a still-fledgling government to initiate action. Action would have to come from the bottom up through individual initiative and through citizen groups such as Franklin's Junto. It did not take long for this spirit of enterprise to emerge in the social as well as the economic sphere.

> Entrepreneurial attitudes and strategies for upward economic mobility pervaded the free population of the British North American colonies throughout the first two centuries of European settlement. These attributes were shared by the vast majority of colonial households; not only by merchants, but by artisans, most farmers . . . indentured servants, unmarried and still youthful day laborers, and even a few exceptional slaves operating in the urban self-hire market. . . . Historians should henceforth stress that the majority of the free population from colonial times forward were active participants in an economic, social, and political system heavily imbued with entrepreneurial values—a system characterized by high savings rates, a market orientation, and positive attitudes toward the accumulation of wealth.[1]

It was British interference with American efforts toward prosperity that had ultimately inflamed popular sentiment against the Crown. Once free of British domination, the period from 1815 forward was characterized by rapid growth, and a general consensus that "improvement," both physical and moral, was the order of the day.[2] While the government focused on improving infrastructure, especially roads and networks of canals, citizens pursued patriotic self-improvement, with physical fitness and reading clubs gaining currency among the middle and upper classes in the growing East Coast cities. These conditions reaffirmed the importance of individual initiative to the future of the nation.

The idea of the entrepreneur, appropriately enough, was much discussed at the time of America's birth. It was an eighteenth-century Frenchman, Jean-Baptiste Say, who first defined the entrepreneur as one who "moves economic resources out of an area of lower and into an area of higher productivity and greater yield." The entrepreneur, in short, is a value creator who figures out how to satisfy a greater number of human needs and wants.[3] Entrepreneurship creates a "win-win" game rather than a "zero-sum game." It was a woman, naturally enough, who invented the metaphor of a pie to describe zero-sum and positive-sum activities.[4] These charts, in the shape of circles, use different-sized wedges to represent various portions of the whole, so they resemble pies. If more slices of the pie are required, some or all of the slices must shrink because the size of the pie does not expand. The entrepreneur is intent on baking a larger pie. This homey metaphor suggests the fundamental importance of growth to the entrepreneurial effort, and the need for the entrepreneur to combine optimism and determination with a practical mindset.

Entrepreneurs recognize opportunities, often where others do not, and establish clear objectives for their efforts. Sometimes the goal is so ambitious that we label them "visionaries." In popular business jargon, such transformative ideas are called "big, hairy, audacious goals," or BHAGs.[5]

But it takes a lot more than vision to achieve entrepreneurial success. Because ambitious goals are, by definition, disruptive of the status quo, the entrepreneur will face resistance. Determination, persistence, and a high tolerance for risk are required, as failure is an ever-present possibility. The entrepreneur must also be "strategic," that is, able to envision key obstacles to success, and to adjust continuously to changing circumstances in pursuit of the desired outcome. More often than not, what the entrepreneur chooses not to do is every bit as important as the tasks actually undertaken.

The first half of the nineteenth century gave rise to a number of commercial entrepreneurs who made an indelible imprint on American life. Cyrus McCormick envisioned, designed, built, refined, and marketed his mechanized grain reaper during the years 1830–1860. The system changed the lives of farmers forever. Increases in efficiency meant opportunities for additional income, but many workers were displaced in the process. McCormick innovated financially, too: he offered his expensive equipment to farmers on a trial basis, requesting payment only when the crops had been successfully, and more efficiently, harvested.

Peter Cooper, in contrast, was a serial entrepreneur. Beginning with a homespun design for a washing machine while still a teenager, he moved on to invent sheep-shearing equipment, a system of manufacturing railroad rails, and eventually a way to turn the rail ties on their heads, producing the I beam. Each product was a commercial success, thanks to Cooper's talent for design and marketing, and his deep sense of what the marketplace needed.

Both these men understood where the new nation was going, not where it had been or where it stood at the present. They understood the inevitable shift from subsistence-level farming to larger production for larger markets. They grasped the newly emerging technologies that made iron a flexible building material with applications from rail ties to ship armor. They saw progress as an opportunity, not a threat to the status quo.

Social entrepreneurs share the mindset of the financial entrepreneur. The commercial entrepreneur targets an audience that can and presumably will pay for a more valuable good or service.

The entrepreneurs and their investors who create a new enterprise will, if successful, receive a financial return on their investment. By comparison, the social entrepreneur targets an audience that is not able to pay for the benefit that will ideally accrue from the entrepreneur's efforts. The objective of the investment is social value, that is, a society in which more individuals are able to contribute their unique abilities to society at large, and enjoy more opportunities to realize their particular dreams. In the process, all members of the society gain a measure of social profit, reflecting the share of enhanced quality of life they now enjoy. In short, "the consensus definition of social entrepreneurship [is] . . . a pattern-breaking effort to create social value."[6]

This is not easily accomplished. A few safety assurances were not the answers to child labor. Six-year-olds working eight-hour days instead of twelve-hour days would not satisfy the social entrepreneur. Ending child labor involved a massive rethinking of an important part of American society. The public believed that business owners should be free to organize their labor resources, hire whomever they chose, and pay what the market would bear. Poor parents had the right to send their kids to work to help support the family. Social entrepreneurs needed to develop a new social consensus: Everyone benefits when young children are educated. The entrepreneurs had to build a connection in people's minds between child labor and their own personal loss. Child labor deprives the child (who is not personally in a position to improve things) and therefore the nation of the gift of that child's potential to himself or herself, and to family, community, and nation.

Social entrepreneurs are rare and exceptionally valuable because they have vision, based in idealism about the value of all life; they are optimistic, convinced that the future holds more opportunities for more people, and they are determined, willing to put in the planning and hard work to turn these possibilities into reality. All these personal attributes, from vision to execution, are essential.[7]

Many wonderful and beneficial activities are *not* included in our definition. Social service providers, social activists, and benefactors are not automatically entrepreneurs. Neither are utopian visionaries or creative innovators whose ideas never actually see the light of day. The efforts of the women social entrepreneurs are distinctly different from the deeds of purely charitable organizations. Charity was and is an important virtue. Helping fellow human beings to meet their basic human necessities in times of disaster, whether natural or manmade, is a cornerstone of our human family. But charity is mostly about survival, not about change or the building of a fairer, more inclusive society. The women social entrepreneurs who built our social profit sector went far beyond responding to the cries of hungry children or wounded soldiers.

They created social profit—a measurable, tangible improvement in opportunities for fellow citizens—through building many of the systems that organize life in a democracy. Their work provided all Americans with a more generous serving of "life, liberty, and the pursuit of happiness" without having to reduce anyone else's portion.

Too many social histories are content to document what happened during our nation's development without sufficient recognition that we require strong individuals to make improvements happen in society. Things don't simply happen. They require agents of change. This is why the individual social entrepreneur is so important to the story of the nation we have become.

FOUR

Republican Mothers in Action

Next to God, we are indebted to women . . .
first for life itself, and then for making it worth living. . . .
—Mary McLeod Bethune

Esther Reed laid the foundation for a tradition of female civic leadership in the new nation. Her broad vision for women's participation in the nation's business was truly exceptional. Most early social enterprises launched by women were based in their own communities, rather than conceived as national efforts. There was plenty of local need, and the majority of women, particularly those ladies of the middle and upper classes, carried out their Christian duties in a community setting. Such settings offered the opportunity for association by women. They could come together and act together. Much of this work was purely charitable in the sense that the women focused on meeting the immediate needs of friends, neighbors, and fellow church members. They did not focus on transformations of large groups or on "big hairy audacious goals," least of all on political goals. Yet without the organizational experience and mutual support offered by local societies, it is difficult to imagine the emergence of the exceptional female entrepreneurs of the 1820s and 1830s.

A group of eleven ladies, six single and five married, formed the Boston Fragment Society in 1812, adopting their name from the biblical parable of the loaves and fishes.[1] Their intention was to help the "destitute and worthy" with handouts of good shoes, shirts, blankets, and, their specialty, hand-sewn layettes made with the best-quality cotton flannel.

The society grew rapidly in its first year to over 400 subscribers (who paid $2 per year) and received over 500 requests for assistance. In the wake of the War of 1812, there was plenty of need, even in the prosperous city of Boston. An illness or accident could deprive even a wealthy family of its income. Members were particularly aware of the fragility of prosperity and in meeting minutes regularly noted their own gratitude for continued security. Not only did widows and orphans need attention in the postwar era, but immigrants from Ireland and Italy were also beginning to arrive, competing for work and taxing the generosity of the well-to-do.

By the 1830s the women of the Boston Fragment Society were providing clothing to enable poor children to attend school, having embraced the notion that these gifts were an investment in the future: "to give education to the young children and lucrative employment to the parents is undoubtedly the best charity."[2] They recognized, perhaps for the first time, that they were indirect beneficiaries of the generosity they extended to those in need, as education, they theorized, would "prevent the recurrence (of poverty) in the next generation."

The Fragment Society is notable both for what it did to help countless citizens of Boston over its long life (170 years to date) and also for what it did not do. Its membership did not change very much. Descendants of many of the original member families still serve on the board today. It did not form alliances with other organizations. It did not alter its belief that "good clothes" could instill pride in poor people. It did not even change its dues structure! There were no entrepreneurs to be found.

Many variations on the Fragment Society idea sprang up across the new nation, some as early as the turn of the nineteenth century. Although few endured as long, or resisted change as effectively as the Boston group, they did provide the social services that were desperately needed in a period when the government, by both design and inclination, did little to address them. The Society for the Relief of the Distressed launched in Philadelphia in 1795 and the Society for the Relief of Poor Widows with Small Children in New York in 1797. The colorful names of groups like these reveal the limited, targeted mission their organizers aspired to fill, none more so than The Female Association for the Relief of the Sick Poor, and for the Education of Such Female Children as Do Not Belong To, or Are Not Provided For, by Any Religious Society. The Daughters of Africa was organized by a group of black women in 1821 in Philadelphia to assure the support of black families in need.

As the names suggest, many associations were religious in nature. This meant both that they were usually organized by women belonging to the same church and that their activities were connected to the doctrine of the religion concerned. Works of charity, for many Protestant sects, testified to the depth of faith of the followers. Such societies often counted on the efforts of younger women from well-to-do families, those not yet engaged in their own households as married women, and membership thus offered an opportunity to confirm the virtuousness of these single women. Of course, the organizations also offered their members fellowship, financial experience, and potentially a window into the needs around them—all at a time, we should remember, when access to such experiences for women was extremely limited.

Virtuousness also became an issue with respect to those targeted for help by the societies. Many concentrated their efforts on the "deserving" poor—women who had the misfortune to be widowed or abandoned, despite leading good Christian lives. Charity stayed within the familiar boundaries of the benevolent ladies. The approach had its critics even then, however, as it tended to insulate the middle-class women from the needs and wants of the chronically poor. Debates surrounding the worthy and unworthy poor continued to shape charitable enterprises throughout the century.

A few enterprising groups found ways to carry out the second great commandment to "love thy neighbor" by addressing the needs of their fellow citizens and of the new nation at the same time. Handouts to the needy laid a foundation for teaching personal generosity and served as an important starting point in the education of children. But democracy required self-reliance, initiative, industriousness, and productivity on the part of each citizen. So republican mothers needed to model and mobilize these additional virtues.

Catherine Ferguson exemplified the combination of Christian duty and republican citizenship. She was more a doer than a joiner, and her optimism and determination inspired others to join with her. Unlike most benevolent ladies, she did not begin with the notion of doing charity according to her means. She defined her work according to the needs she found, and then did whatever it took to generate the resources to meet her goals. Such a "ready, fire, aim" approach to resource development, as we will see, often marks the most impactful social entrepreneurs. Ferguson also instinctively reached out to others and reinvented her projects to overcome the inevitable obstacles she encountered. In the end, her enterprise flourished and inspired hundreds of imitators across many different social classes. Katy, as she was known, is one of America's first social entrepreneurs.

Lewis Tappan, a nineteenth-century abolitionist, wrote an extensive obituary when Ferguson (circa 1774–1854) passed away. He captured the power of her life in a single quote: "Where Katy lived, the whole aspect of the Neighborhood changed."[3] Ferguson was born enslaved and brought to New York City with her mother by their owner, R.B. While she was still a child, her mother was sold to another family, and she apparently never saw her mother again. Her mistress told Katy that if she was as good as her mother, she would do well. The recollection of her own anguish when separated from her mother made her feel compassion for all children, she said. When she was ten years old, she told her master that if he would give her her freedom, she would serve the Lord forever. But he refused.

Katy was never taught to read. "My mistress," she said, "would not let me learn; and once she said to me, 'You know more now than my daughters.'" One of her owner's sons asked Katy to help him with his school lessons. She exclaimed, "I can't!" He replied, "Yes, you can; if I don't read right in the Bible, or if I don't say my catechism right, you tell quick enough."[4]

At age fourteen, Ferguson presented herself at the door of the Presbyterian Church in the neighborhood where she worked. She was warmly received by the Reverend John Mason and R.B. soon received an offer to purchase Katy for $200 from a member of the church congregation. He accepted the offer, and Katy in turn was permitted to work off the debt by her new mistress, thereby gaining her freedom. As a free black woman at age eighteen, she married and bore two children, only to lose her entire family to an influenza epidemic early in her marriage. Free, young, and heartbroken, Ferguson faced the prospect of a life of domestic service. The year was 1788; the individual states were in the middle of the process of ratification of the Constitution.

Many residents of New York City had suffered greatly as a result of the Revolutionary War. Countless orphans and abandoned children were forced to fend for themselves. Poor children, black and white, were often "bound out" to domestic service, where they labored ten-hour workdays six days a week. Ferguson lamented the wasted lives, especially the children who were trapped in this cycle through no fault of their own. Having lost her own family, Katy felt she should mobilize her obvious gifts to help these children. She became a "surrogate" republican mother, a woman who recognized the loss to the nation when children were not provided with the love and discipline that would enable them to become productive citizens in a democracy. Despite the discrimination and lack of education that she had suffered, Ferguson understood that she personally could make a difference in children's lives. Perhaps she did not think of her work in terms of social profit, but her productivity as an entrepreneur is nothing short of remarkable.

She set out to visit orphanages and almshouses (poorhouses operated by local governments), offering to take both black and white children into her home. Over her lifetime, Lewis Tappan reported, she served as a foster mother to forty-eight such children, about evenly divided between white and black. But Ferguson's audacious goal was to offer these and additional children the gift of reading. Reading would enable them to study the Bible and to continue forward in life as far as their God-given gifts would allow. They might escape their difficult circumstances, achieve self-reliance, and gain personal salvation. Katy put her entrepreneurial talents to work.

Her first challenge was simply to reach the children. The only day of the week that might work was the Sabbath, the day when child laborers were not required to work. So Ferguson initiated the nation's first "Sabbath school" in her home in 1793. It was not the Sunday school of more modern times. It was a full class day focused on a mostly secular curriculum. Ferguson accepted black and white students.

Poor children could not, of course, pay for tuition. Ferguson would have to fund-raise to keep her school going. Undaunted, she put her baking talents to work. Her specialty was wedding cakes, and she used the income from her baking enterprise to buy books and to pay additional instructors—to assist in tutoring the children.

Her industriousness gradually inspired outside support. Reverend Mason learned of her work and offered the use of a room in the church to house the school. Isabella Graham, the woman who had purchased Katy from R.B. and whose son-in-law had paid off the last $100 of her indenture, shared Ferguson's convictions about the need to educate all children.[5] Graham incorporated an educational component for children into her own charitable work with the Society for the Relief of Poor Widows with Small Children. The Sabbath school idea was replicated across the city, and gradually a system of Sunday education for working children and adults took shape. No one doubted Catherine Ferguson had showed how to make it happen.

Ferguson's commitment to educating all children has been a hallmark of American society. It is built on the simple idea that all citizens should be educated to their full potential, for their own benefit and the benefit of the nation. We believe that education is one of the best investments we can make as social investors. How many current citizens know that this tradition was greatly expanded by an entrepreneurial, cake-baking, formerly enslaved woman?

Ferguson had a powerful impact on her friend and sponsor, Isabella Graham, who devoted herself to many social profit enterprises following the death of her husband. Graham had arrived in New York City about the same time as Ferguson. She was a Scotswoman who had lived in Canada while her husband was posted there with his Royal regiment. He was later assigned to service in Antigua, where he died in 1774, leaving Isabella with one daughter, Joanna. She returned initially to Scotland, but came to New York in 1789 with her daughter and son-in-law, Divie Bethune, a successful businessman.

She was, by all accounts, a very devout Christian who took the biblical injunctions to care for the sick and needy very seriously. In April 1800, she reported that four members of the board of her Society for the Relief of Poor Widows had remained in New York City to minister as best they could to the needs of the poor during an outbreak of yellow fever that had prompted businesses to close and most "purveyors of charity" to depart the city. In 1802, she obtained a charter from the State of New York for her society, apparently the first female-led organization to receive such a formal designation. In effect, the legislators recognized the legitimacy of her organization and the beneficial impact of its work. Presumably, she made the case effectively that her work would reduce the population of the local poorhouse and thereby at least some of the costs borne by the state.

The following year she received a considerable grant ($15,000) from the legislature, which enabled her to purchase a house that the society operated as a combination shelter, house of industry, and school for children.

The winter of 1807–8 saw the passage of legislation that effectively suspended all trade with England and France. These embargoes, instituted by the various parties, rendered the situation of the poor more destitute than ever. Mrs. Graham adopted a plan best calculated in her view to detect the idle applicant for charity, and at the same time to furnish employment for the more worthy amongst the female poor. She purchased flax, and lent wheels, where applicants had none. Such as were industrious took the work with thankfulness, and were paid for it; those who were beggars by profession never kept their word to return for the flax or the wheel.[6]

In 1814, Graham also founded the Society for the Promotion of Industry Among the Poor and an adult Sabbath school. Her daughter and son-in-law continued this latter project, focusing on black adults and organizing the Society for the Promotion of Sabbath Schools. Ferguson remained active in her own school as well as in the efforts of the Bethunes.

The Ferguson-Graham story illustrates the diversity of the women who built the early social systems in our nation. Benevolent middle- and upper-class white women made important contributions, but so did black women. This "odd couple" exemplifies the spirit of the social entrepreneur with an investment orientation. Although their approaches to fund-raising differed radically, they both pursued funding according to the size of the problem they sought to address, rather than according to their means. In true entrepreneurial fashion, they did whatever it took to raise additional assets to keep the enterprises going.

Both women clearly understood the goal of social profit creation. Ferguson could see the benefits to the community, as well as to the individual children, that education would bring. Graham was an early champion of investing to create self-sufficiency, recognizing that charity alone provided little longer-term improvement in people or society. The Society for the Relief of Poor Widows with Small Children taught mothers to make shirts and then sold them to benefit the widows (a foreshadowing of the Women's Exchange movement that we will discuss in subsequent chapters). Graham's "House of Industry," where spouseless women could live with their children, reflects a similar approach. The house had rooms for spinning wheels, looms, and other equipment. It also provided space where volunteers could teach and care for children while their mothers worked. The scheme had the potential to sustain the dignity and independence of the poor mothers, and teach the children generosity, compassion, frugality, and industriousness. Decades later the Settlement House movement would reinvent similar solutions for newly arrived immigrant families.

Many "societies" played an important role in building a fragile infrastructure to help those in need in the Union. Their economic value, as a supplement to the meager efforts of the government, was enormous. It is difficult for us today to imagine how little official support was available at the time, even in a large city such as New York. Bellevue Hospital opened its doors as a public hospital in 1816 to care for those in need. It cost some $400,000 to construct. Early records[7] note that it served as a penitentiary and an almshouse as well, housing an average of 1,547 paupers during its first years of operation and costing the government about $100,000 per year. Even this early account admits that the institution quickly became "corrupt and mercenary," with continuing epidemics of yellow fever committing "frightful ravages in the filthy wards and loathsome cells." Inspection reports concerning county almshouses prepared by visitors over subsequent decades continue to describe shocking mixes of inmates: men, women, and children, the handicapped, the insane, the criminal, and the non-English speakers, all pitched together without toilets or baths, overseen by keepers, and united in their misery only by their status as paupers. Any mechanism that enabled a poor person to escape the living hell from which there appeared to be no return provided enormous value, not just by relieving the government of the expense of caring for one additional soul, but in keeping hope alive that a poor person could be redeemed and go on to a productive life.

Graham and Ferguson represent opposite ends of the class spectrum. Their success as social entrepreneurs, both independently and collaboratively, illustrates the range of women who took responsibility for creating social profit in the new nation. There were many thousands of women in the "middle" of the income and social spectrum who also organized themselves to do good works during this period. In their associations and societies, they made many collective contributions to the emerging nation and laid a foundation for the next generation of female social entrepreneurs.

Mary Mason founded the New York Female Missionary and Bible Society, the first "cent" society on record, in 1819. Members committed themselves to bringing a penny a week as dues for membership and to pool their resources. They intended to focus on the "combined evangelical, physical, and social needs" of the disenfranchised.[8] Cent Societies reflected the very limited access that most women, even middle-class women, had to money, and the format proved popular. Mason's idea took hold in many cities and in many denominational settings. Cent societies often operated within the framework of Protestant churches, and some offered their donations to the men leading their congregations in support of church operations. Others deployed their funds themselves to support their mission of education and charity for the poor. Mrs. Mason's Cent Society in New York City operated continuously until 1861.

Female voluntary associations provided opportunities for their members as well as for their clients. Societies enabled women to undertake activities not available to them as individuals. An association could, for instance, own property and control bank accounts, activities still unavailable to women acting individually. Leaders of such organizations could invest funds and even lend to responsible merchants to assure their assets earned a return. Women's management of funds through their societies became a source of admiration among (at least some) men, as did their evident fund-raising skills.

Women were indeed resourceful at raising money to fund their voluntary activities. As in the Cent Societies, dues payments were the most common source of support, with some groups permitting men to become honorary members if they paid dues (and promised not to participate in meetings!). Others set up subscription drives throughout their cities to raise more money. They addressed executors of wills to seek contributions from legacies. They organized raffles, although such dangerous flirtations with the evils of gambling were quite controversial. More radically, some groups called on their members to do without their middle-class fashions and accessories, and to donate these savings to the direct needs of their poor clients, reprising the request of Esther Reed some fifty years earlier.

Local women's associations and societies remained important sources of social profit throughout the nineteenth and twentieth centuries. Indeed, they continue as a cornerstone of our civic life today. But in the 1830s and 1840s, they also offered fertile ground for more ambitious agendas in building the new nation. The work of these organizations, whether charity, social service, self-improvement, or community beautification, gradually softened the sharp distinction between the domestic and public spheres that had characterized women's lives at the beginning of the nineteenth century.[9] Entrepreneurial women recognized the potential in this evolution. The well-established tradition of women working together also offered an opportunity to those exceptional women with vision and determination. Leadership women could build on this tradition to create social networks, with the power to shape the new nation. It did not take long for a small number of such leaders to emerge and to mobilize these resources in pursuit of real and lasting improvements in the lives of their fellow citizens.[10]

FIVE

Social Enterprise and the Founding of American Religious Orders

There are different forms of service but the same Lord. To each
individual the manifestation of the Spirit is given for some benefit.
—I Corinthians 12:4–6

W e don't know whether the original signers of the Declaration of Independence or the drafters of the Constitution
were familiar with the work of Katy Ferguson. If they had learned
of her remarkable efforts, those who had argued for a significant
role for women in the new republic would certainly have felt
vindicated.

At about the same time that Ferguson's Sabbath school effort
was spreading across New York City, a woman who probably
better fit the Founders' idea of a republican mother was starting
her family in the same city in high style. Her station in life more
closely resembled that of Esther Reed. Like Ferguson, however,
she was destined to lose her husband prematurely, and in her
widowhood she determined to build an enterprise that was also
devoted to the education of poor children. She shared with
Katy Ferguson a devotion to her religious faith and to children
in need. She, too, devoted enormous energy and creativity to

building an institution that eventually enabled millions of children to become productive citizens. She, too, made her commitments and then sought support to ensure that she could deliver on them.

By 1963, when Elizabeth Seton was beatified by the Roman Catholic Church, some 11,000 Daughters of Charity[1] were at work in the United States, engaged in education, health care, and social works.[2] How could such a successful enterprise have been launched by a woman who chose a life of obedience and service, seemingly the antithesis of entrepreneurship?

Religious convictions were central to the work of many women at the beginning of the nineteenth century. The story of the Good Samaritan reminded Christians that they shared a responsibility for the well-being of their "neighbors." The biblical parable of the talents reminded believers of the importance not simply of charity, but of putting one's own gifts to work. Two of the servants in the story put the talents to work and double their money, to the pleasure of their returning master. The message to believers was clear: It was not acceptable to hoard. They were expected to use the gifts they had been given to increase the "wealth" of God's kingdom.

By having no official church—indeed, the Constitution carefully separated the church and state—America freed the churches to be more socially progressive and active. Jefferson had introduced "disestablishment" legislation in Virginia as early as 1777, and it was officially written into law in 1785. Henceforth, religious groups were simply associations of private citizens. "Private" was the operant word, and individuals enjoyed freedom to associate as they wished without government interference. Religious groups were not permitted to impose their ideas or practices on public or government activities,[3] yet most people in the early nineteenth century had difficulty grasping the notion of virtue without a formal religious framework. The vast majority of citizens were active participants in formal religious organizations. The American variant of the Anglican Church, the Episcopal faith, continued to attract large numbers of upper-class adherents in the major East Coast cities. Whereas many denominations focused on a literal interpretation of the Bible, and on a rigorous dogma of predestination, others advanced the notion of "free will," an idea more in keeping with Enlightenment thinking. In this view, individuals carried a personal responsibility for their own salvation, and good works on earth could contribute to the process.

The Catholic Church had traditionally maintained that good works were an essential part of personal salvation. Moreover, Catholicism also held that assistance to the poor was the most blessed of good works and that voluntary efforts of direct assistance were to be valued even beyond financial gifts.[4] A number of religious orders had developed in Europe that enabled women to devote themselves specifically to these ideals. The orders remained directly connected to the church, of course, requiring a male priest to say daily Mass and to act as spiritual director, but the structure provided considerable independence and "social capital" for the women who joined them.

The Catholic faith had a relatively small number of adherents in America, mostly concentrated in Maryland. Baltimore was the center of Catholic life in America in the first decades of the nineteenth century.[5] Although Maryland welcomed the practice of all religions, Catholic immigrants who began arriving in greater numbers after the turn of the nineteenth century often gravitated to this part of the new nation. Perhaps it was inevitable that an American-based religious order would be created, given the many benefits of religious life for both the sisters themselves and the communities they served. After all, a dedicated source of volunteer female labor provided an invaluable asset to the church itself and to those in need. The founding of the first American order offers a compelling story, both because of its immediate and ongoing contributions to social profit in the new nation and because of the remarkable enterprise of the woman who made it happen.

It took the patience of a saint for any woman to pursue a social enterprise in early-nineteenth-century America, given the constraints on women's independence. But the creation of a religious order proved to be an excellent strategy to ensure systematic assistance to orphans and poor children. Elizabeth Seton's skills as a recruiter, fund-raiser, diplomat, and administrator enabled her to create an enduring and independent enterprise.

Seton does not fit the stereotype of a nun, and she certainly did not fit the profile of most Roman Catholics in America at the turn of the nineteenth century. Catholicism was the religion of the poor immigrants. She was a "high church" Protestant who did her charity work in a setting of wealth and comfort. Her wedding to William Magee Seton in 1796 made front-page headlines. She was the daughter of a prominent physician who served as the first professor of anatomy at Columbia University. Her husband was a wealthy businessman in his father's banking concern, Seton, Maitland and Company. They started married life in a beautiful home near Wall Street, next door to Alexander Hamilton, a family friend.

Elizabeth bore five children in her first six years of marriage, but with ample staff in the household, she found time to assist her father in his public health duties among the poor and to serve as a volunteer officer in the New York Society for the Relief of Poor Widows with Small Children.[6] But tragedy soon struck the young family. Seton, Maitland filed for bankruptcy in 1800, and then in 1803, William passed away from consumption (probably what we know today as tuberculosis). The family had traveled to

Italy in the hope that a more benign climate would enable him to recover, but to no avail. The trip proved momentous for Elizabeth, however, who was greatly impressed by the generosity and warmth of the Italians who befriended her during this difficult time.

She returned to New York with the children, a gentlewoman who, if not destitute, was certainly "decayed" from her previous station of wealth. Soon after her return, she shocked her New York family and society friends by expressing the desire to convert to the Roman Catholic faith. Her official biographer, Joseph Dirvan, describes the reaction:

> The shock of such an announcement to genteel society in New York in 1804 was appalling. The city was frankly bigoted. It had an unofficial "state religion"—Episcopalianism, other Protestant sects were tolerated with varying degrees of scorn and pity. But Romanism! Romans were shiftless, scrubby immigrants who attended the shabby little church on Barclay Street.[7]

It was a fair description of the Roman Catholic population at the time—recent Irish, French, and German arrivals with few manners and even fewer pennies in their pockets—who were thoroughly discriminated against in practice and even in the law, where, thanks to John Jay, it was written that no one could hold elective office in our new land unless he renounced allegiance to foreign, ecclesiastical rulers (most prominently the pope).

So Elizabeth's idea was utterly scandalous, particularly to her in-laws, who still possessed some wealth, as well as to the majority of her friends. Even Elizabeth herself admitted that it took a strong constitution to attend daily Mass amid such a rough crowd, including the local priests, who offered a sharp contrast to the refined and educated clergy she had encountered in Rome.

But she was not deterred. Elizabeth was confirmed in the Roman Catholic Church in 1806. Her decision, it goes without saying, did little to help her in the quest for resources to support her family. Plans to start a school for small children and to take in boarders proved insufficient for the needs of the family, and Elizabeth worried about the "ridicule [her children] were forced to hear of our holy religion and the mockery of the Church and ministers—besides their minds being poisoned with bad principles of every kind which I cannot always check or control."[8]

Elizabeth's decision to abandon her public life, as well as New York City, was not, however, precipitated by poverty or the teasing of her children, but by the decision of her husband's half sister, Cecilia, to join her in converting to Catholicism. Cecilia was sixteen at the time, and dying of consumption. Her family reacted with a fury worthy, as Dirvan puts it, of an ogre in a fairy tale. Cecilia would be sent off to the West Indies against her will; Elizabeth would be cut off from all inheritance for her part in this conversion and her children left to beg in the streets. Elizabeth was indeed disinherited by the Setons, at least temporarily. More dramatically, her supposed proselytizing for the Catholic faith led to assaults against Catholic worshippers at St. Peter's Church on Christmas Eve, 1806. These conflicts abated during 1807, and Elizabeth gradually reconciled with the Setons, but she no longer had any means to support herself in New York. She determined to accept the offer of Father Dubourg, a prominent Sulpician priest based in Baltimore, to move there to start a school.

Dubourg had first met Seton in New York during a fund-raising tour for his St. Mary's College for Boys (a preparatory school). True to his word, he did help her set up a school near the Catholic seminary he directed. Dubourg was a man of many ideas and a perfect partner for Seton. They soon imagined an ambitious goal: the creation of the first American religious order for women.

An order would provide Elizabeth and additional sisters with a formal structure (and hopefully financial support) through which they could pursue their mission. They would focus on improving the lives of poor children through education to prepare them for productive citizenship. Seton believed that this mission would attract women to dedicate their lives to the work of a new order. She would have to obtain the authorization and support of the male clergy, but she felt confident that she would retain the principal management and resource deployment responsibilities as the "mother superior."

She also had to deal with her own five children, concern over whose well-being had brought her to Baltimore in the first place. Nuns were traditionally single women who joined their orders in their teen years. How could Seton be both a physical and a spiritual mother at the same time? She, Father Dubourg, and his successor, Father John David, searched for ideas. They ultimately found a model for the American order to Seton's liking: the Daughters of Charity, a French order founded in the seventeenth century by Saint Vincent de Paul.

The Daughters of Charity was an order active in the world. Members took simple vows of chastity, poverty, and obedience, and "pledged to apply themselves (. . .) to the corporal and spiritual service of the sick poor."[9] There was no veil to wear, no protective grate to cloister the nuns, not even a convent (they were to live in rented rooms in the community and worship at the local parish church). Such flexibility appealed to Elizabeth, and a copy of the French order's mission was obtained to serve as a framework for the new Sisters of Charity of St. Joseph.

Archbishop John Carroll of Baltimore granted permission for a modification of the order, enabling Elizabeth to maintain her family while serving as the first "mother" of the new sisterhood. She took her vows at the end of 1808, and the first American order came into being, helped in great measure by the miraculous (Elizabeth's word) gift of $10,000 that enabled the order to acquire a tract of land in Emmitsburg, Maryland. The gift came from Samuel Cooper, a wealthy convert to Catholicism.

By 1810, Mother Seton had recruited twelve sisters to the order and twelve more were awaiting admission. The sisters established a school for poor children, and it soon included almost fifty students, including thirty boarders. Money was tight at the outset, and Seton began to demonstrate her remarkable entrepreneurial skills. She raised money from loyal friends from New York and Italy to ensure that the majority of students at her school might come from among the poorest of the poor. She also accepted a number of paying students at the outset to help subsidize the operation.

This early success did not come without significant difficulties. She was obliged to deal with the misguided efforts of Father David, who had succeeded Father Dubourg as spiritual director of the order, to merge her fledgling order with the French Daughters of Charity. She also deflected his plan to put her in charge of the school while appointing Sister Rose as "superior" of the order. Elizabeth also endured the death of her youngest child and two sisters-in-law, all from consumption, as well as the absence of her two eldest sons, who were attending boarding school in New York, made possible by the generosity of Antonio Filicchi, whom Elizabeth and William had met in Italy. Adding to her challenges were the first signs of Elizabeth's own failing health, as she, too, began to experience the telltale signs of the dreaded tuberculosis.

The first expansion of the Daughters of Charity serves as a dramatic reminder of the fragile conditions of the nation in the early years of the nineteenth century. As news of the new order spread, Seton received a request in 1814 from a group of Catholic laymen in Philadelphia. They wished her order to take charge of an orphanage that they were prepared to sponsor. Here was an opportunity for the sisters to serve the poor and to extend their work beyond the "mother house." But it required difficult personnel decisions. The trustees of the Orphan Asylum (more formally the Philadelphia Roman Catholic Society of Education and Maintaining Poor Orphan Children) were requesting three sisters and offering payment of $600 per year for support of the operation.

Both Archbishop Carroll and the vicar general raised concerns about the personal safety of the sisters embarking on such an effort. Only weeks earlier, Baltimore had been attacked by British warships, an event that inspired Francis Scott Key to compose the nation's national anthem. But Elizabeth and her colleagues embraced the opportunity to serve, and their wishes carried the day. In September, Sister Rose and two others set out for Philadelphia by coach through southern Pennsylvania to avoid the dangers of travel by ship.

The sisters found many challenges upon their arrival. The orphanage was in considerable debt, as the demand for its services in the wake of an earlier yellow fever epidemic had overwhelmed the budget. But Sister Rose had been well schooled in fund-raising through her work with Mother Seton. Within two years, these debts had been retired and the orphanage was operating in the black. Rose gave ample credit to Mrs. Rachel Montgomery and the members of the Ladies Auxiliary for their support. Montgomery was a convert to Catholicism who had followed Elizabeth's efforts closely, thanks to her friendship with Samuel Cooper. Rose, of course, had learned the value of establishing a women's auxiliary from Elizabeth.

Traditionally, a benevolent society such as the Orphan Society in Philadelphia was established by lay Catholic parishioners and guided by a lay board. The board (potentially men and women) was usually supported by a "subscription society" composed of professional men, and a women's auxiliary, often the wives of the professional men. The men raised funds through subscriptions— membership dues—and provided their professional skills, whether legal or financial, free of charge. The women provided volunteer labor of their own through sewing, tutoring, and occasional direct care of the children. As we have already noted, the ladies proved particularly adept at fund-raising as well, organizing raffles, fairs, games of euchre (a popular card game), and the like. Working-class men and women parishioners often provided much of the maintenance work for an orphanage as their contribution. Elizabeth quickly grasped the importance of this framework and impressed on Rose the importance of cultivating an engaged auxiliary devoted to "good works" as an essential element of a successful parish orphanage operation.

Soon another opportunity was offered to Mother Seton to fulfill her goal of serving poor children and building a permanent organization of dedicated women. The Roman Catholic Benevolent Society in New York City invited her order to take charge of their new orphanage. The bishop himself wrote to ask for Elizabeth's assistance:

> I sincerely wish it may be in your power to immediately grant the laudable request of the said gentlemen [the trustees of the Society], as the object of it would be productive of a great deal of good here.[10]

Not surprisingly, Seton accepted the request with enthusiasm, but not without exercising her own authority on managerial matters, including determining which sister would be best suited to the task of operating in New York. She did not agree to send Sister Margaret to head up the New York operation as requested.

Instead, she made it clear that she knew what was required of leaders in such start-up operations:

> "Was your institution a high-styled grammar school, Sister Margaret would suit better than any," Dubois wrote on her behalf to the New York Bishop, "and great as the loss would be to this house, we would freely part with her";
>
> "For such an asylum as that of Philadelphia the main object is to have a zealous, prudent, economical Mother to govern it. . . . We contemplate to send, at least for a time, the excellent Sister Rose, who is now in Philadelphia—having acquired experience in Philadelphia, she will be calculated to guide the beginners of New York."[11]

Rose arrived and took charge. Her competence was immediately visible as the New York orphanage rapidly expanded from five to twenty-eight charges in the first year. She established a ladies auxiliary, of course, and set about renovating the building. She saw to it that the sisters were provided a modest, but workable, stipend of $36 per year each.

The success of these original expansion efforts led inevitably, during a period of great need, to more opportunities to serve. A formal charter for the Daughters of Charity was obtained from the State of Maryland in 1817, the same year the New York orphanage was established, and within a year came another request, this time for the sisters to operate a school for girls in Philadelphia on the model of their Emmitsburg school for girls. Elizabeth did live to see this opportunity realized, although plans to create similar schools in New York and Boston were not completed before her death in January 1821. By this time, little more than a decade after its creation, the Daughters of Charity had some sixty members working in three dioceses.[12]

During this brief period, marked by uneven guidance from the Catholic Church, Seton pursued her mission with conviction and poise, inspiring dozens and ultimately thousands of women to dedicate themselves to the service of those less fortunate. The efforts of the sisters to educate many thousands of immigrants over generations added immeasurably to the social capital of the nation.[13]

At about the time of Seton's death, a new immigrant arrived in Baltimore. She settled in the Fells Point section of the city, home to a significant number (about 2,000) of black and mixed-race immigrants from various Caribbean islands, many of them French speakers. Elizabeth Lange[14] was about thirty years old, unmarried, and in possession of at least some modest means to support herself. She was a devoted practitioner of her Catholic faith, and worshipped with other blacks in the basement of St. Mary's Seminary Chapel, a church established by Sulpician priests who were refugees themselves, in this case from the French Revolution of 1789. Lange had an even more difficult row to hoe as a social entrepreneur. In addition to dealing with the male-dominated church and practicing her Catholicism in a Protestant nation, she was a black women in a slaveholding state (Archbishop Carroll of Baltimore owned a number of slaves in Elizabeth's time) and an alien who spoke French in an English-speaking city.[15] But she overcame these challenges to create the Oblate Sisters of Providence, the first black religious order in the world. The Oblates continue today to provide education to thousands of children of color throughout the United States, Latin America, and Africa.

Lange was born in the Caribbean, probably in Haiti, a French colony at the time. Her parents were enslaved on a plantation and they took the surname of the French owner. Some sources record that Elizabeth's mother was in fact a "natural" daughter of the owner. The family fled to Cuba during the Haitian Revolution of 1791, apparently with some financial resources (as a result, perhaps, of the above-mentioned relationship), and eventually Elizabeth and her mother came to America, spending time in South Carolina and perhaps in Virginia before settling in Baltimore.

Noting, as had Catherine Ferguson, that there were no formal educational opportunities available to black children in Baltimore, Elizabeth and a fellow immigrant, Margaret Balas, determined to open a "free" school in their home. They taught the girls reading, mathematics, writing, and spelling, in addition to the domestic arts. These progressive efforts were well received by the local free black community, which appreciated the fact that Lange's graduates were able to support themselves in modest fashion. But after a decade of this work, the women had depleted most of their personal resources and Lange turned to the Sulpicians. Together with Father James Hector Joubert, she determined to launch a religious order for black women. An order, they felt, might attract more funding and provide an ongoing stream of women to the calling of educators. It would also enable her to fulfill her great personal desire to dedicate herself more formally to her Christian faith (the term *oblate* translates as "one offered" or "one given to God").

Despite many fears that the white Catholic community would be offended by black women in religious garb, Lange and Joubert received permission from Baltimore's Archbishop Whitfield to begin her novitiate with three additional women. They chose as a name the Oblate Sisters of Providence with Saint Francis as their patron saint, and took their vows in July 1829. The mission or charism of the group was to be the education of black children.

Lange, choosing the name Mary, was named the mother superior, and Father Joubert, the order's spiritual director.

The early years went well, despite some overt discrimination against the black community. The St. Francis school obtained a house on favorable terms from a white member of the Caribbean community to house their program. The original financial plan, based on the European model for religious orders, specified that novices would bring a dowry upon joining. Indeed, two early recruits from the Noel family brought the Oblates several thousand dollars. Lange moved quickly to supplement the dowry funds. She organized fund-raising "fairs" in the black and white Catholic communities. The modest successes allowed the school to grow rapidly to nearly 100 students by 1834. Parents paid tuition according to their means (some black families, particularly those headed by ships' captains, were reasonably well-off) and Lange successfully sought "scholarship" funds to supplement these sums. She soon launched a building fund to create more space for the school and for a chapel. The first black Catholic chapel and school in America were dedicated in the Fells Point neighborhood of Baltimore in 1836, built with the leadership and funds Lange provided. Although it was all very modest compared to the "estate" in Emmitsburg that had been given to Elizabeth Seton, the facilities and programs represented real progress for the black community, and Mother Mary took great pride in their accomplishments.

But storm clouds were gathering over her fledgling enterprise. Few black women could provide a dowry when they joined the order, and Mother Mary proved a difficult and exacting headmistress. Although always willing to set an example by pushing herself to the limit both physically and mentally, she was feared by many of the sisters and "made no allowance for small omissions." She also clung stubbornly to her Francophone roots, refusing to use English for all but the most basic communication. By 1838, there were only twenty-one sisters, and the endowment was funding school operating expenses. When Joubert died in 1843, she lost her most important ally in her always tense relationship with the church authorities. The archbishop of Baltimore at the time, Samuel Eccleston, proposed that the order disband. Mother Mary refused, preferring to mobilize the sisters to beg on the streets of Baltimore to raise money to keep the school afloat. The bishop, in turn, refused to provide them with a priest. During the standoff, Lange marched her sisters some four miles each day to attend Mass at the white St. James Church. The sisters had plenty of reason to fear their white neighbors, as nativist gangs opposed to Catholics (and to free blacks) were widespread in the city in the 1830s. The sisters apparently suffered plenty of verbal and even physical abuse as they made their way through the segregated city, although there is no record that any were seriously harmed.

The rejection of the order by the local Catholic hierarchy impacted both the school and the Oblates themselves. Enrollments fell, and so did income. Two light-skinned Oblates from the original group defected to Michigan where they launched their own white religious order, called the Sisters of the Sacred Heart of Mary, with considerable success.

During such trying circumstances, Lange's leadership skills were severely tested. Her feisty relationship with the local church authorities stemmed in part from her concern that the Oblates did not receive the level of respect that she believed "women of the cloth" deserved. The priests regularly requested various domestic services of the sisters, and whenever money became a question, the clergymen suggested that sewing and cleaning could provide the sisters with sources of income for their own support. Indeed, over the decades, the Oblates did design and stitch large numbers of vestments for clergymen across the nation. But Lange was quick to push back against the creeping domestication of her order by the male clergy. In the mid-1830s, the superior of the Sulpician priests, Father Deluol, requested two Oblates to manage the domestic affairs of the St. Michael's Seminary. Mother Mary consulted Joubert, who was well aware that his colleagues were in general not supportive of the black sisterhood. He counseled her to pray for guidance. In a rare surviving letter, Mother Mary responded directly to Deluol:

> We do not conceal the difficulty of our situation as persons of color and religious at the same time, and we wish to conciliate these two qualities in such a manner as not to appear too arrogant on the one hand, and on the other, not to miss the respect which is due to the state we have embraced and the holy habit which we have the honor to wear.[16]

She goes on to set out the conditions under which she could agree to his request. The most important is that her sisters not be obliged to mix with the servants (the enslaved blacks who actually did the cooking and cleaning and serving at the seminary). She was well aware that most whites made no distinctions between slaves and free blacks. Her letter captures the balancing act in which Lange was engaged, as well as her determination. Her proud and independent spirit might be categorized as arrogance and her leverage on behalf of black children quickly lost if she "overplayed her hand." Perhaps surprisingly, Deluol deferred graciously to her conditions. He responded, "You write the paper which shall contain the conditions under which you will come and I shall sign it."[17]

The clouds did eventually lift from these dark days with the arrival of Father Thaddeus Anwander from Germany. Anwander volunteered to become spiritual director for the order and put his considerable energies into supporting Lange in her recruitment efforts. In 1855, the school had an enrollment of over 300 students, including boys. By this time, Mother Mary was no longer serving as mother superior of her order, having returned to directing the school itself and serving as director for the novices, the women who were embarking on the process of joining the order. She also devoted herself to expanding the Oblate order outside Baltimore. She saw to the opening of a mission in Philadelphia in 1863 and another in New Orleans in 1867. Into her mid-seventies, she was working to establish a group in Missouri.

Today the Oblate order is modest in numbers, with about 300 to 400 sisters. The mother house is still in downtown Baltimore and the sisters continue to educate children in the United States, Latin America, and Africa.[18] Lange lived to the age of ninety-eight and is today a candidate for sainthood in the Catholic Church (an honor already bestowed on Elizabeth Seton). Facing a church hierarchy that in some cases defended and even profited from slavery, she established a system dedicated to the education of all God's children, as our Constitution implies we must in our democracy. Lange's action orientation, based in virtue, inspired generations of women of all faiths to persevere in the work of building permanent, equitable educational institutions. Booker T. Washington and his philosophical opponent, W. E. B. DuBois, as well as white men such as Julius Rosenwald, are direct inheritors of her proud mission.

It is difficult to quantify the social profit generated by subsequent generations of Catholic religious. The numbers of women who followed the examples of Mother Seton and Mother Lange are extraordinary. During the period from 1830 to 1900, over 100 American religious orders were created. The number of nuns reached 50,000. In New York City alone, the number of religious increased from about eighty in 1850 to 2,850 at the turn of the century.[19] Although some of these women practiced lives of contemplation and silence, the overwhelming majority arose each day to teach children or to provide social services to fellow citizens in need, without the expectation of any financial reward.

Lange and Seton exemplified the idealism and optimism of the successful entrepreneur, and they possessed the additional skills needed to overcome the obstacles of prejudice and a lack of resources. Their work illustrates one facet of the many contributions of organized religion to the creation of the American social profit sector. Many women of all religious faiths put their faith into action throughout the history of the nation, and these actions, more often than not, produced significant social profit— better-educated citizens, dignified care for the disabled and elderly, greater amounts of support and compassion for those in need. For our purposes, it does not matter what theological doctrines inspired these women to commit acts of generosity and self-sacrifice. It is significant only to record the important influence that believers in the faiths of Abraham exerted in negotiating a productive balance between personal enterprise and "loving one's neighbor."

SIX

A Market-Based
Social Enterprise Solution[1]

A depository could hardly be called a charity,
as nothing is given for its equivalent. Alms are not offered,
or indeed even thought of . . . only work is given.
—Minutes of the Philadelphia Depository, 1840

The loss of fortunes was an all-too-common event in the free-wheeling new nation. With unlimited opportunities came high levels of risk and instability. Horace Greeley (the fellow who said "Go West, young man!") observed:

> Many who dance in jewels one year are shivering in garrets the next. It was but a week ago that a respectable woman reduced from competence to poverty by sudden calamity, traversed the street of our city for three days in search of food. . . . Such scenes are occurring daily in our city and all cities. . . .[2]

Alexis de Tocqueville noted the same problem during his 1831–1832 visit to America. "In no country in the world are private fortunes more precarious than in the United States," he wrote. Such instability took a particularly heavy toll on women and children. Even well-to-do women fell precipitously on hard times with no means to sustain themselves or their children. Once the furniture was sold (if a woman had retained any to begin with), the charity of friends and the church was all that could be hoped for.

These unfortunate reversals were frequently attributable to the volatility of commerce in the new nation. It was a world of boom and bust, in contrast to the more stable, if severe, world of subsistence farming and trapping of colonial days. The growth of commerce in America during the nineteenth century was a product of many forces: built-up demand following multiple wars in the first decades of the century, both in America and in Europe; technological innovation in the production and processing of crops, especially cotton; and improvements in the Union's infrastructure for transportation and information transmission.

In such a dynamic environment, business entrepreneurs found opportunities everywhere. But every opportunity carried plenty of risk. Newfangled ideas such as railroads and telegraphs required large capital investment and promised uncertain rewards. The emerging consumer economy needed consistent supply and demand to operate dependably, but these conditions seldom existed for any period of time. The dynamics of the cotton trade are illustrative. An end to the Napoleonic wars in Europe around 1815 spurred demand for consumer goods such as quality cotton and wool cloth. Some neat industrial espionage had enabled enterprising Americans Francis Lowell and Samuel Slater to capture the secrets of the power loom and the spinning frame from England. The expansion of the "southwest" (Alabama, Mississippi) by means of generous government land distribution programs (and the importation of thousands of enslaved people from the East Coast, often by forced march) led to greatly increased production of short-staple raw cotton. By the 1820s, Lowell, Massachusetts, had become the industrial center of the United States, employing thousands of mostly young women in its water-powered mills. But an oversupply of goods led to the Panic of 1819. Prices for cotton goods fell; banks stopped extending easy credit and called in loans. Things ground to a halt and hard times affected the well-to-do and, of course, the laborers at the end of the supply chain. Such panics and recessions occurred, it seems, every fifteen to twenty years.

Fortunately, a few social entrepreneurs proved adept at finding ways to build social capital in this difficult environment. One of the most creative approaches borrowed liberally from the emerging consumer economy. Elizabeth Stott (circa 1780–1840) convened a small group of her fellow Philadelphia society matrons in 1832. She had an idea that differed markedly from that of the Boston Fragment Society members. Rather than a straightforward charitable effort, she had in mind a market-driven solution to repair the gaps in the social fabric of her city. She wanted to enable the local female victims of "sudden calamities" to support themselves, and she had a plan to make this implausible idea a reality. On a trip to Scotland (where else?), Stott had visited a "depository." Impoverished Scottish women created handmade items that were sold to the public through a retail shop. Stott imagined applying this strategy to achieve financial independence or at least financial support for "decayed gentlewomen," as the unfortunate ladies were known.

The depository scheme combined a consignment shop with a co-operative. In a co-op, small producers band together to sell their products, rather than each attempting to sell his or her product individually. They all enjoy better marketing clout, better pricing, and better access to the marketplace. In this case, Elizabeth and her friends hoped to create a market for such hand-sewn goods by opening a shop in the fashionable part of town and stocking it on a consignment basis. Proceeds from sales would be returned to the consignors, who would be expected to join the cooperative through a small dues payment. The organizers would also become paying members (subscribers) and when necessary would make dues payments on behalf of consignors. Dues money would be deployed to purchase the raw materials necessary to confect the collars, petticoats, shirts, capes, frocks, handkerchiefs, infant blankets, aprons, caps, sheets, pillowcases, and countless other items that would make up the inventory of the shop. Best of all, the identities of the consignors would not be revealed to the public. The "gentlewomen" could preserve their dignity and avoid the social stigma of working for a living.

Philadelphia was a prosperous city in the 1830s, home to many well-to-do families. Records indicate that there were well over 200 families with assets of more than $150,000 (a number to be multiplied by thirty to forty times to approximate today's equivalent sum). It was also a charitable city, home to some thirty-three charitable organizations attracting hundreds of subscribers. Stott was very much a lady herself, although hardly in the same wealth bracket as the Biddles, Wistars, Sargeants, Girards, and Lippincotts, families whose names still grace the streets and institutions of the City of Brotherly Love. She was apparently a widow, as census records note that her household included a grown son or daughter and his or her spouse, as well as three small children (presumably her grandchildren) in 1830.

Stott convened her society friends to discuss the depository idea soon after witnessing an episode of female desperation in her own neighborhood. She recounted the story to her friends at their initial meeting. While Stott had been shopping, into the store came a woman with several handmade pieces of lace. She sought to sell the pieces to the shopkeeper for a very modest sum, in Stott's judgment, only to be rudely offered an even lower price by the shop owner. Stott was appalled by the helplessness of the woman and determined to put her Scottish experience to work to create a better marketplace. The idea was quickly embraced. The women asserted that their new work was aligned with their religious responsibilities as devout Christians:

> Believing (the Depository) to be founded on the principles in strict accordance with the Divine precepts . . . we trust the blessings of Heaven will attend future efforts and crown them with abundant success.[3]

By the following year, the Philadelphia Women's Depository had attracted 225 subscribers from among Stott's socially prominent friends. Now it was time to face the challenge of making the idea work.

The project had an inauspicious beginning. The first location chosen for the consignment shop proved a disaster, attracting little foot traffic from the high-fashion shops located several blocks away. Then there was the problem of quality control, as not all consignors proved equally adept in the execution of their needlework. Finally, another financial panic struck in 1837 and dampened the market for luxury goods for several years, while adding many decayed gentlewomen to the growing list of needy consignors.

But the women persevered and innovated. Stott and friends created an advisory board, composed primarily of their well-connected husbands. The strategy paid off, as together they identified a superior location closer to the high-end retailers in town. They solved the quality problem with an ingenious solution that avoided any awkward rejection of consigned handiworks. Would-be consignors, rather than having to pass muster with a "jury" of self-appointed experts, would instead be asked to create a "sampler" of their stitching skills. Customers could judge the quality and creativity for themselves and then order items from the (anonymous) consignor(s) of their choice. Prices of the items would reflect the quality of the consignor's work. Carefully preserved records show that in 1840 the depository handled over 2,000 such custom items, and commissions paid to consignors exceeded $5,000. By 1870, this amount would have more than doubled.[4]

On the financial front, Stott's friends served as managers of the enterprise, setting prices (in an era known for bartering), negotiating rents and payments for coal, and keeping the books. They managed their inventory through careful attention to such arbiters of contemporary fashion as *Ladies Magazine* and *Godey's Lady's Book*, despite the fact that these publications editorialized in favor of a strictly domestic role for women. They also hired additional women, often experienced consignor-members, to serve as salesclerks in the shop. When additional capital was required for expansion, Stott organized membership drives for new subscribers and put on periodic fund-raising events such as holiday fairs. Finally, and perhaps most impressively, no monies sat idly in the cash box. They invested their cash on hand with local banks and earned additional income through interest payments.

The managers had the good sense to publish meticulous annual reports, documenting all transactions and educating the public about the structure of the system they had designed. As capitalism grew, increasing numbers of women (and men) labored for wages in manufacturing settings supervised by company "managers." In such a system the workers were (and are) part of the cost of running the business, and tensions quickly arose between their interests and those of the owners or managers. The depository concept, on the other hand, aligned the interests of managers and workers through its parallel ownership design.

Stott had hit upon a brilliant strategy to tackle a problem that others had addressed strictly through charity. She demonstrated the perseverance to make it work, despite several false starts. Her careful records enabled others to learn from her experience. By the time Stott was ready to stand down as head of the Philadelphia depository, the concept had begun to spread to other nearby cities, and national leaders eventually emerged to develop the exchange idea into a national, multimillion-dollar enterprise that could compete against such major retailers as R. H. Macy, Marshall Field, and J. C. Penney. Stott's idea blossomed into the Women's Exchange movement, perhaps the most entrepreneurial of all women's enterprises in the nineteenth and twentieth centuries. By the end of the nineteenth century, Women's Exchanges had become a national movement, selling millions of dollars of goods and services through chapters in some seventy cities across America. Many of these chapters continued to operate successfully well into the 1960s.

Stott exemplifies social entrepreneurship through her vision, ambition, and strategic planning skills. Her leadership captures the can-do problem-solving spirit of our nineteenth-century sisters, who proved very adept at exploiting the tools of retail capitalism for the benefit of their less fortunate sisters. As we all know, it is tough to launch and grow a small business under the best of circumstances. To overcome the legal and social barriers, Stott exercised resourcefulness and vision. For the good of the nation in the pre–Civil War era, few ideas offered greater benefits than the depositories. Families, and particularly women and children destined for the poorhouse—a dead-end existence as wards of the local government and a burden on their fellow citizens—were reprieved. Through the intervention of Stott and her colleagues, significant numbers kept hearth and home together through personal initiative. Instead of experiencing creeping fear and anxiety, these women could retain at least a modicum of optimism and idealism. Increases in the supply of these essential attitudes among the people increased the odds of success for the new democracy.

SEVEN

The Agonizing
Issue of Slavery

*(It is argued that abolition) is a subject with which women should have
nothing to do because it has a political aspect. Its brightest and most
distinctive aspect is a moral and a benevolent one, and in this sphere
it is not denied that women may operate with propriety and efficiency.*
—Minutes of the Lynn, Massachusetts, Female Anti-Slavery Society (circa 1836)

Several major issues confronted the new nation during the
1820s and 1830s, the years that saw the passing of the generation of signers of the Declaration. The issues were difficult because they involved conflicts between personal freedoms and
social needs. They were contentious because they engaged moral
and economic questions. They brought into play the governmental, commercial, and social sectors at an early stage in the
nation's history. The issue of slavery, as we have already observed
in the lives of Katy Ferguson and Elizabeth Lange, was among
the most vexing.

The unanimous signing of the Declaration of Independence
had been achieved only through an agreement among the
Founders to rescind a prior agreement that had prevented the continuing importation of enslaved blacks from Africa by the colonies
of Georgia and South Carolina. Following the Revolution, the

various states pursued their own debates about whether and how to continue the practice of buying and selling workers and their families. This led to an astounding assortment of laws and practices governing the ownership and freedom of enslaved peoples.[1] "Abolition" in some states involved a process that went on for decades as enslaved individuals became free at certain ages. The ladies of Lynn, Massachusetts, understood very well that participants in these decisions often shifted the argument away from moral issues to economic and political considerations.[2]

Women often had difficulty making their voices heard in these convoluted political debates. They did not have a vote to cast, and they were also severely constrained by tradition. There were no established venues for them to discuss economic or political issues, as there were for men, and frankly, few women had any experience or desire for engagement with politics. They certainly had little experience in public discourse, whether at town meetings or large-scale "association conventions." However, a small number of creative, determined women gradually developed their own strategies to influence the debates, and to focus attention on the obvious conflict between the practice of enslavement and the ideals of the Declaration. In the process they developed a veritable tool kit for concerned citizens in the new democracy. As we shall see, certain women among them proved exceptionally talented in utilizing these tools to shape the "voluntary" sector of the emerging nation.

Anti-slavery societies formed in the Union before the ink was dry on the Constitution. They grew rapidly in the 1830s in particular, numbering over 1,000 by 1837. The majority had white members, some were exclusively black, and a minority included both races. Perhaps 10 percent of these groups were composed exclusively of women. Credit must certainly go, in part, to

William Lloyd Garrison, the articulate publisher of *The Liberator*, launched in Boston in 1831. His newspaper gave voice to a countermovement against the "gradualism" favored in so many states. He argued, as did Aaron Burr and others, that the practice of slaveholding should be illegal and that all enslaved peoples should be given their freedom immediately. His efforts provided citizens throughout the Union with powerful arguments and facts to support their case. The urgency of abolition was also bolstered in the 1830s by the growth of religious fervor, often referred to as the Second Great Awakening. Many evangelists preached that believers needed to prepare for the second coming, and to seek personal salvation through their own efforts. Most often this project involved a combination of Bible study and good works to benefit their neighbors. Against this background, the abolitionists' assertion that slavery was a moral issue, a crime against God's law, attracted a significant number of supporters.

Maria Weston Chapman (1806–1885), a prominent Boston matron, embraced Garrison's approach to abolition, and she added her unique entrepreneurial skills to the campaign. She orchestrated multiple media initiatives, public demonstrations, and protests; she initiated direct action on behalf of those in need, built cross-class coalitions, raised large sums of money, and developed model programs. It is not an overstatement to say that her approaches to winning the hearts and minds of her fellow citizens to the cause of abolition became a blueprint for generations of social entrepreneurs to come. Chapman invented the system to change the system.

William Lloyd Garrison had framed the abolition problem boldly:

I do not wish to think, or to speak, or write, with moderation. No! no! Tell a man whose house is on fire to give a moderate alarm; tell him to moderately rescue his wife from the hands of the ravisher; tell the mother to gradually extricate her babe from the fire into which it has fallen;—but urge me not to use moderation in a cause like the present.[3]

His great rhetorical skills drew citizens to his cause. Women could much less easily mount a soapbox and rail against the evils of slavery:

Male abolitionists faced a daunting struggle, but as libertarians the (Weston-Chapman) sisters were often discriminated against because of their sex. In the nineteenth century women had limited rights, and male chivalry alone protected them when they faced pro-slavery mobs . . . But they . . . became "the conscience" of the anti-slavery movement and especially valued as fund raisers.[4]

Maria Chapman certainly acted as the "conscience" of the anti-slavery movement in New England, but her role was hardly as passive or one-dimensional as this quotation would suggest. Chapman was born in Massachusetts, the oldest of eight siblings in the Weston family. She was educated by local tutors and in England. She spoke excellent French as well, a sign of the quality of her teaching and social education. She served briefly as principal of a girls' high school before her marriage in 1830 to Henry Chapman, a prosperous Boston merchant. Maria had children—four of them, although she lost one in infancy.

Chapman and her husband shared a commitment to abolition. This position was not popular among their peers. Most of Boston's merchant class and, sad to say, even the clergy enjoyed many economic benefits from the status quo. Maria, however, was undeterred. She was persuaded that the majority of citizens embraced the idea of justice for all in the new democracy. It was, she felt, essential to mobilize these beliefs through a campaign of education and "consciousness raising" in order to bring about an orderly end to the practice of slaveholding. So in 1833, in the midst of her childbearing years, and inspired by Garrison, she founded the Boston Female Anti-Slavery Society (BFASS) with twelve charter members.

> During the organization's [BFASS's] first year, its members attended lectures, invited clergymen to address their meetings, and sewed goods to raise money for the needy. In early 1834, several members established a primary school for Black girls, and others helped to organize the Samaritan Asylum, a home for indigent and orphaned African American children. Although the Society's first annual report states that these latter projects were undertaken by private individuals, in subsequent years the organization allocated funds for their continued maintenance.[5]

These initiatives were exemplary direct contributions to the African American community in Boston on the part of these benevolent ladies. But Chapman and her sisters were prepared to go much further. She saw the condition of blacks as a direct product of the laws permitting their enslavement. Attacking these laws would bring her into the "political" realm, and potentially put her into conflict with the standards and expectations of many of her peers. Chapman proved remarkably adept at maintaining her social influence while engaging broadly in a vigorous, if not downright unladylike, campaign to change the nation's conscience.

The goals Chapman set for herself and her society went well beyond benevolence. In fact, attendees at a society meeting in 1837 took a pledge to "commit their lives, their fortunes and their honor to the cause" of abolition, reprising verbatim the last words of the Declaration. She wanted the members to take personal responsibility for achieving the Founders' goal of justice for all. Their effort was not about Christian charity, as important as helping one's neighbor was in the new nation, but to "bake a larger pie" so that more Americans could enjoy larger slices of prosperity, as defined by the nation's Founders.

An episode in 1835 demonstrates her boundary-bending forays into the public arena. One evening, Chapman was attending an anti-slavery event featuring Garrison. Pro-slavery demonstrators threatened to burn the hall. The mayor of Boston, Theodore Lyman, arrived at the scene and calmed the torch-bearing mob by promising to break up the meeting himself. He marched into the hall and ordered the meeting ended. By some accounts Garrison was led away by the police. Chapman departed as well, singing loudly and holding hands with her contingent of black and white women friends. They made their way through the angry crowd and down the street to a nearby house, where she reconvened the meeting! As the women faced the angry crowd, she was quoted as proclaiming: "If this is the last bulwark of freedom, we may as well die here as anywhere." By 1836, Maria was frequently the object of shouted insults when she ventured out in her hometown. A short time later, in 1838, a crowd in Philadelphia did succeed in burning the meeting hall where Chapman had spoken in support of abolition.

Such early events in Chapman's career as an abolitionist, rather than a benevolent lady, introduced her to the uses of the Constitutional right to assembly, a right that could be used by enterprising women to expand their engagement in public affairs. Maria also quickly learned about the right to petition elected representatives, and found that her female colleagues were prepared to engage in the hard work of door-to-door campaigning, an

activity that even the most committed male anti-slavery advocates seemed reluctant to undertake. She wrote about the opposition faced by women activists in her book entitled *Right and
Wrong* (1839).[6] She describes the experiences of the women she
mobilized into the "public space" to collect signatures, calling
them "at once touching, ludicrous, and edifying." People expected
"graceful feebleness which the age cherished as an ornament in
the female character," not determined advocates of social change.
She recounts a dressing down from a gentleman who answered
the door:

> My dear young lady, it gives me pain to see your efforts so entirely
> wasted. You only injure the cause you espouse by thus leaving
> your sphere. You actually prevent those who are capable of un-
> derstanding this question [abolition] . . . from entering upon its
> consideration. You make the whole matter seem little, below the
> attention of men.[7]

It is not clear whether Maria viewed this vignette as touching
or ludicrous, but it undoubtedly contributed to her own reputation for impatience. Chapman was undaunted by such patronizing
reviews. Although deeply invested in the politics of the "movement," she did not lose sight of her audacious goal: an end to injustice for black Americans. She expanded her educational efforts
for the broader public and she did so in a most resourceful way.

Maria and her sisters were adept at raising money to support
the good works of the society:

> By 1838 the Westons had challenged the leadership of the Boston
> ladies. The younger ones led youth groups, the older sisters raised
> funds and Maria, who was clever with money, promoted Life

Membership (in her "society") for $5 as against 50 cents for an-
nual membership.[8]

But her masterstroke was to combine fund-raising and education in the "ladies bazaar." This event provided an entirely proper
high-society framework for her social change agenda.

Her fairs became the most profitable fund-raisers and the most
anticipated social events in the city of Boston. Maria was not shy
about announcing their purpose. They were known as the Massachusetts Anti-Slavery Society Fairs from 1834 to 1844 and as
the national bazaars of the American Anti-Slavery Society from
1845 to 1858. They occurred in December, to benefit from the
gift-giving season, and were advertised accordingly.[9] Lists of items
to be offered for sale were published to whet the socialites' ap-
petites and bring in a spending crowd. Goods were promoted as
being of the latest fashion, rare or unavailable at Boston stores.

The Westons understood the craving among the wealthy
Bostonians for sophisticated luxury goods. The British embargoes
on trade with America before and during the War of 1812 had
greatly reduced access to European goods, including many items
rarely produced in the new nation: good stationery and fancy
paper goods; statuary, paintings, and drawings; silver, crystal, and
fine china; jewelry; embroidery; woodwork; and perfume. Chapman's connections to wealthy families in England and France
enabled her to make good on her promises of exclusivity. Harriet
Beecher Stowe judged the fairs "decidedly the most fashionable
shopping resort of the holidays."

Maria's vision for the fairs extended beyond fund-raising.
She had in mind a complete social and educational experience.
She insisted that fair organizers attend carefully to matters of
style and presentation: The hall was always elaborately deco-

rated; refreshments were offered; and the volunteer saleswomen took pains with their dress and deportment. When attendance flagged one year, Chapman came up with a fresh idea. The fair would include a brand-new idea that was all the rage in England, thanks to Queen Victoria and Prince Albert—a Christmas tree. She would take personal responsibility for decorating a large evergreen tree brought indoors, the unveiling of which would be the highlight of the fair. She and her cohorts designed and produced ornaments to cover the huge tree: tiny colored-paper purses, decorated boxes and candleholders, miniature stuffed animals and dolls. The tree was written up in all the magazines of the time.[10]

All the spectacle and entertainment framed the "teaching moment" that Chapman intended. She launched local sewing circles to make items to sell at the fair. She included women from a wide range of social and economic classes. Maria's circles created anti-slavery propaganda by stitching clever sayings on household articles. They labeled writing quills as "Weapons for Abolitionists"; inscribed pen wipers with "Wipe out the blot of Slavery"; stitched on the covers of books of sewing needles, "May the use of our needles prick the consciences of slaveholders"; embroidered on watch cases, "The political economist counts time by years, the suffering slave reckons it by minutes."[11] Potholders were dubbed "anti-slave-holders." Chapman believed mottoes "played an effective role in moral suasion by bring[ing] Truth and Falsehood in continual juxtaposition."[12] In her mind they were an important tool in her mass-marketing campaign on behalf of social justice.

While they sewed, one of the women would read from anti-slavery tracts or stories of slaves' lives. Gradually, they were being "abolitionized," as one of them put it. By 1845, fair advertising invited the ladies in the sewing circles to develop anti-slavery petitions for delivery to lawmakers, and to use the fair to solicit signatures. They were ready and willing. Chapman's social friends who served as sales staff for the fairs also grew familiar with the products of the sewing circles, products that were none too subtle in their "messaging."

Chapman and her colleagues wisely emphasized the domestic nature of the fairs. They all dressed up to sell the wares from beautifully decorated tables and supervised their daughters as salesclerks as well. The sweetly domestic aura helped to dispel the ferocity of the organizers' commitment to the real aim of the event. The women willingly maintained the lighthearted, benign, and even frivolous profile of women's work so they could raise as much capital as possible without raising too many eyebrows. BFASS's sales were extraordinarily profitable and earned tens of thousands of dollars for reform treasuries over the next two decades.[13]

Maria downplayed the financial aspects of her efforts, preferring to focus on the virtuousness of the cause and of the women who pursued it with her:

> It is the moral power, springing from the exertion to raise it [the money]; this increase of light, and energy, and skill, and perseverance, and Christian fellowship, and devotedness to our holy enterprise,—and spiritual strength and comfort,—that we value far more than the largest sum.[14]

She was correct that her fairs had become much more than a highly effective, socially acceptable way to raise money for the cause. They enabled women to develop. Women learned to build and lead organizations and to exercise competence beyond the confines of their domestic lives. The model of Chapman's fairs spread throughout the states. Women's groups duplicated them to fund-raise for abolition and for many other community needs.

They are, of course, still a great part of fund-raising all over America today.[15]

With her successes, inevitably, came conflict in Maria's life, and, let's be honest, there is evidence that she was not always the easiest person to get along with. For instance, some of her critics carped that "social and economic considerations clashed with the primary purpose of the fair, to be a 'light unto the world' doing 'a good work among the people.'" Others complained that the advertising for the fair had gotten so expensive that it would be preferable to just drop the whole thing.[16]

Chapman did indeed display a remarkably modern understanding of the importance of publicity and the media. At a time when information transfer gradually began to accelerate through the publication and distribution of newspapers and magazines, she recognized and exploited the "power of print." In addition to the fairs and such society-page fare as the Christmas tree, she produced an annual volume called the *Liberty Bell*, a coffee-table book of anti-slavery literature: poetry, essays, short biographies, and short stories by the A-list authors of the day: Elizabeth Barrett Browning, James Russell Lowell, Henry Wadsworth Longfellow, and even President John Quincy Adams. It was illustrated with etchings and lithographs by fashionable artists. Chapman even recruited liberal French intellectuals to offer short reflections on the evils of slavery. This miscellany proved highly popular among the East Coast reading public and a useful fund-raising tool as well.

Chapman's whirlwind of activities in the social and political spaces marks her as a true pioneer in social enterprise. She exerted forceful personal leadership in pursuing her avowed goal. She was accused of lacking patience on occasion, and, more than once, of micromanaging her enterprises. Her commitment to her goals undoubtedly wore out even her most committed colleagues, and she could be a bit patronizing, too. In a seemingly unguarded moment, Maria recorded this thought on the value of her *Liberty Bell* publication as an anti-slavery tool:

> "The American public," she wrote, "must be treated like children, to whom a medicine is made as pleasant as it[s] nature admits. A childish mind desires a small measure of truth in gilt edges, when it would reject it in whitty-brown."[17]

Maria's impatience and candor about the nature of her challenge anticipates many driven entrepreneurs who are accused of a "my way or the highway" management style. Those convinced of the justice of their cause have always been known for their audacity, rarely for their patience.

But Maria Chapman's achievements were remarkable for any age, and utterly unprecedented for a woman in the 1830s. She went to great pains to involve a wide swath of citizenry, here and abroad. She balanced her outspoken advocacy with the need to remain within her social framework and to attract others to the big idea. Threading carefully through the constraints of her time, she kept her society's meetings open to local clergy and made sure she and her compatriots met traditional expectations that they do good works. She carried out her commitment to justice while preserving her status as a "woman of standing." It was an extraordinarily deft balancing act.

Along with raising her children and leading her society, Maria eventually took on the editing of Garrison's *Liberator*. Chapman and her sisters remained steadfast and "headed a small but influential clique pledged to raise funds for Garrison."[18] This work clearly provided a convenient way for her to submerge her own uncompromising commitments behind Garrison's male persona of impatience and immoderate behavior in the cause of justice.

When her husband became ill, Maria stepped back from her social enterprise work and tended him. After his death in 1842, she decided to take her children to Paris for their schooling. Her fairs continued through the society. When she returned to the United States in 1855, she was energized with new ideas for capitalizing the abolition campaign. Paris had inspired her to organize evening galas called the Anti-Slavery Subscription Anniversaries. These formal-dress events provided luxurious dining and entertainment, with places reserved for those who made the largest donations to support the campaign.

There is no way to quantify with precision the total number of dollars Chapman raised, nor the number of activists who deployed her fund-raising strategies for the cause of abolition. Nor can we count the hearts and minds that were transformed by her educational campaigns.[19] But we do know that Chapman lived to see the drafting and enforcement of the Emancipation Proclamation and the reunification of the nation following the Civil War.

Unsurprisingly, Chapman did not simply retire to enjoy the fruits of her labors. She moved to New York City and went to work in her son's brokerage business. As she reached the age of eighty, she developed an interest in a fellow influential contemporary, Harriet Martineau, a founder of the discipline of sociology. Maria took it upon herself to contribute to the latter's biography, researching texts from prominent contemporaries who had written about Martineau's contributions to the emerging field of social science. Chapman rightly foresaw that the scientific study of social problems would become a powerful tool for future social entrepreneurs.

Chapman's methods were as significant as her achievements. Not only did she develop a vision of how American society could better reflect the spirit of "liberty and justice for all," she also focused on what would be required to bring about changes. She was fully prepared to engage the more difficult and less dramatic work of figuring out *how* to create social value. On her own terms and driven by her audacious goal, she developed and implemented a remarkable array of strategies that remain essential to success in the social profit sector even today.

EIGHT

Individualism and Social Profit in the Post–Civil War Era

During the war, and as a result of my own observations, I became aware that a large portion of the nation's work was badly done, or not done at all, because woman was not recognized as a factor in the political world.
—Mary Livermore, *Memoirs*, 1897

The Civil War constituted a milestone in the development of the Union and the social profit sector. The majority of citizens rejected the compromises around slavery agreed to by the Founders during the writing of the Declaration of Independence. An armed conflict and the deaths of tens of thousands of citizens were required to establish the power of the federal government to outlaw this terrible practice throughout the nation. The many thousands of citizens who, like Maria Chapman, had taken responsibility for bringing an end to slavery saw their efforts rewarded.

The Civil War did much more than resolve the issue of slavery. It added momentum to the continuing expansion of the Union, and like many wars, ushered in new technologies and infrastructure that spurred economic growth in peacetime. Perhaps nothing added more to the expansive optimism of the postwar era than the emerging transportation infrastructure—the systems of canals, roads, and railroads. It enabled a half million settlers to establish farms on more than 80 million acres during the period, aided by over 30,000 miles of railroad track and countless miles of canals and "turnpikes."

While the westward expansion of the country accelerated, so too did the growth of urban areas, especially in the eastern one-third of the nation. The influx of immigrants from Europe and the Caribbean during the 1840s and 1850s had been steady, but the pace picked up after the war from countries such as Ireland, Italy, Poland, and Holland. Some settlers moved on from the East directly to the Midwest, but the majority remained in East Coast cities, where they sought access to an increasing number of manufacturing jobs created by the Industrial Revolution. Other contributors to urban growth included the many free blacks who moved north in search of manufacturing jobs in industries such as steel, agricultural processing, and mining. The net result was an ample and rapidly expanding labor pool on which the business entrepreneurs of the period could draw to expand their enterprises. The Industrial Revolution was not, however, the only "revolution" under way in post–Civil War America.

The nation was also enhanced by a gradual but meaningful increase in access to formal education for citizens and particularly for women. Although Mount Holyoke had been established by Mary Lyon in 1837, it did not become a "college" in the sense we use the term today until the 1880s. Vassar, Smith, and Wellesley were all created by private philanthropy in the 1860s and 1870s, enabling women to study the liberal arts (as did the men of Harvard and Yale). The federal Morrill Act of 1862 created the "land-grant" colleges (Michigan, Cornell, Ohio State, Iowa, and others), which were open to women from their inception. By 1880, women constituted one-third of all college enrollees,

or roughly 40,000 participants. The generosity of private philanthropists created opportunities for women, particularly black
women, in the South as well (Bennett College, Atlanta Baptist
Female Seminary, which became Spellman College).[1]

Access to professional education for women remained limited
and varied widely state by state, but a few persevering souls
squeezed through the barriers. The University of Michigan graduated a female lawyer in 1871 and a female physician the same
year. By 1897, there were some 250 female attorneys in the nation, enough to form a mutual support organization. The prob-
lematic issue of women studying human anatomy in the presence
of men was partially resolved with the creation of women's medical colleges, such as the Women's Medical College of Philadelphia. There were 115 female members of state medical societies
in 1881. But separate was not always equal, of course.

Graduate educational opportunities for women expanded with
the founding of the University of Chicago in 1889 as a graduate
institution, in contrast with Harvard, Princeton, and Yale where
undergraduate men were the primary focus of faculty attention.
Women were admitted to Chicago's graduate programs from the
institution's beginnings, and a number of very talented women
took advantage of access to programs in political economy and
the new field of sociology.

An additional change occurred in the post–Civil War era that
was to have important consequences for the nation's social profit
sector. Women gradually gained the right to inherit and to control funds in their own names.[2] This was a lengthy process with
wide variations once again from state to state, as the federal government did not engage in these matters directly. Mississippi
passed a female inheritance law as early as 1839, ironically supported by well-to-do legislators in an effort to prevent ne'er-do-
well sons-in-law from squandering family assets, such as slaves,

after marriage to their daughters. New York passed an inheritance law in 1848 and extended it to include joint custody of children in 1860.[3] With the increased control of financial assets came increased opportunities for influence and leverage on social policy issues. Wealth opened new entrepreneurial opportunities and a new degree of independence for a small number of fortunate women. Now they did not automatically need to build a coalition of their peers to make a difference. They could act as "individualists," for the first time, thinking big and, in a few cases, financing their own agendas.[4]

Finally, the landscape of charitable activities evolved over the decades following the Civil War. The scope and diversity of social problems required larger coordinated efforts, particularly in urban areas. Small social profit societies began to reach out to one another in efforts to act more efficiently on behalf of those they sought to serve. The first American Charity Organizations Society (COS) was formed in Buffalo, New York, in the late 1870s and similar coordinating bodies emerged in most large cities.[5] Citizen groups also coordinated their activities with municipal, county, and state government efforts to provide services for the poor, the insane, the incarcerated, and the elderly. Citizen groups provided fundraising support, as well as "visitors" to inspect government facilities (seldom an edifying experience). Social entrepreneurs also took advantage of the nation's enhanced communications and travel infrastructure to locate like-minded individuals and efforts in other parts of the country. National social profit organizations, such as the Young Women's Christian Association (YWCA) and the Woman's Christian Temperance Union (WCTU), were built by these ambitious leaders, using a headquarters and local affiliate model to manage the organizations' work efficiently.

The always powerful influence of organized religion(s) also played across these efforts. Some providers urged support to only the "worthy poor," those felled by fate or circumstance beyond their control. They argued against any assistance to the "unworthy" poor, who brought misfortune on themselves through indulgence in alcohol, gambling, or just plain laziness. Such debates, often characterized as pitting "Social Darwinists" (who saw poverty as a sign of moral weakness) against the Social Gospelers (who believed that environmental factors, rather than moral weakness, were more frequently the cause of poverty), gained in intensity throughout the 1870s and 1880s. During the Third Great Awakening, many evangelizers toured the country offering varied readings on the Christian scriptures, and issues of salvation through good works or predestination were front of mind for many concerned citizens.

This complex mix of urbanization, education, diversification, immigration, industrialization, wealth accumulation, and religious revivalism presented plenty of challenges both to elected representatives of the people and to the people themselves. The federal government, for instance, had demonstrated a willingness to wage war over the "immorality" of slavery and its incompatibility with democracy. Did this imply that the government would now take a more active role in other conditions or circumstances that a majority of voters deemed to be incompatible with democracy as well, such as child labor or family violence? The federal government did undertake an ambitious "welfare" program for the first time in the nation's history, providing pensions to veterans of the Union Army. But with no real bureaucracy to administer a multitude of claims, and politicians eager to reward loyal supporters back home, the program soon got out of hand financially.

A new generation of women volunteers, among them the beneficiaries of college education, perceived many social needs amid the multiple changes in postwar America. There were still children to be educated in the virtues of self-discipline, enterprise, and honesty that democracy required. In fact, there were more of them than ever, and many did not enjoy the security and stability of well-run homes. The parents of these children, whether immigrants or the formerly enslaved, also lacked job skills necessary to provide for themselves and their families. Even those lucky enough to find employment entered a world of mass production and hourly wages that few understood. The new generations of social entrepreneurs took it upon themselves to organize their fellow citizens to address the prejudice, ignorance, and fear that worked against the ideals of the Declaration. These women were themselves highly diverse, but they were united in combating those antidemocratic forces by instilling the ideals of virtue and enterprise on which the nation had been founded.

These women shared the conviction that their greatest weapon was knowledge, backed by the power of publicity. They devised strategies designed to "out" the misguided thinking and values that shaped what passed for acceptable behavior. They reminded elected officials and their fellow citizens that all citizens must practice "self-interest, rightly understood" if democracy was to flourish. Women publicized problems that many preferred to ignore or indeed to pretend did not exist at all—poor sanitation, unsafe milk supplies, the lack of recreational facilities, workplace injuries, and many additional sources of human suffering. By drawing attention to the negative consequences of current practices for certain citizens, the women stirred the pot, discomfited the powers that be, and sought resolution of issues that prevented the protections of the Constitution from being enjoyed by all in a rapidly diversifying population.

Miriam Leslie and Mary Livermore were contemporaries, and despite their differences in upbringing, temperament, and comportment, they both recognized the importance of women's voices in defining a new balance among the government, the business sector, and the social profit sector during this period. Neither was radical in her personal beliefs or aspirations, although it seems likely that both respected those among their sisters who became committed to radical reform of the social contract. Both invested in expanding the sphere in which women could influence the business of the nation, because they were confident that the judgment of women was essential to the nation's prosperity. Together they provide an excellent introduction to the postwar chapter in the story of the nation's social profit sector, because their stories interconnect in surprising ways during the tumultuous years between the end of the Civil War in 1865 and the passage of the Nineteenth Amendment guaranteeing women the right to vote in 1920.

Mary Ashton Rice Livermore (1820–1905)[6] wrote the provocative quotation at the beginning of this chapter, and she spent her life doing something about this state of affairs. She does not fit easily under a label as a "suffragist" or a "temperance reformer" or an "abolitionist." She saw the lack of voting rights for women, the abuse of alcohol, and the toleration of slavery as manifestations of the same flaw in America's social system. Women were simply not full partners in the leadership of the nation. But it is important not to confuse Livermore's work with a 1960s sense of "women's liberation." Although she undoubtedly hoped many women would find engagement in the problems of the nation to be personally fulfilling, her focus was consistently on the good of the nation. She demonstrated in endlessly creative ways her belief that all citizens would profit from a reform of the tacit system that held women on the periphery of power, by limiting their access to education, to the vote, and to the means to defend themselves.

She did more than point out the problem. She leveraged the lessons she learned as a volunteer government adviser during the Civil War into a compelling case for investment in the education and enfranchisement of women. And she cultivated the tools to lead such a campaign. Livermore became a skilled organizer, debater, fund-raiser, and legal thinker. Best of all, she had a gift for communication, in the written word and particularly in public speaking. Although the public "platform" was a space almost entirely controlled by the politicians, evangelists, and salesmen of her day, she managed to earn the contemporary, and un-ironic, epithet: "queen of the American platform."[7]

Mary Rice, born and educated in Boston in a strict Calvinist-Baptist family, spent her early childhood, as she recounts in her biography, pretending to be a preacher. She used the kitchen table as her pulpit, and if no live audience could be found, she would "go alone to the wood shed, arrange the un-split logs in rows as pews, and the split sticks as an audience occupying them, and then mount a box . . . and preach, pray and sing by the hour."[8] As she grew up she turned away from the "hellfire and damnation" spirit of her upbringing, but her skills as an orator continued to blossom.

After her brief formal education (Rice was born a bit too early to take advantage of the expanded opportunities for women noted above), Rice became a tutor for a wealthy Virginia family, and her "education" expanded considerably. She lived on the plantation for three years, listening to lively political discussions about the growing rift between the North and the South, and witnessing firsthand the lives of the enslaved workers.[9] She returned to Boston and met her husband-to-be, Daniel Livermore, while attending the Universalist Church where he was preaching. Universalism, with its doctrine that salvation was available to all believers through good behavior and good works, would have contrasted sharply with Mary's Calvinist upbringing, a point she dramatized to good effect in her writing. The couple shared a deep aversion to slavery and a lively interest in speaking and writing. They married in 1845, and Mary took up life as a minister's wife, giving birth to three daughters while her husband led congregations in Massachusetts and Connecticut. Daniel was frequently in trouble with his congregations for his outspoken views on abolition and the evils of drink, and Mary found that she was often obliged to keep her own thoughts to herself in order to not make matters worse. She contented herself with minding her family while writing stories about the joys of Universalism as well as the evils of drink and slavery.[10]

Eventually the Livermores made a bold decision. They would relocate to Chicago. With their two surviving daughters, they headed to the "Northwest Territory" in 1857. They purchased a Universalist publication entitled *The New Covenant*, and Mary threw herself into writing and editing while Daniel continued his preaching and organizing on behalf of the Universalist Church. She also campaigned actively for Abraham Lincoln, the Illinois native son, in the presidential election of 1860.

The outbreak of the Civil War provided Livermore with a public platform on which to expand her reformist energies. With Daniel's encouragement, Mary accepted the request of Henry Bellows, head of the U.S. Sanitary Commission, to head up the northwest chapter of the commission.[11] The commission, organized in New York City, was composed of citizens concerned about the health and welfare of Union soldiers. Among its prominent organizers was Louisa Schuyler, who was a worshipper at the Unitarian Church of All Souls, where Bellows served as minister his entire life. Schuyler herself was a New York society lady, descendant of a Revolutionary War general and of Alexander Hamilton. She and her sister led active civic lives, founding the

New York State Charities Aid Association that enlisted women volunteers to report on conditions in state-funded "hospitals" and poorhouses.[12]

Although many national leaders (particularly military officers, health authorities, and elected officials) were opposed to interference in the war effort by civilians, Lincoln chartered the group in 1861. The distinguished (male) national commissioners were to (1) inquire into the recruiting process in the various states, (2) inquire into the diet, clothing, cooking, and accommodations—in fact, everything connected with the prevention of disease among the soldiers, and (3) discover methods by which private and unofficial interest and money might supplement the appropriations of the government. Meanwhile, the Women's Central Association of Relief, led by Schuyler, became a component of the commission and sought to incorporate the aid efforts of thousands of local women's groups across the North into a coherent contribution to the war effort.

The work of the national commission consisted of a series of encampment inspections by (male) medical experts, who found no shortage of problems, such as poor drainage, a lack of supplies, unsanitary food storage, and the like. These visits led to the preparation of eighteen "field manuals" for use by senior military officers with guidelines for establishing and maintaining disease-free (or at least healthier) bases and camps. Many of the issues raised in these inspections concerned a role for women. In particular, the commission endorsed the potential of women to contribute as nurses to the medical care of the wounded, as Florence Nightingale had recently done in the Crimea, although little formal training was actually available to women to play such a role.[13]

The challenge of how to organize citizen efforts in support of the war effort was dealt with using a time-tested bureaucratic technique: the creation of committees. In one sense, this was probably a good strategy, as citizen generosity usually came in the form of quilts, blankets, pincushions, butter, eggs, sauerkraut, cider, chickens, and the like (to quote from an early report), donated by local communities in support of local sons "off at war." It made sense to have the regional chapters of the commission (called branches) manage the efforts; the work was to be guided by women referred to as "branch ladies." Branches could also contend with another common issue of the war—women seeking information about the status of their husbands or relatives who had gone missing in battle.

Livermore seized the challenge of bringing order to this well-intentioned, if chaotic, bounty in her region. She demonstrated to the local Western Region citizenry that their boxes earmarked for local soldiers often sat idle for weeks in warehouses because the location of the intended recipient could not be determined. Would it not be preferable to let the logistics authorities send these valuable supplies where they were needed most? In fact, the Chicago chapter was credited with averting an impending outbreak of scurvy by channeling a large shipment of fresh fruit and vegetables to Vicksburg, Mississippi. Livermore's strategy soon became the national model.

The national commissioners also knew enough to leave the fund-raising to the female-led local chapters. Livermore proved an outstanding choice for this task as well. She had a keen sense of money as a result of her publishing experience running *The New Covenant* with Daniel. She organized a series of Chicago "Sanitary Fairs" on the model of Maria Chapman's Abolition Bazaars. She solicited donations of china, silver, and crystal, as well as food and farm equipment. The Chicago Sanitary Fair attracted thousands who bought the items to show their support for the Union. A grateful Abraham Lincoln responded as well.

He donated a copy of his Emancipation Proclamation, which raised $10,000 by itself. Livermore and her allies raised more than $100,000—a stunning sum at the time.

Livermore also traveled to visit soldiers returning from the battlefield, often sitting with dying soldiers and taking dictation as they communicated their final thoughts to their families. She led the creation of the first permanent veterans' hospital in Cairo, Illinois, on the banks of the Mississippi River. This facility became the largest of its kind, serving as an orientation center for new recruits, a critical care hospital for those injured on the battlefront, and a mustering out support facility for those whose service was ending.

Mary's common sense, whether applied to the logistics of food distribution or to the multiple functions of the Cairo hospital, created improvements that saved lives and reduced suffering. She saw the additional value in her leadership as women replicated her fund-raising fairs and food drives in other cities. Finally, she had noted the sad destruction caused by the use of whiskey as the drug of choice for the wounded (actually it was the only drug and by far the largest cost item in the medical budget of the Union war effort). When she completed her commission service in 1867, Livermore was convinced that the nation needed more leadership from women in a range of national political issues. Her entrepreneurial challenge had come into focus.

Livermore organized the first postwar suffrage convention in Illinois in 1869. She wanted a vigorous and open debate on this emerging issue of women's right to the vote[14] and invited speakers both for and against the idea, including the well-known suffragists Susan B. Anthony and Elizabeth Cady Stanton. The delegates embraced Livermore's perspective, resolving in their deliberations that female suffrage was essential to women's full independence and to the improvement of society. They launched the Illinois Woman Suffrage Society and elected Livermore president. The new society sought to advance the rights of women in divorce–child custody cases, to seek equal opportunities for married women in education and property rights settlements, and to pursue the right of women to sign contracts as individuals. But their major goal was to lobby the Illinois Constitutional Convention scheduled for 1870 to draft a state constitution that included the vote for all adults in Illinois, blacks as well as women.

Amazingly, the Illinois legislature did approve property rights enhancements for married women in 1869, but the courts were still not ready to embrace such a progressive view. As happened in most courts in early protection cases, the law was soon overturned by the Illinois Supreme Court. The campaign for a universal suffrage plank in the Illinois constitution ended in failure as well. During the ensuing twenty years before the next constitutional convention could be held, women did make considerable legal progress on issues such as inheritance, contracts, and child custody. The suffrage struggle continued actively as well over the next two decades, and in 1913, Illinois became the first state east of the Mississippi River to grant women the right to vote in presidential elections.

The Livermores, meanwhile, returned from Chicago to New England in 1870, so that Mary could pursue her editorial work. She accepted an offer to become the editor of *Woman's Journal*, published in Boston by Lucy Stone and her husband. The new publication was a weekly newspaper that incorporated *The Agitator*, the magazine Mary had launched following the Illinois suffrage meeting, and a lesser-known periodical called the *Woman's Advocate*. She was supported by an illustrious team of associate editors, including Lucy Stone, William Lloyd Garrison (of abolition fame), and Julia Ward Howe, remembered today as the author of the "Battle Hymn of the Republic." *Woman's Journal* covered the progressive issues of the day with tenacity but reserve, reflecting the personality of its editor. Mary editorialized about the importance of women's access to education, criticizing Harvard for its continuing refusal to admit women to degree programs while citing the University of Michigan approvingly for graduating both a female physician and a female lawyer in the year 1871. (Her own gifted eldest daughter would soon be rejected by Amherst College because of her gender, just as her mother had been rejected by Harvard.) She chronicled the continuing court setbacks and was particularly upset when Julia Howe was appointed a justice of the peace by the governor of Massachusetts, only to have the appointment overturned by the Massachusetts Supreme Court on the basis of Howe's gender.

Livermore also editorialized in favor of fairer treatment and for equal pay for women, filling her editorials with data documenting the numbers of underemployed women and wage inequalities. She noted, for instance, that there were some 35,000 women and girls employed in the "needle trade" in New York City alone, paid 6 cents per shirt that they completed. In this empirical approach to making her case, she foreshadowed the era of "scientific philanthropy." Finally and perhaps inevitably, Mary took up the cause of women's need for protection, often in the framework of their own homes. Marriage, she wrote in 1871, could be a "penal institution" for women, offering virtually no rights to independent actions and no protections from violence or abuse under the law. The number one culprit in the postwar explosion of such cases was undoubtedly "demon drink," and it did not take long for Mary to develop a connection to the Massachusetts temperance movement and to Frances Willard, the brilliant leader of both temperance and suffrage work, who would become a close friend and coauthor of a well-received "encyclo-pedia" of accomplished women.

Livermore, the committed Universalist, also wrote admiringly of the work of Catholic women, especially the religious orders that had, in her judgment, led the way for women in commit-ment to social action on behalf of those in need. In short, *Woman's Journal* offers a primer on many of the issues that would preoccupy female social entrepreneurs from the 1870s until World War I.[15]

Happily, Mary's own marriage was not a penal institution. She had followed Dan in his ministerial work for decades and devoted countless hours as a younger woman to raising their two daugh-ters, including the youngest, Lizzie, who it seems was mentally handicapped. But as her visibility and influence grew, the man she referred to as her best friend stepped up to provide the support she would need to become a national figure. An agent proposed a speaking tour to promote her views. Daniel was all for it. Mary describes the pep talk he gave her:

> "It is preposterous," Daniel said, "for you to continue baking and brewing, making and mending, sweeping, dusting, and laundering, when work of a better and higher order seeks you. By entering upon it, you can advance your views, make converts to the reforms with which you are identified, and make openings for two or three women who can do this housework as well as you. You need not forsake your home, nor your family; only take occasional absences from them, returning fresher and more interesting because of your varied experiences."[16]

Here was the Founders' ideal in practice—a marriage that mod-eled the kind of selflessness they hoped would characterize the (male) citizens of the Republic. Mary was able to put into practice those skills she had honed speaking to the audience of wooden sticks as a child. For some twenty-five years, she spoke "from Maine to Santa Barbara." Her topics ranged from the joys of equality in marriage to the terrible social cost of liquor to the need for better public health measures. Her most popular topic, however, was entitled "What Shall We Do with Our Daughters?" in which she exhorted her audiences to prepare their daughters for a greater place in the affairs of the world. She gave this speech, by her own count, over 800 times,[17] always with passion:

> Is it not pitiful that we rear young girls as if they were "human lobsters" which, when stranded on the rocks or the shore, must wait for some friendly wave to float them again?

Livermore also maintained a vigorous writing schedule, producing a moving account of her experience with the Sanitary Commission during the Civil War entitled *My Story of the War* (1888)[18] and *A Woman of the Century* (1893), the series of portraits of women reformers cowritten with Frances Willard. Livermore retired from the podium in 1895 and published her memoirs, *The Story of My Life*, in 1897.

Livermore died in 1905, some fifteen years before the passage of the Nineteenth Amendment to the Constitution. The *Journal* that she moved east to edit became, for forty years, an important asset in the final push for American women's right to vote. Livermore never perceived a conflict between a woman's right to vote and her domestic responsibilities. As in her marriage, she was a "both-and" rather than an "either-or" thinker. This view enabled her to maintain a wide audience for her progressive thoughts and to remain a devoted advocate of her husband in all her public activities. At the end of her autobiography, she paid her husband a warm tribute:

> We have been housekeepers over fifty years . . . I have been sure
> not only of sympathy and appreciation from my husband, but of
> active, wise, hearty cooperation.

Miriam Leslie, on the other hand, died alone, a wealthy woman, thanks to her remarkable business acumen, and left her entire fortune to the National American Woman Suffrage Association (NAWSA). Livermore is linked forever to Miriam Leslie through the *Woman's Journal*, as a portion of her $2 million bequest was used by NAWSA to purchase the magazine. The *Journal* would serve as the primary educational vehicle for the suffrage movement during the hectic years of 1915–1920, when the final push led to the enactment of the Nineteenth Amendment in 1920.

As a major philanthropist of independent means, Miriam Leslie (1836–1914) was a newly influential kind of woman committed to the greater good. She controlled assets that could make a substantial difference in the future of the nation, and she was prepared to exercise her own, very independent judgment in where these funds should be invested.

Miriam Leslie attended Abraham Lincoln's inaugural ball in 1860, as did Mary Livermore, and she also provided succor to more than a few men in need, although most were not Civil War victims. Like Livermore, she worked in publishing, and she, too, would pass away just before the passage of the Nineteenth Amendment. More important, both women exerted significant influence in the public arena as the nation moved beyond the issue of slavery and struggled to incorporate a new generation of articulate and independent (female) voices in the democratic discussion.

Miriam Leslie engaged in journalism, politics, theater, social policy, the arts, high society, and business. She offered the nation a particular mixture of self-promotion, scandal, business acumen, extravagant beauty, and social conscience. Leslie was simply one of a kind, a nineteenth-century version of Madonna, Arianna Huffington, and Carla Bruni-Sarkozy all rolled into one.

Born Miriam Folline in New Orleans in 1836, she was raised by her father, a cultivated but mostly unsuccessful businessman. Her mother's identity is a subject of dispute. Her father quickly recognized the special asset that was his beautiful, talented daughter, and he made a point of ensuring that she was well-spoken and fluent in several languages (he himself was of French origin). He eventually moved the family to New York City to increase the opportunities for his daughter to meet wealthy suitors. This proved a high-risk strategy, as seventeen-year-old Miriam quickly found the value her outstanding beauty could command without any paternal assistance, exchanging her personal favors for diamonds from an older jewelry dealer. This episode led to her first marriage and its annulment two years later.

Miriam's half brother indirectly provided the next chapter in her education. He had apparently fallen in love with the actress Lola Montez, and when his advances were rejected, he committed suicide.[19] Montez arrived in New York to express her sympathies to his family and offered to take young Miriam "on the road" to advance her acting and singing career. The Montez sisters did indeed hit the road, with Miriam's remarkable beauty helping to attract enthusiastic audiences throughout the East. Eventually, Miriam snared her wealthy beau, marrying Ephram G. Squier, an archeologist by training who happened to own a railroad. This union lasted for sixteen years.

She took up the life of a wealthy lady, translating poetry, traveling, and, according to many accounts, dazzling those in attendance at Lincoln's inaugural ball with her beauty and her diamond accessories. Among those dazzled was Frank Leslie, a transplanted Englishman who had escaped the family printing business in the old country and built a successful illustrated-newspaper empire in America. Squier eventually lost his railroad fortune, but then landed a job as an editor with one of Leslie's newspapers. E. G.'s talented and loquacious wife landed on her feet as well, becoming a writer and eventually editor of one of Leslie's publications, *Ladies Monthly*. When Leslie left his wife and children, Squier offered him a room in their flat and, perhaps inevitably, a scandalous "ménage à trois" ensued.

Frank Leslie's publishing success was based on his method of creating illustrations for his news stories. By deploying teams of artists to work simultaneously on the same engraving plates, he offered his readers immediate illustrations of the "news of the day." The Civil War constituted a journalistic bonanza as the Northern public demonstrated an insatiable appetite for battle scenes, death, and destruction. His *Illustrated Weekly* paper reached circulation above 200,000 in the early 1860s.

The happy trio spent a decade living, working, and traveling the world together with few signs of stress. Eventually, however, Leslie obtained a divorce from his wife; two illustrators from Leslie's shop happened to document E. G.'s dalliance with a girl named Gypsy at a party Miriam had organized, and soon, Frank and Miriam became husband and wife. E. G. met a sad end in the poorhouse, although history does not record whether it was poverty, drink, or disease that drove him there. The year was 1874.

The five years that Frank and Miriam shared before Frank's death in 1880 were happy and productive. They made a highly publicized trip to California and back on the new transcontinental railroad, accompanied by a team of illustrators from the publishing empire. Miriam chronicled their trip in a series of articles that offer detailed profiles of life in Omaha, Nebraska (depressing, unfashionable), San Francisco (beautiful, developed, but still "ruled by the gun"), and Virginia City, Nevada (when the train stops, stay in your car!), among many others.[20] Her readers were captivated by an exclusive face-to-face interview with Brigham Young, leader of the Mormons. She noted that Mormon women were "fashion challenged" but admired them for obtaining an equal voice with men in matters of schooling and other community affairs. Her focus in the interview, however, was the complexity of polygamy. "Don't your wives quarrel?" she asked. "Don't they use every effort of mind, body and soul to attract your love?" Young responded that polygamy required a certain kind of woman and concluded candidly, "Fortunately, there are not many of [your] mind among us."[21]

The Leslies built an impressive compound in Saratoga Springs, New York, home to popular hot springs and casinos as well as a new thoroughbred racetrack. They hosted the movers and shakers of their era in great luxury. Miriam expanded her writings to include advice to the lovelorn and Frank added to his empire of publications. Miriam had her own ideas about the business. "I dreaded breakfast each morning for fear Frank would lay out a plan to launch yet another magazine. He would rather have twenty magazines each with a circulation of one thousand than one magazine with a circulation of 20,000." Sure enough, when Frank died of cancer, his businesses were deeply in debt. He left everything to Miriam, including a large-scale financial mess. To add to an already difficult situation, the good folks of Virginia City, Nevada, had apparently taken exception to her candid assessment of their city in her travelogue article. The local newspaper deployed a set of investigative reporters and assembled a document entitled "A Life Drama of Crime and Licentiousness," which detailed Miriam's numerous breaches of propriety over the years. As Lynne Cheney notes, "It was clear that Squier had breached the clouds of his madness long enough to tell a few tales on his ex-wife."

Undeterred, that ex-wife rolled up her fashionable sleeves and went to work to save the business. She changed her name to Frank Leslie so there would be no confusion about who owned the publications. She borrowed money, fought the inevitable litigation from Frank's children, and resuscitated *Frank Leslie's Illustrated Newspaper*. In September 1881, an unsuccessful office seeker shot President William Garfield in a Washington, D.C., railroad station. Frank saw her chance to settle her debts and reclaim her wealth. The illustrated accounts of the death, postmortem, and embalming of the president's body thrilled the reading public. By shipping papers to Cleveland, where the funeral occurred, she pushed her sales from 30,000 to 200,000.[22] Her newly rebuilt empire flourished, consuming some seventeen tons of paper per week. In the words of a competitor, she was a "commercial Joan of Arc."

Miriam did not, however, espouse the famous virgin's abstemious lifestyle. She did her part to ensure that the tabloid business had sufficient fodder to keep the presses rolling. She persisted in (and continued to report on) a long-running affair with Joaquim Miller, a self-styled knife-toting poet who preferred to answer to "Byron of the Rockies." She recounted her adventures with the Marquis de Leuville, an extravagant dandy who attacked another of her suitors with a whip during a colorful episode in London. She also got involved, during a European sabbatical, with another aesthete, in this case Willie Wilde, the older brother of the celebrated writer Oscar Wilde. She enjoyed Willie's witticisms, his exotic taste in decorating, and presumably the fact that he was some sixteen years her junior (she was fifty-five, he was thirty-nine). They married in London in 1891 and returned soon thereafter to America. All this Leslie reported herself through her own publications to a waiting public. The marriage, needless to say, did not last. In her absence, her managers had made a hash of the publishing business. While she worked to right the ship at *Leslie's Weekly*, Willie drank at the Lotus Club. After only a few months, Miriam had had enough, complaining publicly and unkindly that "she should have married Oscar"[23] and packed Willie back to his mother in England.

By 1902, Frank had had enough with her business ventures. She informed the world that, henceforth, she would be known as the Baroness de Bazus and took up residence at the Chelsea Hotel in Manhattan, a place famous for its artistic residents. She convened regular Thursday salons, featuring the high and low characters of the day. She also wrote, for the first time, in a more aggressive voice, about her life, her personal feelings, and her relationships with men. Her previous chattiness and gossipy informality gave way to a firmer voice:

> I have never been able to train myself into that meek and mild admiration of man as a master that Eve and her daughters so sweetly exhibit. Women must emancipate themselves in the best meaning of the word from the swaddling bands and chains of roses that have tethered their limbs hitherto.[24]

Leslie took up a correspondence with Carrie Catt, the head of the National American Woman Suffrage Association.[25] She informed herself about the complex suffrage movement and its many branches. An idea formed in her mind. She consulted the best legal advisers in the city in structuring her will, anticipating that Frank's children would not like her new idea any better than they had liked her ownership of the publishing empire. The entire estate, over $2 million, was to go to Carrie Catt personally to use in the campaign for women's suffrage.

The bequest was enormous and transformative. Its size equaled the entire Democratic presidential campaign budget for 1916.

The anticipated litigation did reduce the final amount by almost half, in part because Catt refused to compromise with the litigants, writing that she was duty bound to use the funds for their designated purpose. Eventually, Catt set up a commission with a board of directors to oversee the remaining million dollars. They chose to direct it to the strategic goals of Catt's "Winning Plan" that simultaneously targeted state- and federal-level lawmakers. They delegated major gifts to the New York campaign, given its importance. They established the Leslie Woman Suffrage Bureau of Education to produce and disseminate information on suffrage to local associations across the country. Among the Education Bureau's investments was the purchase of the *Woman's Journal*. The bureau also responded to anti-suffrage attacks and compelled newspapers to print retractions and apologies for indefensible slandering of suffragists or their cause. It used freedom of the press to advance this controversial cause—something that required expertise, time, and resources that had been earned through the tabloid press. Four years later, the Nineteenth Amendment to the Constitution became law. Women became full partners in democratic citizenship, thanks in part to the unexpected and well-timed investment of Miriam Florence Folline Squier Leslie, Frank Leslie, and Baroness de Bazus, who earns a place in the pantheon of social entrepreneurs for her one bold move.[26]

The lives of Mary Livermore and Miriam Leslie contain many parallels that offer an excellent way to appreciate the growth of America's social profit sector in the second half of the nineteenth century. The most obvious parallel is simply the diversity in their respective lives. Both women married professional and successful men and devoted large amounts of time to supporting their spouses. They offered this support as dutiful spouses, but also as professional partners or collaborators in their husbands' work. In turn, they each became successful businesswomen in their own right. Work was not a hobby for either woman. It was an integral part of who they were, and they each took great pride in the quality of what they produced.

Their work involved them in the political and social affairs of their day, and each woman made a point of studying these issues in some detail. Their perspectives were not limited or local. They each embraced a national view of the nation's business and reflected a sense of themselves as active agents in the ongoing discussion of national priorities. Even Miriam Leslie, who seems to have come to her concern for the enfranchisement of women late in life, wrote judiciously about topics as diverse as the merits of the World's Columbian Exposition in Chicago in 1893 and the economics of the entertainment industry.

The two women shared tremendous energy. They pursued their work with remarkable drive and determination, traveling constantly. They nurtured what today we might call a "fan base," communicating regularly with their core constituents through both print and the spoken word, and building a national reputation and following in the process. They thus exerted considerable influence over their followers. They were in many respects very modern celebrities who quite outgrew the constraints imposed on women before the Civil War. Their creativity and individualism signal the expanding role of women social entrepreneurs in the second half of the nineteenth century.

NINE

Building National Organizations for Social Profit

*Women's place is Home. Her task is homemaking. But Home is
not contained within the four walls of an individual home.
Home is the community. The city full of people is the Family.*
—Rheta Childe Dorr, *What Eight Million Women Want*, 1910

In 2001, the architectural historian Daphne Spain wrote a book
entitled *How Women Saved the City*, in which she argues that
in the second half of the nineteenth century, women took up the
challenge of bringing order to America's burgeoning cities. She
used the term "municipal housekeeping" to describe their efforts
to support the physical and spiritual lives of America's new urban
residents. This term has proved popular because it captures an
important part of the efforts of social entrepreneurs between 1870
and 1920.

Spain invented another evocative term to describe the strategy
used by these women. They created, she says, "redemptive spaces"
in American cities. These included YWCAs, Girls Clubs, bath-
houses, playgrounds, settlement houses, soldiers' and sailors'
homes, kindergartens, and similar kinds of spaces. Isolated or displaced individuals, travelers, and newcomers could all find physical shelter in such spaces. But the creators wished to provide

much more. They wanted the facilities to provide moral and spiritual support as well—the structure and security of home to those in transition.

The creators of redemptive places certainly had a charitable component in their mission—to provide for the immediate needs of those who might be "homeless," whether physically or spiritually. Many were also motivated by religious intentions, trying to advance the word of God in an ever-more-mobile society. But for our purposes, it is important to recognize the civic value—the social profit—created by a new generation of republican mothers. The stable family, as we noted in Chapter 1, was an important basis for American democracy. The home was the place where self-discipline and generosity were practiced in the relationship of a loving man and wife and taught to the next generation of virtuous citizens. The home also provided grounds for optimism, as its orderliness and security offered residents a sense of control concerning the future. In the 1870s and 1880s, however, this straightforward model came under increasing pressure, particularly in American cities. A set of women identified the destructive potential of such a breakdown and set about inventing new frameworks for social stability.

In the post–Civil War era, American cities grew at alarming rates, fueled by increasing immigration from overseas and by internal migration from farms to cities and from the South to the North. Some 27 million immigrants arrived in America between 1870 and 1920. In 1870, about 25 percent of the population lived in cities. That percentage had doubled by 1920. Among these new arrivals were a significant number of single women, joining the widows of the 600,000 soldiers who had perished in the Civil War.

Problems arose: overcrowding, flimsy housing, crime, and the grime and filth that accumulated from unpaved streets, coal fires, and a lack of water and sewer facilities. There existed no system to dispose of the horses, mules, cats, dogs, and more than occasional human who expired on the crowded city streets on any given day. A lack of housing and sanitation infrastructure was hardly the only deficiency. Also lacking were the services to guarantee protection for weaker members of society and to maintain order for the citizenry. Government, whether municipal or state or federal, lacked the resources (both dollars and expertise), the will, and indeed the mandate to care for such members of society in large numbers.

Into this void stepped a number of intrepid women. A few were genuinely radical, determined to obtain enfranchisement for their sisters and to drive the do-nothing politicians from office. Many women social entrepreneurs, however, were socially and politically conservative. They believed in the domestic virtues of order and cleanliness. To women committed to the Judeo-Christian teachings of love and service to their "neighbors," the disorder and filth must have seemed closer to visions of the Inferno than to the well-ordered Christian home of a competent, devoted homemaker. They also recognized that American democracy itself was threatened by disorder and by fear among those at the margins of society. Immigrant mothers could not raise virtuous children in an atmosphere of fear, whether fear of violence or of hunger or disease for their children.

Social entrepreneurs believed that they were responsible as citizens to "save the city" and American democracy in the process. They worked hard to understand the needs of those they sought to help. They discovered a set of common concerns: safety and security, access to education, and a chance to work hard for a better life. They also discovered a reservoir of optimism, and a drive for self-reliance, just as the entrepreneurial rural settlers had demonstrated in the eighteenth century. The women entrepreneurs set to work developing redemptive places and indeed redemptive systems to nurture the attitudes that they recognized were vital assets to democracy. They expanded their roles as republican mothers to support a more diverse and mobile population of new neighbors engaged in the hard work of becoming contributing members of the American democracy.

Female entrepreneurs recognized the scope of the challenge, but they also grasped the new tools available to them to promote more comprehensive solutions to large-scale problems. Foremost among these were the improvements in intercity communication and travel that made it possible to share ideas and to discover like-minded agents of change. Newspapers and magazines were proliferating; the telegraph and railroad networks were expanding; steamships and the U.S. mail were becoming faster and more reliable. All contributed to the capacity of entrepreneurs to scale up and scale out their efforts. The early builders of citizen support organizations demonstrated a quick appreciation for the potential of these communication technologies to reach new audiences and to gather large groups for planning and inspirational purposes.

But technology had to be yoked to a powerful vision, to a set of robust strategies to communicate that vision to others, and a lot of hard work was needed to create a durable organization capable of delivering consistent support to needy citizens.

Frances Willard (1839–1898) is identified with one of the most difficult and ambitious social profit enterprises of the late nineteenth century—the battle against the abuse of alcohol. Americans were spending over $1 billion on alcohol each year as the nineteenth century came to a close. Meanwhile, total spending on public education in the country totaled less than $200 million.[1] All citizens suffered from such misguided priorities, of course, but women and children bore the brunt of the nation's fondness for spirits. Neglect, domestic violence, and childhood alcoholism were but a few of the social ills directly attributable to the adult male population's taste for tavern life.

It is easy today to think of Prohibition as a rather quaint, and unsuccessful, experiment in social engineering. We have inherited a cartoonlike vision of glamorous speakeasies and rum-running gangsters, on the one hand, with temperance crusaders thumping their Bibles, wagging their fingers, and wearing bad clothes, on the other. But the legislation that created the Prohibition era (1920–1933) was not a triumph of fundamentalist teetotalers. It was a victory orchestrated by the largest and broadest coalition of women up to that point in American history—women intent upon increasing the security of their homes and of the nation. The temperance movement depended for its success on the increased organizational savvy of social entrepreneurs in the post–Civil War era. It is also inextricably linked throughout its history to the drive for women's enfranchisement. These two powerful social change efforts constitute important milestones in the building of the nation's social profit sector because of the numbers of citizens involved and because of the challenge to the role of government that they presented. The "organizational genius" who orchestrated these coordinated campaigns was Frances Willard, the "best-known woman in America" in the 1880s and 1890s.[2]

The Women's Christian Temperance Union was founded in 1874, and Willard became the national president in 1879. When she passed away in 1898, the WCTU counted over 200,000 members, making it one of the largest associations in the nation. As early as the 1850s, women had begun to take matters of "demon drink" into their own hands. They massed outside saloons with hatchets in hand, prepared to smash the liquor bottles behind the bar and the casks in the storage cellar. Not surprisingly, tavern keepers occasionally pulled out their shotguns.[3] Versions of this scenario, first documented in Kewanee, Illinois, were repeated in Michigan, Massachusetts, Ohio, and Indiana. Although men did not initially take much leadership in these early protests, a rare male sympathizer got the picture quite clearly in 1858:

> [These women have a] heaven-born right—that of self-protection—removing out of the way that which was destroying their husbands, sons and brothers—destroying their own happiness and placing their lives in jeopardy.[4]

Because women lacked the right to vote, to control property, or to the custody of their children in divorce, they had little recourse against the domestic violence that was frequently associated with drunkenness. Legal protections did not exist to prosecute rape within marriage, and the "age of consent" for girls in some states was as young as seven. Male law enforcement officers avoided involvement in family matters, and, as Mary Livermore found, the courts were also reluctant to support legislation dealing directly with family matters.

The Civil War disrupted the early anti-alcohol protests. The hardships of war hardly encouraged soldiers to keep any pledges of abstinence offered when they departed for the battleground, and spirits were at least antiseptic. When the war ended, the problem of alcohol grew worse. The number of alcohol dealers paying federal tax increased over 150 percent between 1864 and 1873. In Ohio, it was said that there was one saloon for every twenty residents.[5] In 1873, a group of women in upstate New York once again took up the challenge of "home protection." Under the leadership of Esther McNeil, a foster mother of eight, women in the town of Fredonia drafted an appeal:

> In the name of God and humanity we make our appeal: Knowing, as we do, that the sale of intoxicating liquors is the parent of every

misery, prolific of all woe in this life and the next, potent alone in evil, blighting every fair hope, desolating families, the chief incentive to crime, we, the mothers, wives, and daughters, representing the moral and religious sentiment of our town, to save the loved members of our households from the temptation of strong drink, from acquiring an appetite for it, and to rescue, if possible, those that have already acquired it, earnestly request that you will pledge yourself to cease the traffic here in these drinks, forthwith and forever. We will also add the hope that you will abolish your gaming tables.[6]

After voting their acceptance of this appeal, the women, some 100 strong, headed to Taylor House Tavern. They read the appeal to the proprietor, sang a hymn, and prayed the Lord's Prayer. The women then asked if the owner would accede to their request. He agreed, pending agreement by other proprietors of saloons and liquor stores, so the protestors went to work. Their efforts continued daily and the women's crusade was launched. Eventually, some 200 ladies of Fredonia adopted the name the Women's Christian Temperance Union in 1873.

The pray-ins and sing-ins spread quickly across the Midwest. Hillsboro, Ohio, spawned a group called the Women's Temperance Crusade:

Walking two by two . . . they sang "Give to the Winds Thy Fears. . . ." They visited saloons and the drug stores where liquor was sold. They prayed on sawdust floors and . . . knelt on snowy pavements . . . until almost all the sellers capitulated.[7]

In November 1874, a convention got under way in Cleveland, Ohio, with the aim of uniting the many local efforts into a national organization. Among the delegates was the president of the Chicago temperance union, who had recently been elected secretary of the union of the State of Illinois. Frances Willard, despite relative inexperience in the movement, was elected corresponding secretary of the newly formed National Women's Christian Temperance Union (NWCTU). Annie Wittenmyer, a veteran temperance activist and prominent Methodist church leader, was chosen president.

Willard became active in the temperance movement at a time of transition in her life. Although she was a devout Methodist from a family sympathetic with temperance thinking, Willard had been an educator (and occasional light tippler) until 1873. Born in 1839, she grew up a self-styled tomboy prankster alongside her more traditional brother and sister. She (and her sister) were exceptional among pre–Civil War women in having received a "college" education. When Frances was eighteen, the family moved from Wisconsin to Evanston, Illinois, where she and her sister both attended the North Western Female College. Thanks to the generosity of the family of a college friend, Kate Jackson, Frances then studied and traveled with Kate in France, Germany, and Italy as well as in Palestine, Egypt, and Greece. She returned from her extensive travels with a concern about "what can be done to make the world a wider place for women." Upon further reflection at home, she reasoned that the condition of women had held back civilization—"a stream," she noted, "cannot rise higher than the spring that feeds it." In 1871, she became president of the Evanston College for Ladies (her alma mater, with a new name) where she put her philosophy into practice by initiating student self-government for the young women. Her higher-education career was short-lived, however. When the Evanston College merged with the local university, becoming the Women's College of Northwestern University in 1873, she became its dean. Northwestern's new president, Charles Henry

Fowler, did not share her enthusiasm for female self-governance or indeed for any independent actions on her part. Subjected to petty sniping from both faculty and male students at the university, she resigned in 1874. Northwestern's loss proved to be an enormous gain for the world of social profit.

As corresponding secretary for the new national WCTU, Willard traveled extensively during the early years, visiting local chapters and building the organization virtually single-handedly. Willard demonstrated her rhetorical skills on these nonstop junkets:

> I was reared on a western prairie, and often have helped to kindle the great fires for which the West used to be famous. A match and a wisp of dry grass were all we needed, and behold the magnificent spectacle of a prairie on fire, sweeping across the landscape, swift as a thousand untrained steed, and no more to be captured than a hurricane! Just so it is with the Crusade. . . . When God lets loose an idea upon this planet, we vainly set limits to its progress and I believe that Gospel Temperance shall yet transform that inmost circle, the human heart, and in its widening sweep the circle of home, and then society, and then, pushing its argument to the extreme conclusion, it shall permeate the widest circle of them all, and that is, government.[8]

By 1879, there were more than 1,000 local affiliates and membership of some 25,000 women. As her rhetoric reveals, Willard's goals for the organization were steeped in both religious and civic faith. They were also ambitious. "Gospel temperance" referred to the practice of preaching to alcohol abusers about the virtues of abstinence. This was a fine idea, as far as it went, but Willard believed that it was essential, as she put it, "to make our influence felt at the fountains of power." It was time to transform a system of government that tolerated an increasing lack of self-control on the part of men, and it was up to women to take responsibility, just as the Founders had urged them to do. She was also wise to invoke the authority of religion in her cause. As we have noted, there was a great deal of religious energy in the nation from 1870–1900.[9] At a time of great idealism about the power of government and of religion, it made all the sense in the world to align the cause of temperance with the teachings of the Bible.

Willard was in no way cynical about her Christianity. She was a very devout and spiritual woman who remained comfortable with her Methodist roots throughout her life. But she was also attuned to the temper of her conservative times. She understood that most women embraced a religious framework for their lives, and she spoke favorably about the importance of all religious faiths, Protestant, Catholic, Jewish, and even Eastern rites.

Her audience was also focused on their domestic responsibilities. How could she engage them in a movement to change government policy, when most viewed politics as a dirty, if not corrupt, business? Willard came up with an appeal to women to join the cause of temperance that embraced women's commitment to domestic security and a virtuous home. In what her biographer calls "the revelation" on a spring morning in Columbus, Ohio, the idea of the Home Protection League was born:

> As she knelt before God, it was borne in upon her spirit that the ballot in woman's hand as a weapon of human protection, ought to be worked for and welcomed.[10]

Willard's ingenious interpretation of her "revelation" provided a powerful tool for social change. Here was the means to engage women in the quest to change government policy without having to affiliate with the radical and doctrinaire "reformers" such as

Elizabeth Cady Stanton. Under the banner of "home protection," Willard wisely wrapped the cause of women's suffrage around the obligation to preserve and defend the sacred space of the home-maker, the space where mutual respect, love, and patriotism were practiced. Willard called for women to seek the vote only in local elections that would have direct bearing on the stability and security of their families and communities. She called this approach "limited suffrage" or the "local option." As she wrote in 1880:

> Not rights, but duties; not her need alone, but that of her children and her country; not the "woman," but the "human" question is stirring women's hearts and breaking down their prejudice today.[11]

Willard offered more than pure rhetoric to the cause. She provided a strong management hand. She drafted a detailed plan for the temperance agenda following her experience as secretary of the national WCTU. *Hints and Helps in Our Temperance Work* (1875) is a lengthy pamphlet showing local home protection leaders how to organize and conduct meetings, garner publicity, obtain signed pledges, engage men and children in their efforts, and gather factual information on the impact of alcohol on their communities.[12] Her guidance extended to the most minute details, such as where to order sheet music for performances by the recommended temperance glee clubs, and how to decorate members' parlors in good taste, in order that temperance adherents not be accused of falling short on their domestic duties because of their activism.

Willard put her own ideas into practice in Illinois, following the defeat of the universal suffrage campaign led by Livermore in 1870. She favored the petition drive as an ideal mechanism for women to impact the political process without sullying themselves through direct lobbying. Willard and her Illinois neighbors launched a petition drive in support of the Illinois Home Protection Act, which put alcohol sales under the control of local municipalities and allowed women to vote in local referenda. They collected over 180,000 names, 80,000 of them voters. Willard oversaw the creation of a media-friendly presentation of the petition, formatting it as a single "banner" some 215 yards long, unfurled from the balcony of the State House.[13] Her efforts earned Willard a "first" in the history of the state. She became the first woman to address the Illinois General Assembly on March 6, 1879. She was politely received, apparently, but the bill died.

In New York State, some 70,000 women signed petitions on a white cloth one-third of a mile in length. Women worked by the thousands across the nation to create similar highly visible pleas to public officials. Many lobbied governors to appoint only abstinent men to public office. They created curricula for Sabbath schools on the dangers of alcohol, prevailed upon doctors not to prescribe medicines containing alcohol, and advocated for the study of hereditary influences on alcoholism.[14] In keeping with the Willard strategy, they continued to campaign for "the right and privilege of voting in Municipal elections as a means to better government and that we may no longer be subject to the control of besotted men and the vicious classes."[15]

Frances was elected president of the national WCTU in 1879, adopting the slogan "For God, and Home, and Native Land," capping a three-year campaign to unseat Wittenmyer. She shifted the focus of the organization from a "top-down" approach focused at the legislative level to the building of local affiliates able to reach out to influential local women's clubs and to the emerging labor organizations to support "municipal suffrage" in their communities. She backed up this grassroots strategy by visiting in person "every city in American with a population above 10,000," inspiring the troops and urging the women to assert their moral authority in the crusade.

Her impact can certainly be measured by the size and influence of the national WCTU and its hundreds of thousands of members. She had overcome the initial WCTU opposition to the limited suffrage strategy. She had built the "Temple," the imposing WCTU headquarters building in downtown Chicago. She had recognized the importance of building alliances with the emerging organized labor movement and with male-dominated organizations such as the Knights of Labor. But her greatest influence fell on the many individual members to whom she spoke directly and eloquently through those thousands of speeches across the land, including the South, where many Northern female leaders failed to appear. Her inspirational power can be heard in the vigorous comments of a Louisiana member following a Willard visit:

> Men are full of advice to women about how they should conduct themselves and (men) have decided that brain work is detrimental to the full development of the organization of the female, (but) they do not worry over the effects of tobacco, whiskey, and certain vile habits upon the congenital vigor of both boys and girls. Fathers and medical men ought to look well to the hygienic duties of their own sex. . . .[16]

Willard's focus on local organizations generated hundreds of WCTU "affiliates" across the land, in cities large and small. In Chicago, site of the national headquarters, the local chapter embraced the "do everything" challenge issued by Willard to chapters in major metropolitan areas. By 1889, the Chicago chapter was operating a day nursery, several Sunday schools, vocational training programs, a homeless women's shelter, a medical clinic, a lodging house for transient men, and a subsidized restaurant.[17] Smaller chapters were considerably less ambitious. A reading of the minutes of the Oberlin, Ohio, chapter over a thirty-year period reveals a much more modest agenda, marked by a burst of activist fervor in the 1870s that forced the closing of the local billiards hall, followed by a period of more constrained meetings and discussion and the eventual reopening of said billiards hall a few years later.[18]

By 1886, the first laws against alcohol were passed. It became illegal in New York State to sell or give alcohol to a child under twelve and then for underaged barmaids to be hired where liquor was sold.[19] Related state legislation followed, again with the support of the WCTU. Female children under the age of sixteen could no longer "consent" to prostitution. Males risked five-year prison terms and fines of $1,000 should they be found to have breached this law—a first in the nation. Then the WCTU cooperated with other groups to secure a police matron in all cities over 25,000 inhabitants to assure that females in trouble would be separated from men in prison and be supervised by a female officer. There were still decades of work ahead to bring government policy fully into line with women's needs for "home protection," but Willard's leadership had tilted awareness in the direction of women's interests.

Willard's career was not without controversy. In the 1880s, the number of lynchings of blacks reached an all-time high, and Ida B. Wells, the black suffrage leader and pamphleteer, argued that the WCTU agenda was causing (Southern) white women to stereotype black men as rapists and drunkards. Willard did not help her cause when she offered an equivocal analysis of the lynching scene:

Our duty to the colored people have [sic] never impressed me so solemnly as this year when the antagonism between them and the white race have [sic] seemed to be more vivid than at any previous time, and lurid vengeance has devoured the devourers of women and children.[20]

Frances denied Wells's charge of racism and actively engaged many black women in the WCTU. Some contemporary scholars[21] have concluded that "Willard's success as a political mobilizer has not overshadowed the ethnocentrism and racism imbedded in her ideology."[22] Others object to Willard's portrayal of women as morally superior to men.[23] Some of Willard's contemporaries continued to oppose the connection of women's suffrage to the temperance agenda. Caroline Corbin, who founded the Illinois Association Opposed to the Extension of Suffrage to Women in 1897, claimed that all suffragists were Socialists or anarchists or Bolshevists. Once again, Willard invited such accusations with her professed embrace of "Christian Socialism." This form of "Socialism" seems to have little to do with the overthrow of capitalism in Willard's thinking. She seems to have used it instead to express her faith in the potential of government, when guided by the Christian ideal of loving thy neighbor, to act as a benign and enlightened force for equality, something like the utopian ideal expressed in Edward Bellamy's *Looking Backward* (1888), one of her favorite books.

Willard did assert that men's greater proclivity to drink weakened their dependability as protectors of women and often transformed them into threats. She believed that men fought wars and sacrificed their children for causes that could not be justified. She asserted in her annual addresses to WCTU members, echoing Abigail Adams, that women are more likely to dispel barbarism

127

and to transform the state into a body dedicated to serving as the ideal collective "conscience of the people."[24] Some might even agree with such a "sexist" perspective today.

What cannot be disputed is that Willard was able to mobilize more people to her positions on both temperance and voting than any other figure in the nineteenth century. The WCTU counted roughly ten times the number of members in 1890 as the National American Woman Suffrage Association, the "hard-core" suffrage organization. The Home Protection Movement empowered women to seek local votes on the issues that mattered most to them: temperance, security, and local education.

Nor can it be disputed that Willard reformed a social system that accepted the negative consequences of alcohol abuse as a fact of life. It would be easy to say that she ultimately failed as a change agent because Prohibition is generally seen as a failed public policy. But the changes in public attitudes and laws around drunkenness and spouse abuse, around alcoholism, underage drinking, and drunk driving are her direct legacy and remain in force today. She succeeded in changing the social consensus of her age around the use of alcohol, and we are all beneficiaries.[25] Of equal significance, of course, is her contribution to the passage of the Nineteenth Amendment in 1920. The Home Protection League, endorsing the "local option" vote, engaged millions of women in the pursuit of the right to vote and added enormous momentum to the ultimate achievement of full enfranchisement.

While pursuing her work for temperance and suffrage, Willard never abandoned her love of teaching. In 1886, she authored a guide for young women entitled, boldly enough, "How to Win." It was directed to the emerging group of educated young women with more opportunities before them as the Gilded Age took shape. She argued that these women should develop the ability to support themselves, that being self-sufficient was not "un-lady-like."

In a typical display of her unwavering entrepreneurial optimism, she even envisioned the dawn of a day when men would give up their pretensions to mastery of all things and enter genuine partnerships with women, even though Frances herself would never find such a male partner. She backed away from several romantic involvements with men as a young woman, seemingly sensing that a man, even a loving partner, would inevitably seek to limit her independence. She encountered many controlling men during her professional lifetime, beginning with President Fowler of Northwestern, and extending through the evangelist Dwight Moody, with whom she worked as a platform evangelist for a year or so, and the male hierarchy of the Protestant and Catholic churches with whom she sought to collaborate on temperance issues. These men, it seems, were all inclined to tell Willard what she should and could do, and it took her little time to exit quickly from such entanglements. She enjoyed more constructive behavior in the company of women and inspired great loyalty from a variety of female friends and relatives. She shared a home with her widowed mother and her married sister for decades, and both were active collaborators in her work. Her school chum, Kate Jackson, remained a lifelong friend, and in later life, she took up residence in England with Isabel Somerset (Lady Henry Somerset), who became her host and collaborator on the globalization of the temperance movement. Perhaps her closest companion was Anna Gordon, a talented musician who played the organ, composed hymns, and in effect acted as Willard's booking and travel agent. Gordon traveled with Willard on the temperance campaign, and ultimately wrote the affectionate portrait entitled *The Beautiful Life of Frances E. Willard.*

Frances did not live to see the fruits of her labors, as she passed away in 1898, a full twenty years before both Prohibition and suffrage would be enacted into federal law. But her lasting contribution to the social profit sector was hardly diminished by her premature death. She took the lessons learned from women's contributions to the Civil War effort and created a grassroots lobbying machine in a domestic framework. Through her skilled performances and passionate idealism, she brought generations of women into the political process.[26] Willard, "the most famous woman in America" in her day, is the first women memorialized in the Hall of Statuary of the U.S. Congress.

Despite the efforts of Willard and many others, family units were regularly broken apart not only by alcohol, but by wars, epidemics, accidents, and desertions. The female heads of these households still struggled to sustain themselves after the loss of the family breadwinner, just as they did in the 1830s, when Elizabeth Stott had launched the Philadelphia Women's Depository. Some forty years later, Stott's idea was taken up in New York City by another exceptional woman, Candace Wheeler (1827–1923). Her idea for Women's Exchanges would do more than assist decayed gentlewomen. It would promote the value of work and of self-sufficiency for all women. In the process, Wheeler, herself a gifted artist and businesswoman, established the economic value of a wide range of women's domestic products for the first time in American history. She demonstrated the synergy of the domestic arts, the commercial marketplace, and social profit in a memorable combination that encompassed most major cities in the nation by the turn of the twentieth century. As she put it in a rare celebratory moment toward the end of her life:

> Women began to work profitably and find in it the joy of self-help, of doing, and finally of help for the world.[27]

The visionary Wheeler had her "eureka" moment in 1876, the year of the nation's centenary. The occasion was a visit to the national birthday party, the centennial fair in Philadelphia attended by some 10 million people. Despite a lack of support from the male organizers, American women, led by a committee in Cincinnati, raised $30,000 to build a "pavilion" at the fair dedicated to the accomplishments of American women. It proved popular enough with its slightly incoherent mixture of displays, featuring domestic wares and suffrage propaganda. But the exhibit that attracted Wheeler was found at the English pavilion—a display of needlecrafts produced by the South Kensington School of Art Needleworks. The students were working-class women who attended the school tuition free, thanks to Queen Victoria's royal patronage. They were taught traditional English embroidery techniques, including those employed in the weaving of medieval tapestries. The school had a dual purpose—to teach working women skills that would enable them to support themselves and to preserve a traditional craft that was rapidly disappearing with the advent of machine stitchery. The beautifully executed wall hangings and silk panels inspired Wheeler to launch a similar enterprise in New York City. Under her guidance, the Society of Decorative Art (SDA) eventually expanded to cities across the United States.

In 1876, Wheeler was a forty-nine-year-old wife and mother of four children, happily married to a sometimes successful business-man. Wheeler was not a wealthy lady, having been raised in a strict religious family on a farm in the Catskill Mountains of New York. Her love of arts and crafts flourished once she escaped, as she put it, to marry Tom Wheeler and move to New York City at age seventeen. The Wheelers started their family, and as the children grew up, they all traveled to Europe for extended stays on two occasions (prompted at least in part by financial concerns, as it was considerably cheaper to live in Europe at the time than in New York). Candace was able to study European painting and to take some art lessons herself. Back in New York, the Wheelers became regular visitors at the popular "open studio" events held by New York painters to show off their works in progress. Eventually Tom and Candace Wheeler began to socialize with, and occasionally purchase small paintings from, several Hudson River School painters such as Albert Bierstadt and Frederic Church. On her return from Philadelphia, Candace was confident that her network of contacts in the arts and in society would enable her to develop support for a decorative arts project that would have both an artistic and a social purpose. Wheeler's social concerns at this moment in her life were amplified by the unexpected loss of her thirty-two-year-old married daughter just before the visit to the Centennial Fair. She later wrote that Cannie's death "changed my whole attitude toward life and taught me its duties, not only to those I loved but to all who needed help and comfort."[28]

One year later, Wheeler launched the New York Society of Decorative Art,[29] complete with a board of managers (prominent women including Mrs. John Jacob Astor), a board of advisers (prominent male collectors and artists, including Louis Comfort Tiffany), and a seven-point charter that outlined the mission and objectives. The society would develop and sell on consignment decorative arts produced by women in need. But Wheeler envisioned broader commercial potential as well. The group would solicit design contracts from commercial producers of pottery, china, and textiles that could be executed by the society's consignors. The society would also seek custom orders directly from dealers. Finally, the plan called for offering training to the more talented contributors to enhance their artistic skills. And, in true entrepreneurial fashion, Wheeler would establish SDA "auxiliaries" in other cities.

Wheeler's sense of the marketplace proved correct (as would be the case throughout her long life), and the SDA became an immediate success. In the post–Civil War era, there was growing interest in high-quality decorative objects among middle-class families. The Sanitary Fairs that had proved successful fundraising vehicles for the Union war effort had also nurtured an interest in decorative objects across the North and Midwest. The New York fair, called the Metropolitan Fair, had been perhaps the biggest of all, raising in excess of $1.3 million for the cause. The female consumer was ready to shop and ready to buy as the nation emerged from the recession that preceded the Centennial celebration.

Year one totals for the society included some 6,300 items submitted for consideration and 2,700 acceptances. Net proceeds topped $18,000, with the SDA retaining a 10 percent commission to cover expenses and the remainder being returned to consignors.[30] The SDA was soon obliged to import instructors from England to provide training in European designs and techniques to meet the growing demand for high-quality, handcrafted products. Influential magazines such as *Scribner's* wrote approvingly of these efforts to raise aesthetic standards of individual craftswomen.

The early success of the society is a tribute to Wheeler. She knew how to win commercial design contracts and produce income for skillful women. The focus of the society was not only on decayed gentlewomen. Wheeler welcomed all women attracted to the notion of self-reliance, including middle-class matrons and girls from the local "asylum," who attended sewing lessons without charge. As Wheeler proudly noted in her autobiography, "the idea of *earning* had entered into the minds of women" (italics hers). At the same time, she was content to avoid any conflict with the established hierarchies of the art world. The women's work rested firmly in the domestic sphere. Although Wheeler and colleagues worked to elevate the "decorative arts" to a higher level of quality, these efforts did not challenge the traditional male bastions of painting and sculpture. Nor did she vary from the accepted practice of placing aesthetic judgments in the hands of the men on her advisory committee (some of whom also provided designs and patterns for the consignors to execute).

Wheeler's idea spread rapidly, just as she had planned. She had accepted the position of "corresponding secretary" for the SDA at the time of its founding, placing the socially prominent Caroline (Mrs. David) Lane in the position of president. The corresponding secretary was responsible for spreading the word of the SDA's activities, and Wheeler succeeded in seeding auxiliaries in Chicago, Detroit, Hartford, St. Louis, and Charleston in the first year. The number would reach thirty additional cities by 1880, and the New York chapter eventually opened summer showrooms in popular resorts such as Saratoga Springs and Newport to meet the demand for its goods. As part of her plan, Wheeler encouraged the various auxiliaries to forward their very best items to New York City, where, she assured them, the best prices could be obtained.

But at the end of the first whirlwind year of growth, Wheeler was having second thoughts about her brainchild. She was troubled by the focus on artistic quality that, naturally enough, had come to dominate the society's value system. The number of women whose work passed muster with the society's artistic advisers was limited. As she put it succinctly, "philanthropy and art are not natural sisters."[31] When a fellow board member proposed that they launch a new organization, a woman's exchange that would seek a wider array of women's products to sell, Wheeler made the difficult decision to resign from the

NYSDA. "Everyone disapproved of me," she wrote, "I remember the stony glare of Mrs. John Jacob Astor when I tried to explain my defection."[32]

She launched the New York Exchange for Women's Work in partnership with Mary Choate.[33] The two women devised a feature that proved a genuine breakthrough for the women's exchanges, vastly expanding their scope and scale. In addition to accepting traditional goods such as clothing and home furnishings for consignment, they would include "services" in their offerings. They wanted to assist all women in the pursuit of self-help, so that, as Wheeler wrote:

> A woman of brains, industry and opportunity might make and sell whatever she could do best, and yet not lose her place. . . . Women (would) work profitably and (find) in it the joy of self-help.[34]

Wheeler and Choate envisioned an extensive system of women's enterprises, still within the domestic framework, that would be both socially and financially productive. Their new breakaway idea was not an easy sell. Several organizational meetings with prominent matrons failed to produce an initial set of investors. Apparently, the moment of enlightenment finally arrived when an exasperated Choate responded sharply to an attendee who asked whether Mary was "certain that the Exchange would succeed." "No, Madam," she replied, "but if all the shopkeepers in town today had waited to be assured of success, where could you do your shopping in this big city?"

With that, at least a few investors apparently came forward and the New York Exchange was born in 1878. Within a few years, the exchange was selling several thousands of dollars of handmade merchandise per year, including foodstuffs and jewelry.

Wheeler's sense of the middle-class-home marketplace served the new project well. She guided the women in the production of the most up-to-date fashion and home decorating objects. Such was the success of Wheeler's new enterprise that the work attracted the attention of women in cities where auxiliaries of the Society of Decorative Art had been established. A decade later, the writer of a Directory of Exchanges for Woman's Work exclaimed: "There is hardly a city of any considerable size that does not have its Woman's Exchange."[35] The exchanges in Cincinnati, Baltimore, Richmond, and New Orleans attained particular distinction for the scope of their product lines and their marketing.

The exchanges were expanding in a gilded age of retail. A greater variety of goods and services was on offer in major cities than at any previous time in the nation's history. Entrepreneurs such as the Gimbel brothers, William Macy, John Wanamaker, and dozens of others stood ready to provide the shopping public with a new level of glamour and variety. As many scholars have hypothesized, home decoration—feathering one's nest, to borrow a turn of phrase from the period—took on added significance as a way to shelter those who could afford it from the filth and disorder of the urban street scene. Retailers created picture windows positioned on the city boulevards that offered carefully "designed" displays of goods. Customers were entertained with holiday decorations, organ concerts (the Wanamaker organ in Center City Philadelphia has recently been restored), and ever-more-elaborate restaurants and tearooms. How were the women's exchanges to compete?

The leaders proved remarkably dexterous at steering their social enterprises through the shoals of commercial competition. Some exchanges sought to compete with department stores at their own game. They adapted the "departmental" model themselves, dividing their merchandise (and management structure) into groupings of clothing, home furnishings, food items, and so on. The New York Exchange rented a picture window on Fifth Avenue to display its wares, arraying the products in carefully designed settings to inspire shoppers with ideas they could transfer to their own homes. Many exchanges found their greatest competitive advantage through the development of food services such as home-cooked catering, carryout meals for shut-ins, party baskets, and the like. The Cincinnati Exchange served 100,000 meals in 1894 alone.

During the early days of the New York Exchange, Wheeler and Choate were approached by a woman who had moved with her husband and children to New York to seek work. She was having no success. A quiz ensued during which the woman enumerated all the things she was not very good at—singing and dancing, drawing and painting, sewing and mending. Finally, Wheeler hit upon the right question: Did she cook anything special that her family liked? Sure enough, her face lit up. She made the best chicken pot pie in North Carolina! "Excellent," responded Choate, "deliver six pies tomorrow morning." Wheeler recalled this story over a lunch with Choate some twenty years later, as both of them were tucking into the very same chicken pot pies that had become the all-time best-selling item at the New York Exchange restaurant. Exchange-sponsored cookbooks featuring recipes from the home cooks purveying to the exchange restaurants proved a popular retail item as well.

Through it all, the exchanges did not vary their cooperative structure. They continued to return about 90 percent of all sales to their consignors. According to data published in 1958, exchanges paid out over $6 million in fees to consignors over the years. During the difficult times, including the Great Depression, these modest sums made the difference between stability and destitution for hundreds of thousands of women. This we know personally for a fact: David's maternal grandmother supported her four children, following the death of her husband in 1917, by working as a caterer through the Detroit Women's Exchange.

How did Wheeler help to steer this remarkable expansion of the exchange system? First, she understood exactly how to position the exchanges to match the temper of the times. As did the Societies of Decorative Art, the exchanges provided independence for women while remaining firmly based in the domestic arts and in domestic space. They also held fast to their charitable Christian roots. Wheeler even asserted that good home decoration had a moral purpose: "The perfectly furnished house . . . not only expresses but MAKES character," she wrote.[36] Unlike the suffrage, and occasionally, the temperance movements that included public protests and demonstrations, the exchanges provided a safer route to self-help for women.

Second, the ever-resourceful Wheeler took advantage of the networks created by associations that shared her fundamentally conservative views. The Women's Christian Association (WCA, which became the YWCA), the WCTU, and the Women's Educational and Industrial Union (WEIU) all served as conduits for the exchange idea to travel across the country. The newsletter of the WCA, *The Evangile*, carried a detailed article about the New York Exchange that led to the founding of the Cincinnati chapter. The WCTU, as previously noted, boasted some 200,000 members nationally, and affiliates in Denver and Santa Barbara launched exchanges as part of their chapter activities.

The conservative stance of the exchanges provoked more than a little criticism during the violent labor–management conflicts of the 1890s.[37] Many women were pressured to support the organized labor movement and join the fight for better wages and working conditions, especially for women in factories. Yet Wheeler and the other leaders could point up the advantages of their model. As the nation became aware of the intrinsic conflicts within capitalism between labor and management, the cooperative exchange offered a more harmonious, and less adversarial, model of production and marketing.

As is so often the case with generosity, the ladies who originated and sustained the exchanges profited as much as their consignors did. Many acquired considerable business knowledge through their management duties. By the end of the nineteenth century, these positions had gained some social status as well. Newspapers spoke favorably of the competence and self-help commitments reflected in the exchange enterprises. Female-run businesses, in the form of small shops, catering businesses, and the like, had become commonplace by the beginning of the twentieth century, in no small measure because of the knowledge gained through exchanges.

Candace Wheeler became one of the most successful businesswomen of the late nineteenth century. At about the time she terminated her formal association with the SDA in New York, Louis Tiffany invited her to join a design and decorating collaborative he was assembling. She would be in charge of fabrics and decorative needlework. Tiffany's commitment to domestic design was among the first for a male artist. Apparently in need of money, Wheeler accepted (with her husband's permission, as Tiffany had specified in his offer). Thanks to the lengthy lists of wealthy friends and acquaintances shared by Wheeler, Tiffany, and their fellow collaborators Longwood deForest and Samuel Colman, the firm obtained a variety of prestigious commissions for both commercial and private residential decoration, including a commission to decorate the home of Samuel Clemens (Mark Twain), who became a lifelong friend to Wheeler, and another to redecorate the White House in 1882.

The collaboration was certainly instructive for Wheeler, who continued to learn and to develop her own skills as an artist. But her work supervising the execution of designs by Tiffany did not hold her attention for long. In 1883, she formed her own women's design partnership with her daughter Dora, calling it Associated Artists (AA). She was motivated once again by her interest in art as a tool for self-sufficiency: "After four years, I felt a call to devote myself to art in a way which would more particularly help women. . . ." This objective was realized through the educational efforts of the AA group, which recruited new graduates of public schools and trained them extensively in hand-embroidery techniques, using a technique that Candace Wheeler had developed and patented.

Perhaps the high point of the AA was reached when Wheeler obtained the (paid) commission to decorate the Woman's Building at the World's Columbian Exposition in Chicago in 1893. The scale of the project was vast. The Hall of Honor was 200 feet long by 67 feet wide with a 70-foot ceiling. The Board of Lady Managers for the Expo, chaired by the imposing Mrs. Potter Palmer of Chicago, wanted a 400-year history of women's accomplishments from across the world. Wheeler oversaw the collection and judging of tens of thousands of contributed objects, encompassing paintings, glass, wood carvings, pottery, jewelry, metalwork, and various categories of textiles. There would be a nursery exhibit, a cooking-school exhibit, a knitting-mills exhibit, an African American exhibit, and a grand library featuring works about women collected by women's groups in all the states. Wheeler worked with the New York State managers to assemble a collection of 2,500 volumes authored by New York women. She also enlisted her daughter and several friends to compose and execute the enormous murals that decorated the ceiling and the end walls of the library.

Even this staggering project did not deplete Wheeler's continuing inventiveness on behalf of the arts and her fellow artists. She supported the launching of a design movement, commonly known as the Arts and Crafts movement, across the nation. As in the case of the Society of Decorative Art,[38] the goals were both aesthetic and social. Chapters across the nation, inspired in part by John Ruskin's tracts glorifying traditional handwork and crafts over manufactured goods, pushed back against the commodification of design and worked to raise the appreciation (and the financial value) of artisans' contributions to the decorative arts.

Wheeler's idealism and entrepreneurship also guided the creation of an artist's colony in upstate New York near her original home, in partnership with her younger daughter, Dora, and son, Dunham, an architect. Onteora, as it was called, eventually encompassed several hundred acres, an impressive "clubhouse" and commercial inn, and dozens of cottages for family and visiting artists. Both before and after Tom's death in 1895, Wheeler spent large periods of time at the camp and established rug-making classes for the rural women in the area. She also began to write extensively about her design ideas and her needlework techniques in her later life. Her own textiles are today in the permanent collection of the Metropolitan Museum of Art.[39]

Women's exchange operations endured well into the 1950s. The benefits to countless women are a cause of celebration for all of us. There is no finer example of female entrepreneurship on behalf of the greater good than the seventy-two exchanges that operated across the nation for well over 100 years. Whether measured in dollars distributed or self-respect earned, the exchange system proved to be one of the great engines of social and economic progress in our nation's history, brought to us all by enterprising female social entrepreneurs.[40] Writing about the Associated Artists project, the art critic Clarence Cook assessed Candace's leadership: "She was a large-hearted woman—she wanted to help young girls who desired to be employed and give them a fair return for their labor. . . . Mrs. Wheeler's next qualification for the work . . . was a clear business head and an eye steadily fixed on her well-understood purpose . . . to foster a truly American style of art embroidery." Wheeler's third qualification was that she "is an artist and it is her love of art that has incited her to her undertaking."[41] Cook concludes: "The first new path . . . in embroidery in modern times has been pioneered by the taste, the ingenuity and the indomitable energy of an American woman."

A third "municipal housekeeper" comes closest to Daphne Spain's definition cited at the beginning of this chapter. Grace Dodge (1856–1914) was a serial creator of "redemptive spaces" for marginalized citizens, and the spaces she created were both physical and spiritual. She ended her remarkable career as a social entrepreneur as national president of the YWCA, perhaps the prototype organization that Spain had in mind, since the Y's mission was to build and operate places of shelter for women alone in strange cities. Yet Dodge's most impressive contribution to social profit, in our judgment, was the standard she established for the education of social entrepreneurs. She applied her lifelong commitment to the science of teaching and learning to herself. Unlike so many well-intentioned but self-important philanthropists, Grace did not presume that she understood how to be an effective agent for the greater good. Instead, she modeled the behavior of an ideal student, seeking first to understand before providing solutions. The result was an unusual cross-class learning adventure that defied the conventional stereotype of the benevolent lady.

Grace Dodge did not launch a religious order. But she did attract thousands of devoted women to her organizations and became an important agent of social change through her audacious approach to social problem solving. Audacity is not a word often associated with Grace Dodge. She was a self-effacing, conservative Victorian lady with a leadership style to match. But Dodge proved a remarkably adept builder of social profit. She focused her life and her talents on the needs of "working girls," and on those who aspired to teach the next generation of American citizens. She pursued this vision with great patience and persistence. She demonstrated again and again the value of being better prepared and better organized than anyone else when she undertook a project, and her leadership emerged naturally from this base of knowledge and self-discipline. Not the life and soul of any party, perhaps, but Dodge certainly was the person to have on your side if you were in need of an advocate. Through her exemplary commitments, she ultimately benefited students of all ages and built our nation's human and intellectual capital in the process.

Grace Dodge, according to an insightful and utterly charming biography,[42] inherited her businesslike approach to life from her family. She was the daughter, granddaughter, and niece of successful businessmen with interests in mining, transportation, food, and legal affairs. Although destined by the family's standing to lead the life of a socialite, Grace enjoyed considerable attention from her father as his eldest child. He ensured that she understood his household affairs, if not all his businesses. This was no mean task, given that the Dodge family included five younger siblings, two homes, and several household employees.

When Grace was fifteen in 1871, the family doctor prescribed a trip to southern France for her mother. Off went Dodge's parents for three months, leaving Grace in charge of the household to deal with shiftless relatives, an outbreak of measles among her siblings, and a series of unpleasant plumbing disasters. She signaled her lifelong competence in managing complexity by performing admirably. Following her parents' return, she went off to Miss Porter's School in Connecticut, a finishing school for daughters of wealth and privilege. Although she loved the riding lessons (she had owned her own pony since childhood), Grace did not fit in. She was a tall girl with a face "filled with character," and not much at ease amid her peers concerned with the latest gossip and fancy dress balls. Grace was more interested in the headline-grabbing efforts of the post–Civil War reformers who were leading temperance and religious revival movements. She was fascinated by Anna Howard Shaw, who had just announced her intention to travel to Alaska to deliver the word of God to lumberjacks.

Such adventures were out of the question for Grace, but she was clear about what she did not want to do. She did not want to return to Miss Porter's, and she certainly did not wish to be presented to New York society at a traditional debutante ball. She preferred to meet important people who were engaged in the world of charity and service. Remarkably, her father acquiesced and arranged for her to meet Louisa Schuyler, who helped to found the original Sanitary Commission group in New York City in 1860. Schuyler was sufficiently impressed by young Grace to offer her membership on a subcommittee of the State Charities Aid Association, an organization that Schuyler had founded to provide citizen oversight of the state welfare institutions (the infamous poorhouses). Dodge embraced this new responsibility and immersed herself in the work of the Committee on the Elevation of the Poor in Their Homes.[43] She learned much from Schuyler over the subsequent five years, including important leadership lessons for how a woman could "manage" the service work of others rather than limiting herself to personal good works.

During this period, Dodge met Emily Huntington, who was in charge of the Wilson Industrial School for Girls. Huntington's enterprise was devoted to teaching domestic arts—cooking, cleaning, sewing, hygiene—as well as the social arts of greeting and entertaining, to the "daughters of the poor." Grace visited the school and quickly became a partisan of Huntington's efforts. Dodge was taken by an approach to education that focused on the needs of the learners, rather than on the expertise of the instructors. The Wilson School engaged the students in the learning process through role playing. Dodge admired the skills of the teachers and threw herself into learning their pedagogical strategies.

She organized an association in 1880 to prevent the Wilson School approach from "degenerating into careless and erratic methods of teaching."[44] She and Huntington named it the Kitchen Garden Association (KGA), a nod to the "learning by doing" approach that Huntington had borrowed from kindergarten classes and applied to industrial education. The association prepared instruction manuals devoted to Huntington's methodology, sponsored teacher preparation classes, and offered dozens of direct teaching programs. The *New York Times* reported in April 1881 that over 2,000 young people from different social classes were enrolled in the KGA in New York City alone. Eventually, the KGA became a worldwide movement, with chapters in India and England, and the professional teaching of "industrial arts" was launched.

Dodge also began teaching traditional Sunday school classes at the urging of evangelist Dwight Moody, a favorite of her father who stayed with the family while leading his New York City revival meetings in 1876.[45] Her classes at the Madison Square Presbyterian Chapel attracted girls from the working classes, and she soon discovered that they had many questions for her beyond their Bible lessons. They were curious about how this wealthy woman lived, what her home was like, and what she thought about men. Most of the attendees were being raised by mothers who worked long hours outside the home. They themselves had gone to work in factories or shops at an early age and were as ignorant about the lives of wealthy women as Grace was about their lives. Soon Grace found herself sharing her "household" knowledge with her charges.

This early effort (Dodge was twenty-three in 1880) provided in-service training for Grace's next project. By 1881, the informal girls club that Grace had organized among her Sunday school students was running out of steam. They had lost their place to meet and attendance was dropping, a sign that Dodge had grown a bit too didactic for their taste. Fearing the end of the "club," a girl named Irene Tracy asked Grace if she would come to the factory where Irene worked (the factory manufactured silk ribbons and bags) to talk about "life." Grace replied that if Tracy could find twenty girls willing to attend such a discussion, she would agree. Here was an opportunity for Dodge to test her own capacity as an educator outside a church framework, and to bridge the gap between wealthy and working-poor social classes.

The first meetings were awkward and showed Dodge the deep distrust these girls felt toward "women of leisure." The girls pressed her to admit that such women had little respect for working girls. In her typically straightforward way, Grace acknowledged that this was often true. She was well aware, through her social connections, of the prevailing attitude of her social peers. Most felt that working girls/women displaced men from work, and were working primarily to indulge themselves in finery.[46]

Over time, Grace won the confidence of the factory girls through her openness and sincerity, traits that were to be the hallmark of her career. She learned to do more listening than speaking, a radical pedagogical strategy even today. Dodge focused the discussions on what we would now probably call an "empowerment" approach. She offered few rules or regulations other than that the girls should attend regularly and should be interested in learning more about the world. Grace used her social connections to persuade guest speakers to address topics the girls wished to learn more about. Although most presenters focused on household management issues, budgeting, investing, balancing accounts, and the like, others dealt with more personal matters such as female health, job skills, and relationships.[47] The girls wanted to discuss whether it was possible have a home life and work life.[48] The ironic tone of the following journal entry of one of the members suggests that they found no simple answers:

> Trying to be twins when she wasn't born that way. . . . Men are a great deal wiser in this respect; they never try to do two things at once. . . . What would any sensible person think of a man who worked ten hours in a shop, and then went home and made his shirts and his coat and trousers and trimmed his hats and washed his linen and swept the parlor?[49]

Dodge was deepening her understanding of women's lives beyond the safe confines of privilege. She saw that the girls aspired to be wives, mothers, and homemakers despite their twelve-hour workdays, six days per week. She was also learning how resistant her well-to-do friends were about educating these girls at all. Most dismissed the effort as simply a waste of time. She sought advice about how to grow the group from a (female) foreman in the factory where the girls worked. She was warned not to patronize the girls, but rather to "offer an opportunity for the girls to govern and do for themselves."[50]

Dodge had the wisdom to embrace this advice. It pointed toward a kind of education that honored the knowledge and commitment of the students, something she believed in already. The guidance was vindicated by the girls' decision to name their club. "Let us call ourselves the Working Girls Society and show New York that we are not ashamed of work."[51] They made their goals cooperation, self-governance, and self-reliance. They proposed to use their meetings to learn, to socialize, and to build a sense of camaraderie. The formula seemed to work, as the club soon reached 150 members strong.

A room was rented to hold regular meetings, and the girls decorated it to their own taste, using "turkey red paint and curtains," vivid color to demonstrate their independence and vitality.[52] It remains unrecorded what Grace thought about the decorating scheme for the clubroom, but we can imagine that she kept her mouth shut. She surely appreciated the symbolic importance for the girls to have a space that they could call their own outside their crowded tenement dwellings.

Dodge focused her personal attention on the entrepreneurial challenge of growing her nascent organization. She set about educating her peers about the value of these empowering activities that the working girls had developed. She obtained detailed coverage of the clubs' activities in the press.[53] She sought opportunities to speak in public at women's clubs, women's colleges, and church groups throughout the Northeast, always stressing the talents and industriousness of the young women in an effort to position them as "worthy poor" in the minds of her frankly biased peers. As a natural alliance builder, she quickly perceived the potential of cooperation with the settlement house movement and other emerging social service organizations.

By March 1885, only thirteen months after the original organizational meeting, the New York Post reported on the first annual meeting of the Association of Working Girls Societies, noting that attendance topped 1,000 representatives of clubs in New York City, with delegates from Philadelphia and Yonkers, New York, attending as well. Grace had done her job in New York. Five years later, in April 1890, there were 2,155 attendees at the national convention of Working Girls Societies, representing seventy-five clubs in industrial cities in the East and Midwest. One year later, the meeting of the New York City clubs attracted 2,000 members and over 7,000 guests from throughout the country to Madison Square Garden.

Grace probably felt a bit uncomfortable with the slogan adopted at this meeting ("agitation, education, cooperation"), but she rejoiced in the girls' struggle for dignity and independence. The original model developed by Dodge in partnership with her working girls dominated most of these clubs. Meetings were devoted to "practical talks" on subjects chosen by the members. Wealthy women often played important roles in enabling the clubs to operate as their members wished. The relationships formed between the ladies of leisure and the working girls were seldom comfortable. Few of these volunteers possessed Dodge's skills as a listener and a mediator. But the relationships also created many advantages for both sides. In describing the impact of these cross-economic relationships, one young member said they had "completely changed my life and where I once saw no beauty and considered life one long grind, now I find plenty to interest mind and heart."[54] As the history of the clubs indicates, many upper-class women came belatedly to appreciate the value of educating the working girls, as they continued to invest and to build the beginnings of a social safety net even before the labor movement and the New Deal.

The clubs supported themselves through membership dues and initiation fees (25 cents per year and 20 cents one-time initiation were the original amounts). Dodge, as we might anticipate, had instilled a tradition of careful bookkeeping and scrupulous attention to detail in the affairs of the clubs. Wealthy club "sponsors" were cultivated to offer additional "angel investments" to provide growth capital. These donations were also logged into budget books and members managed the gifts that came in. A group of these investors developed the Alliance Employment Bureau in 1891 to help girls advance their careers as jobs became available. These investments paid significant dividends in the form of improved job placements for the members. The bureau actively sought job listings, trained girls for jobs, and paid for their travel and room and board as transitions occurred. The bureau refused to work with firms or households that did not offer girls and women fair wages.

The high point for Dodge undoubtedly came in 1893 at the World's Columbian Exposition. Dodge was invited to author a chapter in a souvenir book entitled *What America Owes to Woman*. Here was a chance to present the value of the Working Girls Clubs to a national audience. The National Association of Working Girls Societies was created, she specified, to "knit together the Clubs and to protect their interests." It would assist all clubs in procuring top-notch teachers and medical specialists to educate the members, and "make known the aims of the movement and ensure the alignment of goals as new clubs formed." She underscored the accomplishments of the clubs in an effort to demonstrate to her readers that investments in these working girls were paying off for society at large. She lists the Choral Union, a newspaper, the Mutual Benefit Fund, the Summer Holiday program, and the Auxiliary Society as but a few of the socially beneficial activities of the clubs. The Auxiliary Society had as its goal the creation of additional clubs across the land.

Dodge chose to step down from the national board in 1896, having devoted fifteen years of her life to the education of working girls and the professionalization of those who would presume to teach them. The working girls societies testify to Dodge's success in building a self-sustaining system of education and self-help for her "girls," one strong enough to grow and evolve after the originator had withdrawn from active leadership.

By 1900, the twenty-one clubs in New York City were led by councils composed of members. Clubs organized courses on bookkeeping and typewriting, adding job skills for an ever-changing economy. They established national savings plans and mutual aid societies just as Grace had envisioned a decade earlier. In 1901, the New York Association launched the Manhattan Trade School for Girls. The school was so successful that it was taken over by the City of New York in 1910 and opened a new era in practical free education for women. Finally in 1911, the national federation developed a guaranteed insurance program with modest monthly contributions by members, a forerunner of modern unemployment insurance. The clubs made an enduring contribution to women's work lives and to the nation as a whole over subsequent decades. They offered an alternative to unionization.[55] They promoted relationships between women of different social levels and dispelled many prejudices in the process. As in the case of the women's exchanges, this collaboration built a sense of independence and self-help for all concerned.

Dodge, meanwhile, continued the pursuit of her larger goal, the elevation of teaching to the status of a profession. Her leadership of the highly successful Kitchen Garden Association led to an appointment to the New York City Board of Education in 1886. Dodge distinguished herself once again by the seriousness with which she undertook these responsibilities. She reviewed textbooks, keeping scrupulous notes on each, visited classes, and reviewed examinations used by the teachers. She compiled lengthy reports on the activities of her committee that became the standard for the board's work. She also joined the board of the Industrial Education Association (IEA), the successor organization to the KGA, and became the acting president. The IEA provided immensely popular classes at its headquarters near Washington Square, training teachers to teach the skills needed to gain employment in the rapidly industrializing nation. Using funds provided by George Vanderbilt, Dodge hired Nicholas Murray Butler to be president of the IEA in 1887, writing in her request to Vanderbilt that she believed the organization needed "brains" as it grew its teaching function. Butler proved to be a strong and ambitious educator who pushed for the IEA to formalize its collaborative relationship with Columbia University.

The IEA became the New York College for the Training of Teachers and eventually, in 1889, the Teachers College of Columbia University, which remains one of the preeminent schools of education in the country. Dodge became a trustee of Teachers College and chair of the Finance Committee (thus the de facto head of development for the new college). Once again, her personal records testify to the energy, drive, and thoroughness she brought to this daunting task. By her own account, Grace wrote 32,371 letters, as well as 10,680 leaflets and reports, seeking private funding support for the fledgling college. In 1894, she noted tartly that "no secretary" had been made available to her to support her efforts.[56]

She was very successful nonetheless, raising some $100,000 between March and July of 1894 alone, and she remained a trustee of the college until her death in 1914.[57] But her relationship with Butler and the faculty of the college was distant at best. On one occasion, she was rebuked by Butler's successor, James Earl Russell, for criticizing the curriculum for kindergarten teachers, which she felt lacked appropriate emphasis on the moral and spiritual grounding of educators. So she turned her attention to another leadership opportunity, one where her particular skills and beliefs as a "humble servant" could add more value.

In 1905, Dodge offered her services as a mediator to the American Young Women's Christian Association. The "YW" had been started in England in the 1850s, and American chapters initially sprang up in the major cities on the East Coast of the United States. These chapters focused on providing shelter and services to women traveling alone. As the idea spread to the Midwest, it attracted many student members and a decidedly evangelical bent modeled in part on the Young Men's Christian Association, resulting in a distinct organization called the American Committee. Grace, whose father had been a strong leader of the YMCA movement, offered to help the two factions find a way to unite and take better advantage of their considerable membership (over 100,000 at the time).

The circumstances were ready-made for Dodge to deploy her lifetime of servant leadership. She convened a "joint committee" that met daily for ten months, with Grace presiding at every session. Her self-discipline and thoroughness had not varied from her time on the New York City Board of Education. In a letter written as the deliberations got under way, Dodge cited her lengthy experience with young women and noted that "from all these friends, I have learned a great deal." She also expressed her personal belief that "the spiritual life of young women needs to be more emphasized." Dodge's talents as a mediator and alliance builder (apparently she called for a moment of prayer every time the discussions became heated) brought the sides together, and in 1906, Grace was chosen to become the national president of the new organization, the YWCA of the United States of America.

During the eight years that she served in this capacity, Dodge led the organization with her customary dedication and zeal, believing that the YW could provide great service to the working girls to whom she felt so attached. As usual, her primary strategy was education, and the YWs organized a variety of job-training programs and placement bureaus for young women under her leadership. But she also used education to strengthen the future of her organization through systematic staff training. She set up the National Training School for YWCA "secretaries" (the executive staff), apparently lending her own gracious home until she could raise the funds to build a national headquarters, which she did on Lexington Avenue in New York City. The current YWCA website notes that hundreds of future leaders of the YW came through these training programs, each one presumably influenced by Dodge's charge:

> Get each young worker to feel that she has a part to play in the world's history, and that the world will be either better or worse for the fact of her living in it. Keep up her courage, give her thoughts outside of herself and her work, and by all this lay the foundation for a true womanhood; in a word, teach each member to become "mistress of herself."[58]

Grace passed away on December 27, 1914. A biographer summarizes her life in touching terms: "Her life was so nicely attuned to the Infinite Goodness that she could detect the latent goodness in a person."[59] Here in a nutshell is Dodge's entrepreneurial triumph. She sensed that many working girls had enormous potential to contribute to the growth of the nation. She believed that skilled teachers could develop human capital to its highest level. What was missing was a system to ensure that this value creation happened consistently for all citizens, but particularly for working girls. She wanted professional training for teachers as had been achieved for doctors and lawyers. No less an entrepreneur than J. P. Morgan admired Dodge's gifts:

> Grace H. Dodge had the finest business brain in the United States, not excepting that of any man.

TEN

Investors in
Social Profit Enterprise

Miss Garrett's contribution consisted in securing the adoption of these
requirements (for a medical school curriculum) through the use of force
majeure, *or perhaps more correctly,* force monnetaire [*sic*].
—A. M. Chesney, *The Johns Hopkins Hospital and*
the Johns Hopkins School of Medicine, A Chronicle, 1867–1893

The social profit sector was shaped in the final quarter of the nineteenth century by new levels of wealth creation in the nation. We all recall the names John D. Rockefeller, Andrew Carnegie, and Cornelius Vanderbilt, but there were many additional entrepreneurs whose leadership in the Industrial Revolution created large personal fortunes. Their generosity created great institutions of enormous social value to the nation.

The ability to inherit wealth enabled women social entrepreneurs to play a new role in the creation of social profit. Rather than selling ideas to improve the nation and seeking investors to support their ideas, wealthy women could act as investors themselves. They could choose to fund the ideas of others or their own ideas as they saw fit. Most took the responsibilities of wealth seriously. Their investments yielded gains in our nation's stock of human and intellectual assets that we continue to benefit from today.

Many wealthy women were philanthropists rather than social entrepreneurs. A philanthropist is not automatically entrepreneurial. A rich and generous person may have no audacious goals or commitments to social change; he or she may have no interest in making a strategic plan to achieve a particular objective or in doing any more work than simply writing a check. But some early female philanthropists define the meaning of "informed investors," and we admire their creative contributions to the greater good. Although none enjoyed the privilege of a college education, as many women in the next generation would, they shared a voracious appetite for self-education. They invested first in themselves, using their funds and their connections to study the important issues of the day. Each of these women reached far-sighted conclusions about what needed to be done to strengthen the nation and acted on her own judgment. As we will see, these judgments were not timid; they were seldom aligned with the more conservative ideas of those who advised them. This first generation of women social investors exhibited a taste for high-risk, high-reward investments. They made plenty of mistakes, as any high-risk investor is likely to do. But in the social profit sector, as in the business world, money talks, and we can still hear the voices of Mary Garrett, Caroline Phelps Stokes, and Olivia Sage loud and clear today.

Mary Elizabeth Garrett was the only daughter of John Work Garrett, the president of the Baltimore and Ohio Railroad. He was a prominent citizen of Baltimore, where he served as a trustee of the university created by his fellow transportation baron, Johns Hopkins. Mary was exceptionally close to her father. She often accompanied him on his business travels and soon became his "secretary," meeting prominent businessmen and observing, if not sharing in, his business dealings. She had a front-row seat from which to observe the rapidly developing infrastructure of

the nation. Her father navigated the competition with the Chesa-
peake Canal, survived attacks on the railroad's trunk lines by
Confederate troops, and judiciously built an integrated network
of rail lines for both passengers and cargo. A confidant of Lincoln,
close friend of George Peabody and Johns Hopkins, and himself
a leader in employer-employee relations (he established pensions
for his workers), he enabled Mary to see the big picture in a way
that few women of her era did.

   She was thus accustomed to the management and governance
systems of the new economy. She also observed how these same
systems were deployed in the building of institutions such as colleges and universities, thanks to her father's involvement with
Johns Hopkins. Mary was particularly interested in the issue of
women's education, a topic that had generated considerable controversy in the 1870s and 1880s. When the time came, she was
ready and willing to risk her funds on educating girls and women
to the same level and in the same curricula as boys and men. The
separate-but-equal philosophy implicit in the creation of institutions such as Vassar (in 1861) and Smith (in 1875)[1] was not
acceptable as far as Mary Garrett was concerned.

   There was plenty of new "scientific" information being produced at the time that argued against advanced education for
women. The argument over women's education boiled down to
the issue of female physiology. Education for girls and women
was acceptable only if it allowed for their special circumstances
and avoided placing undue strain on the delicate constitutions
of female students. Under the influence of Charles Darwin (*The
Origin of Species*, 1859), behavioral differences between males
and females that had previously been understood in social terms
now became the domain of science, of evolutionary biology, to
be precise. Darwin theorized about differences between male and
female behavior in the human species. "Woman seems to differ

159

from man in mental disposition, chiefly in her greater tenderness and lesser selfishness," Darwin wrote. "Man's competitiveness, ambition, and even his selfishness seem to be his natural and unfortunate birthright. The chief distinction in the intellectual powers of the two sexes is shown by man's attaining to a higher eminence, in whatever he takes up, than can woman—whether requiring deep thought, reason, or imagination, or merely the uses of the senses and the hands."[2]

Darwin's musings created an opportunity for lesser lights to legitimize their prejudices. In ways he never could have imagined, his work was used to justify claims about women, and later about those of African descent, and their biological readiness to live on equal terms with (white) men. Dr. Edward H. Clarke, a member of the Massachusetts Medical Society, Harvard professor, and author in 1873 of *Sex in Education*, found numerous physical dangers for overeducated women. Clarke reports:

> There have been instances, and I have seen such, of females in whom the special mechanism [the uterus] we are speaking of remained germinal,—undeveloped. It seemed to have been aborted. They graduated from school or college excellent scholars, but with undeveloped ovaries. Later they married, and were sterile.[3]

The education and intellectual excitement of girls, he notes,

> produce an excessive performance of the catamenial function; and this is the equivalent to a periodical hemorrhage. Sometimes they produce an insufficient performance of it; and this, by closing an avenue of elimination, poisons the blood, and depraves the organization. The host of ills thus included is known to physicians and to the sufferers as amenorrhoea, menorrhagia, dysmenorrhea, hysteria, anemia, chorea, and the like. Some of these fasten them-

selves on their victim for a lifetime . . . Fortunate is the girls' school or college that does not furnish abundant examples of these sad cases.[4]

The reason for these difficulties, Clarke continued, was that brain work made demands on the whole body and diverted energy from the "divinely-appointed field of operation. . . ." The "energy" that women's brains and reproductive systems had to draw on was finite, a zero-sum situation. Extraordinary demands on brains would occur at the sacrifice of the reproductive organs. With just so much energy to go around, a price would be paid if balances were disrupted. One case he reported involved the youthful death of his young female patient who had out-achieved the men as well as the women in her class.

Clarke's conclusions grew darker and darker. Women could be highly educated but at grave consequences to the advancement of the human race, as well as their own personal health and well-being. Women's reproductive systems would necessarily be "aborted or deranged by the withdrawal of force that is needed for its construction and maintenance." Educated women would drift into what he identified as a "hermaphroditic condition . . . a dropping out of maternal instincts, and appearance of Amazonian coarseness."[5] Needless to say, Clarke considered the "identical education" of women not merely unwise, but nothing less than a "crime before God and humanity, that physiology protests against, and that experience weeps over."[6] A close friend of Mary Garrett, M. Carey Thomas, admitted that many women college students were "haunted . . . by the clanging chains of that gloomy little specter, Dr. Edward H. Clarke's *Sex in Education*."[7]

Historian Sue Zschoche identifies the challenge posed by Clarke's book. Women's opportunities were defined by her physiology, what Clarke called her "organization," not by public opinion, personal prejudice, or biased legal doctrines. It should be "the empirically revealed, ironclad laws of biology that determine and define true womanhood".[8] In an age of rising authority of scientific research findings, this argument robbed supporters of women's equal education of the vocabulary they needed to defend it. If they rejected Clarke's stance, they seemed to reject the legitimacy of the new biology.

It might seem simple to dismiss such biological reductionism,[9] but Clarke's work spawned a cottage industry of gender theorists. Clarke's first edition of *Sex in Education* sold out in a week and ran through sixteen editions. The editor of *Popular Science Monthly*, Edward L. Youmans, knew a hot topic when he saw one and published dozens of articles on variants of the Clarke hypothesis.[10]

At its extreme, the new evolutionary biology seemed to provide little more than a thin disguise for outright misogyny. French sociologist Gustave LeBon believed that women's inferiority could be proven by the differences between male and female brain structures:

In the most intelligent races, as among the Parisians[!], there are a large number of women whose brains are closer in size to those of gorillas than to the most developed of male brains . . . All psychologists who have studied the intelligence of women . . . recognize today that they represent the most inferior forms of human evolution and that they are closer to children and savages than to adult civilized man. They excel in fickleness, inconstancy, absence of thought and logic, and incapacity to reason. Without doubt, there exist some distinguished women, very superior to the average man, but they are as exceptional as the birth of any monstrosity, as, for example, of a gorilla with two heads. . . .[11]

Ironically, the new discipline of sociology, often identified with Harriet Martineau, contributed some unhelpful (and clearly flawed) conclusions to the debate, based on the use of the field's new "survey" technology. Surveys had shown, for instance, that college-educated women married less often and had fewer children than their education-spared sisters. Furthermore, 42 percent of all women admitted to mental institutions were college educated, compared to only 16 percent of all men.

Mary Garrett would have none of this flawed reasoning. Despite the theorizing of evolutionary biologists that seemed to intoxicate the reading public, Garrett held out for equal treatment. She was her powerful father's daughter, and if Darwin himself had shown up to tell her that women and girls should not be exposed to vigorous education, she would have assumed she could change his views. She used her financial assets during her life to change educational policy even when university faculties and their boards of trustees opposed her positions. She showed that persistence, personal preparation, and, of course, money would prevail. And they did. Mary Garrett lived "a life on her own terms."[12]

At their father's death in 1884, John Garrett's college-educated sons inherited his businesses. Mary, who was not college educated or married, received $2 million and all three of his estates. Her inheritance made her one of the wealthiest women and also one of the largest female landowners in the country. Garrett's first project was Baltimore's Bryn Mawr School for Girls, created with a gift of $500,000 in 1885. The name reflected her admiration for the women's college that had recently been founded in Pennsylvania. Like the college, the school offered a curriculum normally reserved only for male students: mathematics, sciences, modern and classical languages, and physical education. The centerpiece of the campus was a large gymnasium, a symbolic and to many a shocking testimony to Garrett's belief that *mens sana in corpore sano* (a healthy mind in a healthy body) applied equally to men and women. Critics called on her to invest in a model school of domestic economy to prepare girls for house-keeping and homemaking. But the *New York Times* wrote: "Being a thoroughly practical business woman, as well as a philanthropist, she undertook the matter (of the curriculum) personally."[13]

In this endeavor, as in more momentous efforts to come, Garrett was supported by a group of close female friends who came to be known as the Friday evening group. The women shared many traits: Most were wealthy, well educated, well connected, and interested in the substantive matters of the day. This was particularly true concerning matters at Johns Hopkins University, as all but one of the women were daughters of trustees of the institution. In 1893, the most compelling topic at Hopkins was medical education. The president, Daniel Coit Gilman, had spoken at length about the inferior state of medical education in America, when compared to the leading programs in Europe. He vowed to do something about it. He proposed the creation of a medical school at the "graduate" level, beyond college. The Hopkins Medical School would require students to acquire basic scientific training before being admitted.

Given her insider knowledge of Gilman's interest, Garrett offered the trustees a series of gifts if they would consider a coeducational science program at Hopkins, but her overtures were rejected outright. Gilman's plans stalled in 1890 because of a drop in the value of B&O Railroad shares (which made up a large share of the university endowment, as Garrett knew very well). Here was Mary's opportunity. She offered to raise $100,000, or roughly 25 percent of the funds needed to launch the medical school. But she would do so only if the trustees agreed to admit women to the program on exactly the same terms as men.

This was, as we can now appreciate, a genuinely radical notion, particularly in a field as sensitive to gender issues as medicine. Up to this point, women had not been allowed even to appear in the same classes as men. Despite a variety of protests, the trustees agreed to the bargain and Garrett set about making good on her promise. She twisted arms from one end of the country to the other, reporting to her Friday evening group through "Dear Girls" letters. Her persistence is captured in this epistle:[14]

> Dear Girls, Mr. Childs rec'd me of course most cordially; of course he wd have preferred it to be a pure friendly visit and when I said I had come to tell him . . . about our scheme, . . . he exclaimed that he was interested & that he had told us he would be very happy to contribute $1000 toward. As nice as I could, I told him that we should very much like him to help it very early; told him of what had already been promised, of how much good it would do if he wd start the Phila Fund with a very early subs. (I indicated that the $10,000 basis w'd be a very delightful one) that it w'd influence not only in Phila but all over the country . . . He w'd of course have preferred not to be asked for . . . the ten thousand, but he was really as nice as possible . . . I am inclined to think that he will increase his subscription.

Needless to say, the campaign was a success, in no small measure because Garrett chipped in some $47,000 of the eventual total of $109,000. It was now up to the trustees to make good on their end of the deal and complete the additional fund-raising required. Garrett and her colleagues gave the trustees until February 1892 to reach their target. But it soon became evident that they were not going to succeed, and once again, their difficulties offered Garrett an opportunity.

She announced that she would complete the funding with an additional gift of her own, to the tune of some $307,000. But this additional generosity would come at a price. This time around, not only would women be admitted on the same terms as men, but all candidates would have to furnish evidence of scientific training, in the form of course work in biology and chemistry, and a women's council would be created to offer guidance to female students, their faculty, and administrators. Some hard-nosed bargaining ensued, with President Gilman and senior faculty concerned about the potential for ongoing intervention in academic affairs. But agreement was ultimately reached in a document extending to several thousand words.[15] Garrett was satisfied that her "donor intent" was secure. The medical school opened in the fall of 1892, and the rest, as they say, is history, although it has taken until our current decade for medical school enrollments to reach gender parity nationwide.

Garrett was not finished, however. When Columbia University sought a gift in support of its medical school, she imposed the same conditions that she had at Hopkins (they also complied). Garrett's behavior in relation to Bryn Mawr College was even more assertive, if not shocking in today's academic world. Approached by the trustees of the college for a gift to develop a campus master plan, Garrett imposed a different kind of condition. Her gift would be contingent on the offer of the presidency of Bryn Mawr to Garrett's close friend and Friday night group member, M. Carey Thomas.[16]

Thomas was certainly qualified for the post, having earned a PhD at the University of Zurich, one of the few universities in the world at the time that allowed women to compete for the PhD. She was appointed dean of the college at Bryn Mawr at the age of thirty-one. But still, Garrett made a bold move and it paid off. Early in her academic career, Thomas affirmed her position on the still-contentious issues surrounding women's education. She wrote in "Should the Higher Education of Women Differ from That of Men?":

> Women while in college ought to have the broadest possible education. This college education should be the same as men's, not only because there is but one best education, but because men's and women's effectiveness and happiness and the welfare of the generation to come after them will be vastly increased if their college education has given them the same intellectual training and the same scholarly and moral ideals.[17]

Thomas served as president of Bryn Mawr from 1896 to 1922, and Garrett, having contributed generously to the cause of women's suffrage following her pioneering educational work, eventually retired to the campus herself. Garrett's leadership shows a remarkable story of radical investment in institutional change.

Mary Garrett created opportunities in the lives of women and in scientific education in a simple and powerful way. She did not simply *respond* to requests for funds. She defined the future for the institutions she knew and loved.

Caroline Phelps Stokes was Garrett's match as a social investor. Both women shared a sense of confidence in their own observational abilities. They appreciated the importance of research to substantiate their observations and were prepared to invest their considerable assets to fund such research. These investments in intellectual capital, in the creation of knowledge, opened an important chapter in the role of the social profit sector, creating the foundations on which the social scientific enterprise is built.

Caroline Phelps Stokes (1854–1909) was another fortunate daughter of another large, wealthy family. Her grandfather and father had made their fortunes in the mining industry, and both Caroline and her older sister, Olivia, inherited considerable sums. Caroline spent her own life in philanthropic activities that made a dramatic change in the education of African Americans and Native Americans in the United States. The family had a tradition of social involvement, dating back several generations. The girls' grandfather, Anson Phelps, was instrumental in the establishment of Liberia, the idealistic effort to repatriate formerly enslaved blacks to Africa at the end of the Civil War. Caroline demonstrated her social consciousness at an early age, writing in a school essay at age eleven: "The poor people suffer very much. . . . I think the tenement houses are dreadful places, almost as bad as prisons."

The Stokes sisters traveled widely, both in the United States and overseas. They treated the trips as educational opportunities rather than idle diversions. In 1896–1897, they completed an around-the-world voyage that included stops in India and in Africa, where they visited Christian missions, witnessing firsthand the dire conditions of women and children in poverty. Their travels in America took them to the West where they had their first introduction to the impoverishment of Native Americans on ever-smaller tracts of land.

The sisters were properly philanthropic during their lifetimes, using their funds to honor their Christian beliefs and their interest in educational diversity. They supported the construction of impressive chapels at Columbia University in New York City, Berea College in Kentucky, and Tuskegee Institute in Alabama. Caroline also continued her family's commitment to the city of Ansonia, Connecticut, which had been named for her grandfather's family. She donated a public library there in 1892.

At the time of her death in 1909, Caroline followed through on her childhood worries about housing for the poor. She established a fund to construct improved tenements for working poor people. Her major investment, however, was education. She set up one of the first family foundations in America, the Phelps Stokes Fund, donating almost $1 million toward the following mission:

> The Fund's charter interests include the education of African Americans, Native Americans, Africans, and needy White youth. Its logo, four open books, symbolizes the importance of education in promoting the fullest development and use of human talent.

It may be difficult for us today to appreciate the boldness of this very "individualistic" investment. The value of investing time and money in the education of blacks, American Indians, and the poor, like the identical education of women and girls in 1880, was not at all widely accepted in 1909. The bequest was directed to promote the "fullest development and use of human talent." Consequently, it funded not only individual scholarships but research and knowledge production on the most effective ways to achieve the development of human talent among these disenfranchised groups.

One of the fund's first studies, "Negro Education in the United States," completed in 1917, detailed the differences between white and black schools and presented the inadequacies of the segregated system.[18] This enormous two-volume, three-year undertaking, in cooperation with the Office of Education within the U.S. Department of the Interior, documented the flaws in the effort to sustain "separate but equal" schools, fifty years before *Brown v. Board of Education*. Through the dissemination of these studies, the fund also raised awareness among Americans that the nation as a whole would be well served by improvements in the treatment of these peoples.

The Phelps-sponsored research contradicted the assertions of evolutionary biologists concerning the feasibility of educating people of African descent. Dr. Samuel Cartwright, who had studied medicine under Declaration signer Benjamin Rush, a strong abolitionist, had identified in 1851 two types of mental illness experienced by African Americans. He named one of them "drapetomania," an illness that caused the enslaved to flee from their masters. This condition, "as much a disease of the mind as any other species of mental alienation," was common among slaves whose masters had "made themselves too familiar with them, treating them as equals." The need to submit to a master was "built into the very bodies of African Americans . . . written in the physical structure of his knees, being more flexed or bent, than any other kind of man."[19] The other disease was characterized as the "unique ailment differing from every other species of mental disease, as it is accompanied with physical signs or lesions of the body"—resulting in a desire "to avoid work and generally to cause mischief." Dysaesthesia Aethiopis was also stimulated by a lack of aggressive governance and therefore more common in freed blacks than in slaves.[20]

In 1868, Dr. John Van Evrie in *White Supremacy and Negro Subordination* contended that educating Negroes would certainly do irrevocable harm to their brains. This effort would alter their center of gravity, Van Evrie asserted, and they would find it impossible to stand erect or to walk.[21] Caroline Phelps Stokes provided that her bequest would fund "scientific and practical study of the Negro and his adjustment to the present civilization." The fund made its first grants of $12,500 each to the Universities of Virginia and North Carolina to support a research project undertaken by the Southern Sociological Congress in cooperation with the Young Men's Christian Association. The project aimed "to study and improve social, civic, and economic conditions in the South solving the race question in a spirit of the helpfulness to the Negro and of equal justice to both races."[22] New studies funded by philanthropy and carried out by African American and white scholars would begin the process of pushing back on the nineteenth-century deprecation of the black race.

In 1903, a young University of Chicago–trained sociologist, Monroe Nathan Work, had already assembled several thousand Library of Congress holdings related to Africa. Over the next twenty years, he would compile A Bibliography of the Negro in Africa and America. This document is still regarded as the most reliable and comprehensive listing of sources by and about people of African descent published before 1928. In 1906, the Library of Congress bibliography contained 522 alphabetically arranged unclassified entries. Over a lifetime of diligence, Work's bibliography grew to include some 20,000 references on the American black, about 3,000 references on the American black outside the United States, and 10,000 references on the black in Africa.[23] Work joined the faculty at Tuskegee Institute around 1908 and began the annual publication of the Negro Year Book, as well as a chronicle of lynchings of blacks across the South.

Caroline Phelps Stokes was supporting the Tuskegee Institute at the time of her death. She had established a scholarship in honor of J. J. Roberts, the first president of Liberia, and contributed to the campus chapel. She made a special bequest to Tuskegee in her will, as she did for several other institutions. Most important, however, her nephew, Anson Phelps Stokes, who served as secretary of the Stokes Fund, was a member of Tuskegee's board of trustees and served briefly as board chairman. He became one of the greatest supporters of Monroe Nathan Work as he compiled, edited, and published A Bibliography of the Negro.[24]

As Caroline had envisioned before she died, the fund did more than simply fund research. It partnered with the General Education Fund established by John D. Rockefeller to support the historically black colleges and universities (HBCUs) that educated the majority of black college students in the country in the first half of the twentieth century. The fund also supported many grassroots organizations dedicated to opportunities for blacks. Among many others, the Phelps Stokes Fund nurtured the Citizens Housing Council of New York, the Boys Choir of Harlem, the Harlem Youth Development Foundation, and the Jackie Robinson Foundation. Each of these organizations is now independent and has embarked on significant projects that create opportunities for minorities both in the United States and in Africa.[25] The American Indian College Fund, today's largest social profit organization devoted to supporting Native American education, also traces its origins directly to the Phelps Stokes Fund.

Caroline Phelps Stokes invested in a future where science could liberate citizens from prejudice, rather than serve to reinforce it. In her deep and careful conservatism, she believed that the argument of the Declaration of Independence would prove correct when opportunities for all were equalized. Her wealth enabled her to create a unique asset, a permanent fund that would enable continuing investments in the greater good into the future. This investment has spawned a cascade of additional investments over the decades, confirming her sense that a foundation could serve as a continuing asset for the nation.

Caroline and Olivia Phelps Stokes, like Mary Garrett, represent the beginnings of female individualism based on financial wealth. Caroline's will specified that funding should be directed to the support of African education as well as American education. The fund followed this injunction and issued comprehensive surveys of education in West Africa (1921) and East Africa (1923), prepared

INVESTORS IN SOCIAL PROFIT ENTERPRISE

by African scholars as well as fund staff. When Olivia died a decade later, she left additional funds earmarked for the creation of a post-secondary institution in Liberia. The institution, called the Washington Agricultural and Industrial Institute, continues to operate today. The Phelps Stokes sisters saw America in a global context, though they would not have used that language. Their view of a better America extended beyond our nation's borders to include the well-being of a larger human family, a view that is only today becoming widely shared. Their transformative investments extended across an ocean that up to this time had been better known as the major highway of the slave trade.[26] Their imaginative personal investments in human capital have produced outcomes that moved the vision of the Founders a little closer to lived reality for important groups of Americans.

The third major investor in social profit enterprise at the beginning of the twentieth century is perhaps the most "individualistic" of all. Her fortune was by far the largest, her ideas the most eclectic, and her legacy an important component of our social profit sector today. Hers is a remarkable story, given that she did not have a penny to her own name before the age of seventy-eight.

Olivia Sage became one of America's richest women in 1906 when her husband, the railroad tycoon Russell Sage, died. He left her roughly $50 million, having generally refused to share his wealth during his lifetime. Olivia was only too happy to make up for lost time in mobilizing his great fortune on behalf of the greater good.

Olivia was an intelligent and curious woman who had always taken it upon herself to be well informed about the social issues of the day. One year before her husband's death, Mrs. Sage (as she insisted on being addressed) had published an article[27] in which she explained her beliefs concerning the responsibilities of wealth:

Woman is responsible in proportion to the wealth and time at her command. While one woman is working for bread and butter, the other must devote her time to the amelioration of the condition of her laboring sister. This is the moral law.

She went so far in her piece as to assert "that 'missionaries' were needed among the idle rich [ladies] more than among any other class of citizens" to ensure that these teachings were understood. Such opinions expressed in public, we can imagine, did little to endear her to the wealthy ladies in whose circles she traveled with Russell.

Mrs. Sage was clearly ambivalent about wealth during her thirty years of marriage. She came from a modest background herself, having had to "work" as a teacher to support herself as a young woman. Once married to a wealthy man, she did not spend great amounts on her clothing or on entertaining to impress her friends. She seemed more anxious to support the propagation of her Christian faith through contributions to the Bible Society. But she did succumb to some social pressure among the established families in her husband's business circles, such as the Rockefellers, Vanderbilts, and Morgans. She spent both time and money to document her family's connections (on her mother's side) to the original settlers on the *Mayflower* voyage.

Olivia Sage had enjoyed an exceptional education for a middle-class woman in the 1840s. Despite her family's modest resources, she was enabled by her uncle to attend the Troy Female Seminary, later known as the Emma Willard School for Girls. This institution was recognized for its academic rigor, insisting that the young women study, and then be publicly examined by faculty, in classical and modern languages, history, mathematics, and even human physiology. Olivia surely became accustomed to using her mind as a young woman and was given to speaking her mind on numerous topics throughout her life. A friend commented that her home "looked like the newsroom of a daily paper." She had serious problems with her eyesight by the time of her husband's death, but no matter, she struggled through mountains of newspapers and magazines as well as the annual reports of countless charitable societies and associations, often having material read aloud to her. Once she had a fortune to back up her opinions, she was ready to let her money do some talking as well.

Despite her reserved personal nature and her advanced age, she prepared to back up her call to women of wealth with her own actions. She invited Robert de Forest,[28] her family lawyer, to advise her. Together they arrived at an original idea: She would immediately create an independent foundation with a broad purpose, "the improvement of social and living conditions in the United States of America." She would invest $10 million to launch the effort. Moreover, the Russell Sage Foundation (as she insisted it would be called) would include four women among its nine trustees: Sage herself, Helen M. Gould (daughter of Jay Gould, a former business partner of her late husband), Gertrude S. Rice (a founder of the Charity Organizations Society of New York City with Josephine Lowell), and Louisa Schuyler (mentor to the young Grace Dodge).[29]

No one could accuse Mrs. Sage of failing to think big. She wanted to fund the research necessary to document the causes of poverty and illness. She had heard lots of heartbreaking tales from well-intentioned matrons about the lives of the poor. Now it was time to find facts that could be used to build effective programs, and she was prepared to pay the bill. John D. Rockefeller Sr. and Andrew Carnegie had taken a particular interest in the physical and life sciences. Mrs. Sage was determined, despite the resistance of her adviser, to support efforts to bring the same type of systematic inquiry to solving the complex social problems that impaired the quality of life for too many citizens:

> Margaret Olivia Sage . . . set an example with the simple and breathtakingly general language of the charter she obtained from the State of New York in 1907. The Russell Sage Foundation, her charter read, was established to promote "the improvement of social and living conditions in the United States of America," by "any means" the Foundation's trustees deemed appropriate, including "research, publication, education, the establishment and maintenance of charitable or benevolent activities, agencies and institution, and the aid of any such activities, agencies or institutions already in existence."[30]

The originality of the Russell Sage Foundation is expressed by Daniel Murphy, president of the New York State Conference of Charities and Correction at the time, praising the newly established foundation as "one of the most significant gifts of modern philanthropy. This is practically the first instance in our civilization where so munificent a sum has been contributed to scientific research in the social order."[31]

And so, under Olivia's watchful eye, the Russell Sage Foundation became America's first combination "think tank"[32] and general-purpose foundation. The board asked difficult questions: What are the core problems in the lives of poor city dwellers? Does help offered encourage laziness or inspire self-reliance? How do we know? Together with their founder, the leadership of the foundation undertook one of the most important projects ever funded by any foundation, the Pittsburgh Survey. They initiated this data-gathering project in 1907 and concluded it in 1914.

The immediate outcome was the publication of the six volumes of data and analysis,[33] providing the first systematic study of the living conditions of the working poor in a modern industrial community.

The picture that emerged from the work of the (predominantly female) foundation staff was quite dramatic. Their careful interviews revealed that most industrial accidents, often blamed on workers, had other causes: a lack of safety devices on machinery, hazardous working techniques imposed by employers, and the like. The study detailed the lack of space; the lack of access to fresh air, fresh water, and food; and the absence of sanitation facilities in homes and workplaces. The systemic inadequacies of the urban infrastructure and the dangers of the workplace were revealed for all to see.

The impact of the survey was not limited to Pittsburgh. The survey was widely studied in other cities and created, according to Jane Addams, a great zeal for social change in the country. Subsequent surveys were funded by the Sage Foundation in Topeka, Kansas; Atlanta, Georgia; Scranton, Pennsylvania; St. Paul, Minnesota; Ithaca, New York; and Springfield, Illinois. The data and analyses stemming from this work were used by a generation of change agents to inform the drive for workmen's compensation, improvements in housing for the working poor, and formal limits to the length of workdays.

The Sage Foundation also sponsored the creation of knowledge in the emerging field of public health. This field represented the intersection of scientific understanding of disease and the behavior patterns of society. As in the case of "social science," public health represented a revolution in thinking and problem solving. The Sage Foundation–sponsored study in Topeka, Kansas, offers an excellent illustration of the application of the new science of germs to the well-being of society.

The study, entitled *A Public Health Survey of Topeka*, was funded by the foundation and published by the Topeka Improvement Survey Committee in 1914.[34] The section devoted to the milk supply of the city illustrates the confluence of knowledge about infectious diseases, the commercialization of milk as a consumer staple product, and the well-being of citizens. The study enabled trained investigators to visit dozens of farms where Topeka's milk was produced. It enabled the staff to trace the supply chain through middlemen and retailers. Samples were collected and analyzed. Individual farms were rated on multiple factors, as mandated by existing laws. This framework had been made possible by advances in the understanding of the causes and transmission of infectious diseases, thanks in part to the work of the French biologist Louis Pasteur in the 1860s. He had also demonstrated that harmful pathogens in liquids such as milk and beer could be eliminated by heating, a process that came to be known as pasteurization.

By 1914, the sources of contamination of milk supplies were well understood.[35] There were, in fact, many laws and regulations governing milk production, bottling, and transportation on the books. The picture that emerged in Topeka was, however, not a pretty one. The committee staff illustrated the report with multiple photos of the substandard facilities where the dairy cattle were fed, pastured, and milked. The report revealed that many of the rules were simply ignored and that the single milk inspector on the government payroll could do little to affect a system involving hundreds of small farms, distributors, and retailers. The careful documentation of the exhaustive study, which also included detailed reviews of the wastewater and storm sewer deficiencies, among many other problems, served as a blueprint for action for a generation of concerned citizens in a moderately sized midwestern city.

By 1921, the Russell Sage Foundation was the nation's chief supporter and coordinator of research, program development, and management training in social services—and for many related public policy areas, including housing, zoning, city planning, public health, and labor relations. The foundation's departments of Charity Organization, Recreation, Child-Helping, Surveys and Exhibits, and Delinquency and Penology set standards for their fields, supporting the growth of the national organizations in the fields and publishing the standard texts.[36] The foundation drafted model legislation not only for child welfare and improved working conditions for women, but also for anti-loan shark statutes and reform of the juvenile courts. In short, the work of the Sage Foundation provided the basis for a new generation of social entrepreneurs.

Olivia Sage's philanthropy was not limited to her foundation. She retained tens of millions of dollars in her own name, and her personal entrepreneurship is every bit as inventive, if less organized, as that of her foundation. She underwrote the design and construction of an airplane by a woman. The female engineer-aviator, Lillian Todd, succeeded in building the plane and Olivia spent a cold and windy day on eastern Long Island hoping to witness the maiden voyage of the aircraft. (It did not go well.)[37]

She became one of the early champions of the humane treatment of animals as an element of a just society. She believed that "the tender-heartedness of woman will naturally lead her to use her influence in bringing about a humane treatment of animals."[38] At a time when horses were the primary source of power for transportation in New York City, Sage personally funded the creation of some 2,000 watering stations throughout the city in 1915, in partnership with the Women's League for Animals. She campaigned for, and ultimately paid for, a veterinary hospital that would treat the animals of poor citizens free of charge and underwrote an ambulance service for animals throughout the city.

At the organizational level, she served as a board member of the Women's Society for Animal Protection in New York and through her personal involvement and investment drove the organization's expansion to the national level, creating the American Society for the Prevention of Cruelty to Animals (ASPCA). She campaigned actively against the use of bird feathers in women's fashion. She criticized the "barbarous fashion of wearing for her adornment the plumage of small birds," and in a robust assertion of her individualism, she defied her adviser de Forest by purchasing a 75,000-acre island off the coast of Louisiana for use as a bird sanctuary for migratory species. She donated the island, called Marsh Island, to her foundation in her will, and it remains a wildlife preserve to this day.

Another of her personal priorities involved the Long Island town of Sag Harbor, New York, where her mother had been born. In this case, her efforts ended badly, despite an abundance of good intentions. While Russell Sage was still living, Olivia had purchased her family's former home and renovated it as a summer house. Olivia loved the town, and after Russell's death, she began a campaign to restore it to prosperity, as it had fallen on hard times with the end of the whaling industry, coupled with a fire that had shuttered the only industrial business in town. She created a "kitty" to help the town poor, purchased new uniforms for the firemen, and paid for the renovation of the Presbyterian Church steeple. More boldly, she funded the building of a grand new public library, a new high school, and the creation of a city park. The park was particularly symbolic, as such creations figured prominently in the "city beautiful" movement of the time. Mrs. Sage had it designed by a New York City firm, with modern playground facilities on the site of a former horse-racing track, thus embodying the ideas of social improvement that the Russell Sage Foundation had researched and championed.

At first, her generosity was gratefully received by the citizens and town fathers, but over time the town residents apparently came to resent what they saw as her single-handed engineering of town improvements. Having failed to engage the community in her well-intentioned vision for a "model" Sag Harbor, she gave up her efforts and her beloved summer home.

Sage's personal philanthropy also extended to higher education, although it is difficult to sense that she brought the same passion to these projects that she did to her work with animals or in Sag Harbor. She made significant donations during her lifetime to Harvard, Princeton, Syracuse (her father's alma mater), and Rensselaer Polytechnic Institute (RPI). She repeatedly sought evidence from Syracuse that the scholarships for women she had provided were being put to their intended use. In her will, she left gifts ranging from $800,000 to $1.6 million to each of the institutions noted above, as well as to the historically black colleges Hampton and Tuskegee, and to Bryn Mawr, Vassar, Smith, and Wellesley. These were generous and important gifts at a critical time in the evolution of American education, but they broke no new ground, nor did they show much personal involvement on her part.

Even her creation of Russell Sage College seems to have engaged her only a little. We could find no evidence that she invested her personal knowledge or leadership in its creation. The college was launched on the original campus of the Emma Willard School that Olivia had attended. She provided a gift of $250,000. The college was successful from the start, offering a practical curriculum designed to educate competent women for the workforce. It endures to this day and now includes a junior college and a graduate division. But Olivia did not leave a significant bequest to Russell Sage College for Women.

Olivia Sage was a complicated, not to say contradictory, woman. Many sniped that she was overbearing. She had an enormous affection for certain species of animals and worried publicly about their well-being. In one oft-repeated tale, she arrived for a dinner party soaked to the skin, having taken public transportation rather than bring her own horses and carriage out in the rain. She seemed unfazed by the fact that the "public" transportation was a horse-drawn streetcar. Her concern for animals did not apparently extend to rodents with luxurious fur, as she was reputed to own no fewer than twelve fine fur coats at the time of her death.

She was modest and outspoken at the same time, schoolmarmish, pedantic, and sometimes arbitrary. She hated idleness and drove herself at a very advanced age to handle her responsibilities as a wealthy woman with pride and humility. As any number of developers can attest, she is hardly alone in her failed efforts to bring prosperity to a town she loved. She failed in some of her philanthropic efforts like any good risk-taking entrepreneur.

Olivia's investment enabled the Russell Sage Foundation to underwrite a revolution in the social profit sector. The sector would henceforth pursue the difficult work of strengthening America's commitment to mutuality, aided by a growing body of knowledge, both social and scientific. This knowledge could provide a documented basis for social action, rather than relying on touching stories of individual hardships. Perhaps more important, it could overcome misguided and prejudiced generalizations about groups of people based on anecdotal evidence. In short, the investments of Sage, Garrett, and Phelps Stokes produced knowledge that could mobilize the benefits of scientific understanding for the largest number of citizens.

The women investors confronted increasingly large and complex institutions shaping American society in the last quarter of the nineteenth century. They demonstrated the intelligence and intellectual energy to ask difficult questions concerning the uses of new knowledge. How would the scientific breakthroughs generated by Darwin, Pasteur, Gregor Mendel, and others benefit all citizens, not just a few lucky ones? How could the new methodologies of data collection and analysis yield insights that could be applied to help citizens in need, rather than simply filling the shelves of scholarly libraries? They arrived at these challenging questions by exhibiting intellectual curiosity, a willingness to remain engaged as active learners, and the physical stamina to see for themselves what was happening in the world.

ELEVEN

Social Science, Social Service, and Social Profit

Striding, like some modern Colossus, the southwestern shore of Lake Michigan, Chicago, the capital, the metropolis of the wealth producing West, rears her stately head, the most remarkable city in the world.
—"Chicago of Today," 1893

The importance of the Northwest Territory increased significantly with the election of Illinois native Abraham Lincoln to the presidency in 1860. Mary Livermore added to the profile of the territory through her remarkable civilian leadership during the Civil War. In the postwar era, Chicago came to symbolize the many disparate trends and aspirations that characterized the period, a city of great energy and wealth, as well as a volatile, conflicted, and corrupt aggregation of needy souls. By the 1890s, it was the home of some of the nation's most successful businesses. The names are synonymous with American enterprise: Philip and Herman Armour, and Gustavus Swift (meatpacking), Cyrus McCormick (farm equipment), and George Pullman (railroad cars), as well as the merchants Marshall Fields, Richard Sears, Alvah Roebuck, and Aaron Montgomery Ward. It was also home to one of the first "skyscrapers," as architect Louis Sullivan deployed the gearless elevator technology of the

Otis Elevator Company to produce the ten-story Auditorium Building in 1889.

Chicago was characterized by size and diversity on the human level as well. It was the home of over 1 million residents by 1890, an increase of some 700,000 residents since the great fire destroyed the city in 1872. Most of these newcomers were immigrants from throughout Europe, supplemented by tens of thousands of black Americans arriving from the South, all seeking a better life and a small piece of the American Dream.

Theirs was not an easy path to wealth or security. Survival was often the order of the day. The juxtaposition of a large human population and a large industrial sector made for a toxic mix. Competition for precious Lake Michigan water led to rapid pollution from both the community and industry. Slaughterhouses and railroad yards made smelly, filthy neighbors for those crowded into flimsy housing. Brutal winters and more brutal political corruption in city government only made matters worse. Chicago soon became a flashpoint for increasing tensions between employers and their workers. The Haymarket riot of 1886 and the clashes at the Pullman Company in 1894 characterized an era of frequent public violence, exacerbated by racial and ethnic conflicts and periodic financial panics that brought the economy to a standstill. For many citizens, the first public bathhouse that opened in 1893 to serve the 80 percent of residents without running water was of greater utility than the better-remembered events of that year—the openings of the University of Chicago and of the World's Columbian Exposition.

Against this backdrop, it seems unlikely that Chicago would be chosen as the site for America to celebrate the 400th anniversary of its founding. But indeed it was, winning out in the competition against New York and Washington, D.C. In the midst of a deep recession, Congress chose Chicago as the site to celebrate "America's coming of age—a grand rite of passage" for all the world to admire. Chicago would host the Expo by creating from scratch a "magic kingdom" of utopian cleanliness, orderliness, and efficiency.

The symbolism of the effort was unmistakable—a monument to the power of technology, planning, and design.[1] The millions of square feet of buildings laid out on 686 acres along newly created boulevards (swept daily, in contrast to city streets) were painted white.[2] Chicago's answer to Gustave Eiffel's tower that had been unveiled at the Paris Exposition Universelle of 1889 was the 264-foot-high, revolving wheel, complete with seats to ride on, created by engineer George Ferris and placed on the Expo's "midway" boulevard. During the six months that the Expo was open, it attracted some 27 million visitors.

Despite great expense and imagination, the Expo did not manage to escape reality completely. It attracted a wide variety of thought leaders representing a spectrum of opinions about contemporary social issues. The Woman's Building was equally divided between exhibits devoted to the latest kitchenwares and to women's struggles for equal rights and representation. Activists also organized the World's Congress Auxiliary that sponsored a series of symposia featuring well-known speakers and thinkers— male and female, religious and secular. The agenda focused on the great social issues of the day: female suffrage, equal rights, temperance, public health, municipal government, and the rights of black Americans, among them. Finally, labor organizers Samuel Gompers and Clarence Darrow took advantage of the Expo to hold a rally on behalf of the working poor that attracted some 25,000 participants to the Lake Michigan waterfront.

In retrospect, it is not surprising that the energetic and chaotic city of Chicago in the 1890s became a focal point for a new generation of women social entrepreneurs. There were great needs for social services; there were people with money who cared about America's "second city," and the city enjoyed a growing number of female college graduates who took themselves and the nation's problems seriously. Social enterprise in Chicago also profited from the inspirational leadership of America's first female winner of the Nobel Peace Prize, Jane Addams. Addams had opened Hull House in 1889, an idealistic experiment that offered female college graduates an alternative to returning home to await a marriage proposition or to care for aging parents. The goal of the settlement house, as it came to be known, was to bring a small measure of cleanliness and order to the neighborhood where it existed. The volunteer women (and men) could live together and work among the poor in a community dedicated to providing what the government did not or could not—language lessons, job training, child care, parenting and hygiene lessons, art and music lessons, and countless additional forms of support. Addams, a graduate of the local Rockford Seminary (not a religious institution), embodied the spirit of the social gospel approach to poverty. People were poor because of their circumstances, not because of any moral defects, and she had every faith that they could prosper through the support of citizen-to-citizen generosity. Addams's settlement houses solved a complex set of needs and wants across social classes. Hull House became a mecca for smart, educated, socially minded college graduates seeking opportunities for service and validation of their desire to use their education for the good of the nation. Many of these disciples eventually launched settlement houses in their own urban communities. Soon a College Settlement Association (CSA) was organized to serve as a clearinghouse for lessons learned among the dozens of settlement houses across the nation.

But Chicago's importance in the development of American social service enterprises is not limited to the founding of Hull House. It is also home to the University of Chicago, a distinguished university founded only one year before the Columbian Expo in a neighborhood adjacent to the Expo site. From its inception, the university was a unique institution. A student wrote during the institution's first year: "In many ways, the University of Chicago is wholly unique. It is at once an experiment and an assured success." Backed by John D. Rockefeller's funds and led by former Yale religion professor William Rainey Harper, Chicago planned to distinguish itself from its East Coast rivals by focusing on graduate, rather than undergraduate, education. Further, it would be a coeducational institution, admitting men and women on an equal basis. And finally, it would focus on public service, with many ties and commitments to the city where it was located.

Harper, Rockefeller, and the many local sponsors recruited to support the founding of a Chicago university envisioned an institution that would serve society by advancing intellectual inquiry. This mission attracted scholars and researchers who were inventing the new disciplines of political science, sociology, and political economy, all fields that sought to create insight into social problems and social policy through scientific methods. These thinkers, among them Thorstein Veblen and John Dewey, welcomed the connection between social theory and social action, and Chicago encouraged faculty to use the community as their laboratory for data gathering and hypothesis testing.

The first generations of female graduate students who pursued advanced degrees in the social sciences thus did not see a bright line between their academic pursuits and social action. On the contrary, these women were encouraged to use their social scientific skills to address the problems of the day.[3] They could seek causes and test solutions in the real world of Chicago.

As we can imagine, one of their favorite locations for fieldwork and intellectual debate was Hull House on Chicago's West Side. As part of its commitment to the community, the University of Chicago developed a continuing education division, called the Extension Division, from the outset. An enterprising minister and part-time sociology lecturer, Graham Taylor, persuaded President Harper that there should be a program for the training of "social workers" and others involved in community betterment. The program was a popular success, and a number of the newly minted female social science PhDs found teaching work in the program, even as they struggled to find academic appointments in their fields. After Harper's death, the university severed ties with the social science–based outreach program. Taylor and others reinvented the program as the Chicago School of Civics and Philanthropy, supported in large measure by tuition and from 1908 to 1915 by grants from the Russell Sage Foundation. The school established a research division, and the faculty and students put their scientific methods to work with Chicago neighborhoods as their laboratory. Over the years 1910–1920, they produced a series of illuminating studies, published in the social scientific journals of the day, that detailed and quantified the "lived reality" of the Chicago poor: a report on housing conditions of immigrants published in the *American Journal of Sociology* in 1910; a study entitled "The Delinquent Child and the Home" in 1912; and a book-length study of truancy published by the University of Chicago Press in 1917. Such was the quality of the research and teaching of the largely female faculty that the school was re-incorporated in the university in 1920 as the School of Social Service Administration.

The seamless connection of academic work to public service was crucial. The housing study led directly to the creation of the Chicago Immigrants' Protective League, devoted to protecting new arrivals from the unscrupulous scammers who preyed on them. Faculty members Sophonisba Breckinridge and Grace Abbott both assumed leadership roles in the league. The delinquency study led to the creation by the authors of a vocational placement program for boys released from reform school. The impressive results led to a jointly funded partnership between the School of Civics and the Chicago public schools called the Bureau of Vocational Supervision. Potential school dropouts were identified, interviewed, and provided with job placement assistance and a counselor.

The authors of the various School of Civics' studies offered a not-so-subtle indictment of public officials and the failure of government to care for those in need. It was difficult to determine the extent to which these failings were attributable to corruption, laziness, or a political philosophy that resisted government responsibility for creating equal opportunities for all citizens. Whatever the case, the Chicago researchers believed their research presented a call to action for those who cared about their community, and they embraced the responsibility with the same passion they brought to their research.[4]

The life and work of Florence Kelley (1859–1932) were profoundly shaped by the social science made possible by the previous generation of female social profit investors. She distilled her unusually varied experiences as a young woman into a set of audacious goals that transformed the nation. Her sometime collaborator, Supreme Court justice Felix Frankfurter, had this to say about Kelley: "She . . . had probably the largest single share in shaping the social history of the U.S. during the first 30 years of this century."

Kelley grew up in a prosperous Quaker-Unitarian family in Philadelphia. It was not a happy family, burdened by the deaths from infectious diseases of five of Florence's seven siblings before the age of six years and the subsequent depression of her mother. There is little doubt that these premature deaths of her siblings account, at least in part, for her lifelong commitment to improving health care for children. Her father served as a "radical Republican" U.S. congressman for three decades, championing educational and political opportunities for blacks and supporting the Morrill Act that created the coeducational land-grant universities.

Florence was bright, inquisitive, and self-motivated. She entered Cornell University in 1882 without the benefit of much formal education other than her readings of her father's library, but she worked hard, authoring a senior project entitled "The Law and the Child." She also profited from a year away from school following a serious bout with diphtheria, during which she lived in Washington with her father and enjoyed access to the Library of Congress. Upon graduation, she apparently sought admission to the University of Pennsylvania for graduate study in classical languages but was not admitted. When she accompanied her brother and mother to Switzerland, where her brother was treated for an eye ailment, she found access to graduate education in government and law at the University of Zurich. She also found a coterie of radical students, primarily from Germany and Russia, who embraced the critiques of capitalism formulated by Karl Marx and his protégé, Friedrich Engels.

Kelley spent the period from 1882 to 1886 in Europe. She set about translating Engels's 1845 tract, *The Condition of the Working Class in England,* and married one of the young Socialists, a Russian Jewish medical student named Lazare Wischnewetzky, bearing three children in as many years. She also managed to accompany her father on a "business trip" to northern England in 1883. This purpose of his visit to the Black Country, as she later called it, was to inspect working conditions of miners. In her autobiography, however, Kelley recalls most vividly a visit to a private home where the mother and children hammered out individual chain links on an anvil in the living room for a living. The links were collected by a "businessman" who dropped off more chunks of raw iron for processing on each visit.

When the Wischnewetzkys returned to New York in 1886, it was not easy for the transformed Philadelphia society woman to find a suitable setting for her unconventional ideas or her unconventional family, which now also included Lazare's mother. She did eventually reconcile with her own family and became an "independent scholar" while tending her young family, researching issues of child labor while Lazare sought opportunities to use his medical training without much success. In 1889, Kelley published *Our Toiling Children*, her exposé of child labor in the United States—in many ways an American equivalent of the Engels work she had translated.[5] The book was difficult to ignore. Her message was simple and clear. Children were being exploited by the owners of the means of production right here in the United States. But the power of the book derives from Kelley's combination of careful, documented research and skillful rhetoric.

Kelley begins with a provocative statement: "The only children to enjoy a childhood are the children of the propertied classes. The child of the workingman is a drudge." And she goes on, using data obtained from various state census materials, to prove that at least 1.2 million children under the age of twelve years are currently working for wages in the United States. She then begs the reader's forgiveness for having to report on the ghastly consequences of this situation. She organizes subsequent chapters according to the types of disaster that befall working children: fire, explosions, unguarded machinery, suffocation, and the like. She buttresses each story with data from official sources, rather than with the word-of-mouth tales of tragedy that we might expect from a propaganda piece. Kelley also examines tenement life and the hidden child workers doing "piecework" at home. She documents the decline of health and morals among working children who easily fall prey to tobacco, alcohol, and sex for money. She also demonstrates, in considerable detail, the negative impact on school attendance of child-labor practices and asserts that children's absence from school creates the greatest deficit of all for the nation.

Kelley concludes with the argument that society must invest in the education of its children in order to continue to grow. To those who would object that the nation cannot afford the cost, she cites the economists of the day, who were apparently in the habit of announcing the weekly growth of "capital" (what we might today refer to as gross domestic product, or GDP) produced by the booming national economy. It is evident, she asserts, that society has the wherewithal but lacks the moral courage to invest in its future. The work was published by the Woman's Temperance Publication Association (WTPA).[6] Kelley had clearly touched a nerve at an uncomfortable time for the expanding manufacturing industry. Her dogged commitment to gathering documentation to support her arguments made her assertions difficult to ignore. She had demonstrated the power of accurate and detailed information as a tool in the work of social enterprise.

At the time of the publication of *Our Toiling Children*, Kelley was not able to give her full attention to the fire she had kindled. Her husband had become increasingly abusive, and Kelley made up her mind to leave him. On the recommendation of friends and with borrowed money, she headed for Chicago with the children. She hoped to hide the children long enough to obtain custody of them under Illinois law. Her new life was shaped forever when she found shelter, as well as work and a welcoming community, at Hull House. The children were to live with the family of Henry Demarest Lloyd, a well-known journalist with a beautiful home north of Chicago in Winnetka.[7]

Kelley and Jane Addams soon developed a powerful friendship. Kathryn Sklar writes:[8] "Addams taught Kelley how to live and have faith in an imperfect world, and Kelley taught Addams how to make demands on the future." In particular, by Addams's own admission, Kelley increased the awareness of Hull House residents concerning the treatment of the working poor by their employers. Her ability to use her social scientific training to bring transparency to social inequities proved a powerful tool that she deployed with increasing success in the supportive Chicago environment.

In her first year of residence, Kelley was asked by U.S. commissioner of commerce and labor Carroll Wright to take charge of the Chicago portion of a federal study of slums in American cities. Hull House proved an ideal setting for such an undertaking and Kelley the perfect project leader. She and her assigned federal researchers soon documented a hidden world of "sweatshops" surrounding Hull House. There were hundreds of workers, mostly women and children doing piecework in the tenements. They labored for small wages over endless hours out of view of the public and the local authorities.

Kelley did not allow these data to disappear into an unread government report. Quite the contrary, she leveraged her findings through two important projects. The first was the drafting of the Factory and Inspection Act. Kelley sought legislative protection for the workers she had discovered by proposing state-mandated limits on work hours for women. For the first time, she put into action the many lessons learned from her father about the legislative process. She resurrected a rather moribund coalition of women's groups called the Illinois Women's Alliance that engaged representatives from the state WCTU, female trade unionists, the Ladies of the Grand Army of the Republic,[9] and of course her settlement house colleagues. Off they went to Springfield to buttonhole legislators to explain the scope of this terrible problem. Kelley also volunteered to serve as a guide for the legislative commission established in the wake of her findings. As she recounts with some satisfaction in her autobiography,[10] the commission was composed of mostly rural legislators looking forward to an opportunity to visit Chicago on a paid holiday. She saw to it instead that the commissioners visited every ghastly sweatshop and climbed every tenement staircase that she had encountered in her work.

The result of her labors was the passage of the Kelley-drafted Factory and Inspection Act in late 1893, limiting the use of sweat shop labor by manufacturers. This was the first such legislation in the nation. Perhaps of even greater significance, the law contained a provision to enable its enforcement, as early laws dealing with social issues were often simply ignored. Kelley was appointed chief factory inspector for the State of Illinois by Governor John Altgeld and, with a modest staff, was empowered to report on violations of the new law. As happened repeatedly in those days, the law was eventually overturned by the Illinois Supreme Court on the grounds that it limited the freedom of workers to contract for their services with employers, but not before Kelley had made the lives of the state attorney general (the state official charged with enforcing the law) and a variety of business leaders very uncomfortable with her diligence. (The U.S. Supreme Court finally found such legislation constitutional in 1908.)

Kelley was undeterred, persuaded as she was that efforts to create basic protections for child workers and women (maximum work hour limitations, limits on "outsourcing" work, and eventually a minimum wage) would eventually benefit all workers. Between 1893 and 1895, she continued to push her Hull House colleagues into greater activism at the policy level, despite Addams's inclination to focus on serving the needs of neighborhood residents. She worked with colleagues Helen Gates Starr and Julia Lathrop on an innovative application of her social scientific methods. Using the data they had gathered for the U.S. Department of Commerce study, they plotted income and ethnicity data in color-coded fashion on maps of the neighborhoods surrounding Hull House. The picture that emerged—ethnic clustering, income discrepancies, a hidden population of ultra poor living in the backs of tenements—brought the world of urban neighborhoods to life for all to see. As testimony to her respect for Kelley's work, Jane Addams proudly called the project, entitled *Hull House Maps and Papers*, "our child."[11]

At this time, Kelley also reached out to Ellen Henrotin, the chairwoman of the General Federation of Women's Clubs (GFWC). Women's clubs, composed of well-to-do women and dedicated to improving their communities through charitable works, were active in cities throughout the East and Midwest. The GFWC was hardly a hotbed of socialism, but Kelley persuaded Henrotin to mobilize hundreds of GFWC chapters around the nation to work on behalf of improved working conditions and wages for laborers. The GFWC eventually championed worker rights and campaigned for a juvenile justice system that had been initiated by Kelley's Hull House colleague Julia Lathrop. Henrotin and Kelley also launched the Illinois Consumers League, built on the model of the New York League, to enlist concerned consumers on behalf of the interests of workers. As things turned out, the work of the Consumers League would occupy Kelley for the remainder of her life.

Kelley was offered the position of executive secretary of the National Consumers League in 1899. Although the post required a move to New York City, she accepted. At age forty, she had truly found her calling. She understood the potential power of consumers in the new "consumption economy" of the Gilded Age, and she was convinced this power could be put to use to offset the exploitative practices of producers. She set about building the organization with her trademark indefatigable drive. Between 1900 and 1904, she expanded the organization to include sixty-four local leagues across the East and Midwest. Her annual report from a decade later lists presentations she made to ninety-eight organizations spread across nineteen states and the District of Columbia.[12] She argued that consumers could force producers to behave ethically simply by choosing certain products over others. Seeking ways to combat the continuing sweatshop approach to manufacturing, she created the NCL "consumers league label," to be affixed to manufactured goods produced without the labor of children under sixteen years and in compliance with state labor laws. The "white label," as it came to be called, proved a powerful tool in the battle for just working conditions. Local chapters of the NCL employed local inspectors to verify work practices, and Kelley acted as national inspector, personally visiting hundreds of manufacturers across the nation. Her labeling system caught on and her "impetuous fire" became the "embodiment of the public conscience on the subject of child labor and its attendant evils."[13]

Kelley also led the NCL into legislative activism beyond the boycott strategy. She focused initially on child labor issues, her original area of expertise, and subsequently on laws to limit the work hours of women.

When Kelley moved to New York City, she took up residence at another settlement house, in this case, the Henry Street "nurses" house established by Lillian Wald in 1893. As had been the case in Chicago when Florence met Jane Addams for the first time, she again encountered a congenial colleague whose professional knowledge (in the emerging field of public health) would compliment and enrich her own. Wald (1867–1940) was the daughter of German-Polish Jewish immigrants who arrived in America in the 1840s.[14] Her father was in "optical goods," and the family eventually settled in Rochester, New York, the center of American glassmaking at the time. Lillian was raised with an older sister and brother and one younger brother. By all accounts, hers was a loving, multigenerational family unburdened by the sadness of Kelley's childhood: a grandfather who loved storytelling and literature and an uncle who simply loved life and good jokes.[15] Her mother, Minnie, was ultimately asked by the mayor of Rochester to cease feeding so many vagrants out the back door of the family home, because the neighbors were complaining.

Lillian Wald attended a proper finishing school and at age sixteen sought admission to Vassar. She was refused, apparently because she was judged too young. A chance encounter with a nurse during her sister's childbirth experience led her instead to the New York Hospital Training School for Nurses, where she was admitted in 1889 and graduated in 1891. The program was new and unusual in the sense that most students were from the middle and upper economic classes (and mostly Protestant), rather than working-class women. She took her first professional position at the Juvenile Asylum in upper Manhattan. She lasted one year, observing what she felt was the appalling treatment of the orphans in the institutional setting, and then attended the Women's Medical College. But when she ventured downtown to teach a home health class to a group of Jewish immigrants, she found a new and compelling calling.

Although Manhattan lacked Chicago's stockyards, it also had its share of growth challenges in 1893: Of its 1.5 million residents, 1.3 million lived in tenements described as "a five story walk up building with limited plumbing." (Wald later joked that she was told there were only two indoor toilets on the Lower East Side when she was searching for a building in which to locate her settlement.) Of the tenement dwellers, 1.2 million were either foreign born or first-generation Americans. Five hundred thousand new immigrants were arriving each year. Lillian knew little about them, but she learned quickly when she visited the home of a child enrolled in a reading class she was teaching.

> Through Hester and Division Streets we went past odorous fish stands . . . past evil smelling uncovered garbage cans; . . . The child led me on through a tenement hallway, across a court where open and unscreened [water] closets were promiscuously used by men and women, up into a rear tenement, by slimy steps whose accumulated dirt was augmented by the mud of the streets . . . up into the sickroom. There were two rooms and a family of seven not only lived here but shared their quarters with boarders. . . .[16]

In her first memoir, *The House on Henry Street*, Wald referred to this experience as a "baptism of fire."[17] She was struck simultaneously by the appalling conditions and by the dignity of the people she found. Despite the filth and degradation, she noted that "they were not degraded human beings, judged by any measure of moral values." She was immediately preoccupied with the challenge of how she could help such decent people. She concluded in discussions with colleague Mary Brewster that she should take up residence among these people and, as she put it, "contribute our citizenship." They apparently arrived at this idea without any particular knowledge of the Hull House enterprise of Jane Addams. By September 1893, they had located a suitable house/tenement of their own and joined the Russian, Romanian, and Irish immigrants on New York's Lower East Side.

Their education and medical training soon made the women a source of both curiosity and multiple services. It did not take long before a larger space was required to match the needs and the idealism of Wald and her colleagues. In 1895, with the financial assistance of Jacob Schiff, the wealthy, well-connected "uptown" Jewish banker who was president of the investment bank Loeb, Kuhn, she opened "the house on Henry Street," which became known as the "nurses' settlement house." She had met Schiff, who served as benefactor and surrogate father for Lillian for many years, through her work teaching home health-care skills to Jewish immigrants.

Lillian's ambition at this point in her life was to mobilize her nursing knowledge for the benefit of her poor neighbors. As simple as this notion appears to us today, it was a revolutionary idea and challenging to implement. There was the matter of credentials, as the field of professional nursing was still in its infancy.[18] Neither doctors nor patients automatically recognized the medical value of interventions from female nurses, most of whom had historically lacked any formal training beyond their "female gentleness and compassion." Second, trained nurses did not, at the time, operate as free agents. They were assigned to individual doctors or worked for religious or charitable organizations and were deployed only by their supervisors. Wald wanted to deploy nurses to help those in need in their homes, where most sick people were to be found, and she envisioned them responding directly to those in need when called upon, rather than awaiting a call from a third party. Finally, she did not wish to operate a charity, but rather a service organization operating on a sliding fee scale, tailored to each family's ability to pay.[19]

She went to the woman who had underwritten the reading program for immigrants, Mrs. Solomon Loeb, to explain her plan for a mobile nursing corps. Mrs. Loeb's daughter, who was Lillian's age and married to Paul Warburg, became a best friend and benefactor of Lillian's effort. The Visiting Nurse Service was launched in late 1893. Wald relates multiple stories of the early years of work in *The House on Henry Street*: encounters with quack doctors, with pompous physicians, and with suspicious families. But the value of the nurses' contributions was easily recognized by those they served, and the program expanded rapidly. With considerable pride, and questionable use of statistics, Wald notes that in 1914, Henry Street staff treated some 3,500 cases of pneumonia with a mortality rate of 8 percent. She obtained records for the same period from four large New York City hospitals that treated some 1,600 cases with a mortality rate of 31 percent.[20]

Wald believed that community-based nurses were, indeed, better placed to offer care for many kinds of disease than were institutions such as hospitals. Her nursing philosophy was colored by her enduring belief in the value of the family and the innate dignity of each patient. Medical care that took advantage of these assets increased the chances of successful outcomes, in her judgment. Thanks to her fertile imagination, the opportunities to improve public health through the intervention of trained nurses proliferated throughout the decade. She turned her attention to the role of public health interventions in the public schools of New York City. At the time, the Department of Health assigned a doctor to examine schoolchildren for signs of infectious disease on a regular basis. Those displaying signs of such disease, whether trachoma, ringworm, or lice, or more serious influenza or TB, were promptly sent home. The greater the diligence of the Health

Department doctors, the more depleted the classrooms became. Moreover, parents were provided with no information on follow-up treatment. Their children were simply sent home and often did not return.

Wald argued for an experiment in which she hoped to demonstrate that a trained "school nurse" could provide on-site treatment for many children, in the case of trachoma or ringworm, for instance, and also advise parents on the proper follow-up for children diagnosed at school. The goal, of course, was to have the children back in school as quickly and continuously as possible. The one-month experiment proved the value of this approach to the satisfaction of the Department of Health, and the following year, 1902, the first school nurse was placed on the public payroll. Wald soon built on the success of this program by persuading the Metropolitan Life Insurance Company to partner with her "public health nurses" as she now called them. The company would provide nursing services directly to their industrial policyholders, thereby improving the health and productivity of workers insured through Metropolitan policies.

Yet another intervention occurred in 1903, when Lillian established a milk station at the settlement. In an earlier chapter, we noted that the quality of the milk supply was a major public health issue. Pasteurization was a controversial practice in 1903 in New York City, but Wald knew her science and saw how to apply it to the greater good of more citizens. She created her station to monitor the milk quality, and equally important, she ensured the presence of a nurse at the station to teach mothers the basics of milk sterilization in case they obtained milk from unreliable sources. By 1911, the City of New York had accepted responsibility for the creation of fifteen municipal milk stations.

Wald established the National Organization for Public Health Nursing in 1912 in order to standardize the training for this new field that mobilized scientific understanding of infectious diseases to benefit the greatest possible number of citizens. She was elected president in 1913.

Remarkably, these creative and long-lasting achievements in improved public health constitute only a small part of Wald's legacy as a social entrepreneur. Like Jane Addams before her, Wald could not escape the powerful influence of Florence Kelley. They quickly became robust allies when Kelley took up residence on Henry Street, with Wald's optimistic compassion buffering Kelley's powerful mind and outspoken convictions. In fact, Kelley arranged for Wald and other Henry Street residents to visit Addams in Chicago in the fall of 1899, and Wald was quick to acknowledge her admiration for Addams's determination and inspirational leadership.

Kelley, as we know, focused her initial Consumers League work on organizing new chapters and on the consumer boycott strategy. She also pushed the organization more gradually into legislative activism in support of women and children's labor laws. The idea for a national legislative campaign to protect child laborers was born, the story goes, over the breakfast table on Henry Street in 1905. Kelley and Wald were in the habit of reading the morning papers and commenting on the news of the day for the benefit of the other residents. On this morning, the papers carried a story that the U.S. secretary of agriculture, a Mr. Wilson at the time, was embarking on a trip to the South to investigate a boll weevil infestation plaguing cotton farmers. Florence commented ironically on the concern of the federal government for the cotton crop in light of all the human suffering across the country. Lillian's eyes brightened. Why, indeed, should the government not care equally about raising the next crop of children? Surely they were more valuable assets than the wheat, corn, cattle, sheep,

pigs, and fish that the government was taking the trouble to protect. In short order, Wald had used her connections to Jacob
Schiff to arrange a trip to Washington, D.C., to make the case
to President Theodore Roosevelt.

Politics being what they are, it took years (seven to be exact)
and a change of presidents before President William Taft signed
an official act creating the federal Children's Bureau, charged
with collecting and codifying all information pertaining to the
well-being of children. In the intervening years, Wald and Kelley
worked tirelessly as members of the Steering Committee of the
National Child Labor Committee (NCLC).

The NCLC had originated in 1904 through the efforts of a
Southern labor activist, Edgar Murphy, and the New York Child
Labor Committee. The goal was to elevate the problem of child
labor to the national level. Wald and Kelley formed a notable
coalition of influential leaders for the Steering Committee: the
presidents of Harvard and Vanderbilt universities, the publishers
of the *New York Times* and the *Atlanta Constitution*, the Catholic
cardinal of Baltimore, and the Episcopal bishop of New York
City. Labor leaders and settlement house workers also partici-
pated. The women were determined to educate these and other
people of influence about a system of labor that had tipped dan-
gerously toward private wealth accumulation and away from "self-
interest, rightly understood." Their efforts relied heavily on the
documentation provided by Kelley in *Our Toiling Children*. Sadly,
their cause was greatly aided by the tragic Triangle Shirtwaist
Factory fire in 1911.

The first efforts of the NCLC targeted children's work in coal
mines and glass factories, particularly dangerous industries for all
workers, but especially for children. (Children were a convenient
size to drop into exploratory holes drilled to sample potential coal
deposits, for instance.) The committee determined to bring a

new technology to bear on the documentation process. Lewis Hine was hired to photograph the workplace abuses of children. Arriving in New York from his home in Wisconsin, Hine found "the air full of the new social spirit" of Lillian Wald and Florence Kelley. To prepare for his assignment, Hine read *The Bitter Cry of the Children* by John Spargo, who quotes Kelley's 1905 article, "The Needless Destruction of Boys: Night Work in New Jersey Glass Works."[21] Hine was sufficiently moved to assert: "Truth meant the portrayal of social conditions in such a way that the appeal for reform would be effective."[22]

Hine became a photographer–social investigator with NCLC sponsorship from 1908–1912. The result was a collection of photos that he entitled "Lost Youth." The photos show children working in mills in Massachusetts, North Carolina, and Georgia; "newsies" selling daily papers in St. Louis, Missouri, and Hartford, Connecticut. They show child miners in Pennsylvania and Tennessee; basket makers in Indiana, and cigar rollers in North Carolina. They show children picking shrimp and shucking oysters in Louisiana, and cutting sardines in a canning factory in Maine. He captures child bootblacks, salesclerks, and bowling-pin setters. Hine also documented children's injuries and their work hours, noting their ages, years of employment, and sometimes their physical size and weight. Additional photos capture the children's vices, given their unsupervised hours and their squalid home living conditions.

As the women had imagined, Hine's photos were snapped up by the popular press. They provided a powerful tool in transforming public opinion. Support for federal intervention to protect children from exploitation by employers, whether factory owners or theater impresarios, seemed overwhelming. Mysteriously, however, the votes could never be assembled to pass the appropriate legislation. Some of the opposition was geographic in nature, as those legislators from agricultural states, often in the South where Murphy had worked, were accustomed to a strong rural tradition of children working on farms. Long days picking crops were an expected part of life for all farm families, including their young children. The idea of federal intervention and mandated working hours smacked of the worst kind of socialism. Additional opposition came from traditional legislators opposed to any governmental involvement in private enterprise. Work rules were time and again rejected by the Supreme Court as unconstitutional interference in the free enterprise system.

One might be tempted the think that after President Taft established the federal Children's Bureau in 1912, Wald and Kelley would declare victory in their fight to improve the lives of children. But they kept up the pressure, relying once again on their ability to collect factual information about the dimensions of the problem and make it public. They devised yet another creative partnership strategy to gather their all-important data. Wald realized that they had an unlikely ally in their cause: insurance companies.[23] The companies' agents visited tens of thousands of homes throughout the city on a yearly basis as part of their work. Lillian recognized that this routine offered a natural partnership with home health nurses who could document living conditions and health problems across the population. She approached the CEO of Metropolitan Life Insurance, who embraced the idea immediately. By 1915, there were working partnerships in some 1,200 American cities.

The collaboration produced a wealth of information about the problem of child labor. The NCLC partnered with the *Woman's Home Companion*, the most popular ladies magazine of the day, with a circulation in excess of 600,000. Each issue contained an article on child labor for two years running. The committee wrote to thousands of public libraries all over the nation, ensuring that each one acquired a copy of the committee's annual report each year. In all, the NCLC had produced over 2 million pages of documented reporting on the condition of children.[24] Most important, a public and political consensus was gradually built that engaged the federal government in the protection of children.

Throughout their lengthy battles to end the exploitation of children, both Wald and Kelley continued their efforts for the fair treatment of adult workers as well. Kelley had not forgotten the court defeat she had suffered at the hands of the Illinois Supreme Court. She mobilized the National Consumers League to take legal action to enforce the protections for workers that had been enacted in various states. The most famous case involved legislation passed by the Oregon legislature that limited the (formal) workday for women to ten hours. In *Muller v. Oregon* in 1907, the Oregon Supreme Court upheld the law, and laundryman Curt Muller, the plaintiff, appealed the decision to the U.S. Supreme Court. Notified of the impending case by the Oregon NCL chapter, Kelley and her colleague Josephine Goldmark, an NCL staffer, went to work. They collected documentary evidence from the leading medical professionals of the era that work beyond ten hours could jeopardize the health of women (most women's workday did not stop after ten hours in a factory). Attorney Louis Brandeis (who happened to be Goldmark's brother-in-law and later a distinguished U.S. Supreme Court justice) argued the case for the state and won on the basis of this "scientific" documentation, setting a legal precedent for the admissibility of this type of evidence. It was an "epoch-making event," as Kelley put it, and did much for the reputation of the NCL as a force for the legalization of work-hour legislation. The Brandeis brief, as the research document was called, was published as a pamphlet with support from the Russell Sage Foundation and widely circulated.[25]

Wald continued to pursue her work "on behalf of the alien" on the Lower East Side of New York City, and at the state level as well. Her health training convinced Wald of the value, both mental and physical, of physical exercise for children, and she set about raising the funds necessary to create play space at the Henry Street facility and to expand nearby Seward Park. She also tapped her well-developed business acumen to create Clinton Hall near her Henry Street home. Wald had great respect and enthusiasm for the diverse cultural assets that the newcomers brought to the Lower East Side community. Noting that the local population had no place to hold events such as weddings or festivals, or indeed to gather for any public meetings, she created a public company, the Social Halls Association, to build and operate a nondenominational hall. Shares were sold at $100 apiece to local merchants and to her many uptown supporters, and the new facility opened in 1905. A theater, the Neighborhood Playhouse, also funded by Lillian's uptown Jewish supporters, enabled various ethnic groups to mount traditional plays and performances, demonstrating what Wald stressed were the reciprocal gifts exchanged between newcomers and the resident population. By the 1930s, there were a dozen branches of the Henry Street facility in New York City. Her modest original home for young women dedicated to serving the health needs of the poor had burgeoned into a community center offering some sixty programs ranging from art, music, and theater to classes in homemaking, child care, the English language, and multiple vocational skills.

Wald expanded her commitment to "aliens" to the state level as well. She persuaded Charles Evans Hughes, the governor of New York, to create the Commission of Immigration to examine the condition, welfare, and industrial opportunities for aliens in the state. Her appointment to the commission enabled her to visit "labor camps" across the state where the immigrant workers lived while employed building the state's admired network of canals and bridges. The commission report in 1909 led to the establishment of a sanitary code for the camps, as well as stricter enforcement of age requirements for the workers.

Abolition of child labor became a plank in the platform of the Progressive Party launched by Teddy Roosevelt in 1912 (he lost). In 1916, the U.S. Congress passed legislation making it illegal to conduct interstate commerce in goods produced by underage child labor. It was ruled unconstitutional by the Supreme Court two years later.[26] In 1924, Congress passed a constitutional amendment making it legal for the federal government to regulate child labor, but it died when a majority of states failed to ratify the change. Ultimately, the national consensus concerning children and work was codified in the Fair Labor Standards Act in 1938.

The 1920s proved quite inhospitable to the efforts of Florence and Lillian. Although the Henry Street Settlement expanded its programming and outreach to the immigrant population, both women were frequently named as Communist sympathizers by post–World War I fear mongers. Given the nation's ultraconservative stance in the wake of the Russian Revolution of 1917, Wald and Kelley took these criticisms as a point of pride. Kelley was the target of particularly virulent personal attacks in a publication entitled *The Woman Patriot*, which referred to her as "Mrs. Wischnewetzky, Moscow's chief conspirator."

Over a forty-year period, these two remarkable women demonstrated what it takes to reform a social consensus from outside the system. They exhibited compassion, drive, fierce intelligence, and the imagination to deploy the latest social, scientific, and medical knowledge in the service of marginalized citizens. In the field of social science, they "diversified its research questions, investigative practices, and political commitments."[27] They mobilized their fund-raising skills and their coalitions to push the nation toward a new definition of social justice. In the end, they redefined both state and federal protections for the health and safety of children. Their leadership defined the Progressive Era, as historians now call the period from 1880 to 1910.

In a review of *The House on Henry Street*, historian Salwyn Shapiro said it best when he wrote that Wald's work is "in line with the 'cooperative individualism' that is the distinctive mark of the Anglo-Saxon world."[28] We are not giving either the Angles or the Saxons credit. The credit for building "cooperative individualism," for achieving the delicate balance essential to the practice of "self-interest, rightly understood," goes to American women social entrepreneurs.

TWELVE

Partnerships with
the Federal Government

Democracy is that form of government and spirit among men which actively insists that society must exist to give every human being a fair chance.
—Julia Lathrop, presentation to the National Conference of Social Work, 1919

The generation of post–Civil War women social entrepreneurs that included Wald, Kelley, and Addams raised difficult questions about the role of government in the protection of vulnerable citizens. They asked, in effect, whether America's highly decentralized, laissez faire (hands off) philosophy of governance remained appropriate in a newly urbanized, diversified, and industrialized nation. And they answered their own question with a strong no. The scale and complexity of problems such as child labor, domestic violence, sanitation, and disease required interventions that exceeded the capabilities of even the most devoted private citizen groups. At a minimum, engaged citizens needed a partner to provide tools, in the form of regulations, resources, and, ideally, expertise to support their efforts. The logical partner for social enterprise was the government, particularly the federal government. As women increased the pressure, the government did take on increased responsibilities for the welfare of certain groups of citizens, and officials turned, not surprisingly, to women to lead these efforts.[1]

State and local governments held the primary responsibility for social issues, for better or worse, throughout the nineteenth century. When social entrepreneurs targeted government as a potential partner in their efforts to create social profit—universal education, limited work hours for children, protection for immigrants, abolition of slavery, suffrage for women—they focused as we have seen on state and local elected officials. As early as 1803, the Widows' Society headed by Isabella Graham received $15,000 in direct support from the New York State Legislature, presumably because legislators recognized that her charitable work reduced the potential population of state-run facilities for the indigent. Louisa Schuyler created the New York State Charities Aid Association around the time of the Civil War to assist in providing funding and "quality control" for state-supported institutions such as hospitals and poorhouses. Similar organizations and collaborations existed in other states as well, with Massachusetts and Pennsylvania offering the most developed examples. The appointment of Florence Kelley as state factory inspector responsible for the enforcement of newly passed employment legislation marked an important milestone in the alignment of the goals of social entrepreneurs and state governments.

The federal government, on the other hand, kept a very low profile on issues of morality and social justice. The Civil War and the Emancipation Proclamation marked important milestones, however, as the federal government acted decisively to extend federal protections to more of the populace, rather than deferring to the individual states. This stance encouraged a new level of partnership with citizen social entrepreneurs. Louisa Schuyler, Mary Livermore, and dozens of additional women engaged directly with the federal government in managing the U.S.

Sanitary Commission (USSC) as part of the war effort. Ultimately, the USSC coordinated some 7,000 soldier aid groups led by women across the nation.[2]

In the post–Civil War era, the federal government showed a willingness to extend its engagement in the well-being of individual citizens in ways not previously seen. Civil War veterans of every economic level were provided with generous pension benefits from the federal Treasury (states chipped in as well). The federal Freedmen's Bureau contributed approximately $1 million to a school-building effort aimed at black children across the Southern states. In the best cases, this increased willingness of elected representatives to spend limited federal resources in support of traditional social profit enterprises leveraged private volunteer resources. The school construction effort attracted some $15 million in direct citizen funding from Northern aid societies between 1865 and 1870. The federal Freedmen's Bureau, far from discouraging private citizens, complimented the efforts of hundreds of Freedmen's Societies that sprang up across the Northern states to raise money and provide support to the formerly enslaved. The nation's Centennial celebration in 1876 offers another example of a constructive partnership, as the modest federal investment in the birthday party attracted considerable volunteer support in both dollars and labor.

These federal efforts were not, however, universally successful. It soon became apparent that the federal government was not well prepared to develop and manage far-reaching efforts. The pension plan for Civil War veterans became the poster child for these weaknesses. The cost of the plan ballooned in the 1880s and 1890s, reaching close to 45 percent of total federal expenditures just before the turn of the century. The obligations created a significant federal deficit, and in the minds of many citizens, they symbolized the incompetence of the federal government in the administration of social support programs. The programs were indeed poorly run. America lacked a trained civil service cadre of professional administrators in government. Vague wording in legislation aimed at extending or refining benefits offered many opportunities for program administrators who owed their jobs to political patronage to bend the rules in favor of favored constituents. In short order, the pension program became a target of critics who saw in it the dangers of big government and party patronage politics.

Toward the end of the nineteenth century there was no social consensus that the government, particularly the federal government, should be responsible for extensive social programs. Could "the state" be counted on to act in benign and caring ways for the weaker members of society? Should government mandates for the care of those in need be expanded? Or should the political apparatus be viewed with suspicion by citizens concerned with the well-being of orphans, the poor, the elderly, the mentally ill, and victims of discrimination?

While progressive groups pushed for a more active federal role, most middle-class citizens still preferred the traditional American paradigm of citizen-to-citizen mutuality with a strong emphasis on the church: Families cared for their own and for their extended families, citizens cared for communities, and employers, for better or worse, cared for workers. And (women) citizen volunteers cared for those "at the margins."

Women social entrepreneurs, however, were not easily dissuaded from their belief that America's tension between rugged individualism and citizen mutuality was, in fact, out of balance. While the nation's political leaders struggled to deal with budget and competence issues, the women kept up the pressure. Backed by the insights garnered through their social science training, and propelled by increasingly sophisticated use of the media, the social entrepreneurs insisted on a better and closer collaboration with government. The temperance movement forced elected officials to confront the damage to families and to society as a whole caused by the unregulated use of alcohol. Scientifically informed citizens brought to light the damage done by unregulated sanitary practices and food and water supply chains.[3] Implicit in these challenges was the idea that free enterprise had overwhelmed mutual responsibility.

The issue of child welfare is illustrative. Between 1860 and 1890, the number of orphanages grew 300 percent.[4] Children were often "outsourced" by families in financial difficulty to orphanages for limited periods of time. Various states employed different funding and management plans for such institutions, some of which were state-run, although most were privately operated with the state subsidizing operating expenses on a per capita basis (clearly a plan that encouraged the growth of orphanage populations!). In the first decades of the twentieth century, a new generation of "social workers" argued against the institutional model. These trained specialists had inspected hundreds of institutions and found overwhelming evidence of poor management, neglect, and occasional abuse of the children. The officials running taxpayer-funded asylums and state (reform) schools were primarily patronage jobholders. They lacked training in the management of social welfare institutions. What was needed was competence, professional training in the new social sciences of public health, mental hygiene, and child development. Yet such training would only add to the government's costs and increase the burden on taxpayers. Given the messiness and complexity of operating social services through a government bureaucracy, one can imagine that the politicians targeted by criticisms of the status quo were none too eager to fight to retain or grow their welfare responsibilities. Child advocates argued that children should be kept with their families at all cost, and that it would be cheaper and more child-friendly to provide subsidies directly to mothers so they could stay at home to care for their children.

The women social entrepreneurs were not satisfied with petitioning their elected officials before returning home to wait hopefully for action on their request. By now, leaders such as Florence Kelley and her colleague Julia Lathrop were legally trained and well versed in political dynamics. Women held the high moral ground in public debates in part because they were women with traditional knowledge of and responsibility for virtue in children, and in part because they were not tainted by the self-interest that ran rampant in the political arena. Women could still not vote in most states in the first decade of the twentieth century, and they therefore escaped any responsibility for the failures of the state. Women also enjoyed the fruits of their own extensive investments in the building of networks and associations. They could count on a vast reservoir of volunteer labor to collect information, organize it as requested, and mobilize ideas for change at the grassroots level. The government, on the other hand, was chronically short of resources, both financial and human, to address growing human needs.

Once engaged in the political arena, female entrepreneurs were well prepared to fight for the hearts and minds of their fellow citizens on the battlefield of public opinion. They proved particularly adept at coalition building, a skill that seemed to escape their male counterparts in the emerging organized labor movement. Even when the inevitable factions arose, as in the case of the YWCA or various associations of women's clubs, leaders found ways to move forward and to engage additional women's organizations in their own efforts. Candace Wheeler used the YWCA and WCTU to expand the Women's Exchange movement. Florence Kelley deployed a similar strategy in building the reach of the National Consumers League. Virtually all leading social entrepreneurs understood the value of reaching across class boundaries in their organizing efforts, moving more or less comfortably from middle-class parlors to working-girls' clubs, from university classrooms to tenement buildings. The powerful General Federation of Women's Clubs (GFWC), launched in 1890 by Jane Croly, numbered over 1 million middle- and upper-middle-class urban members by 1910. It served as a kind of omnibus partner for many social profit efforts. The federation established permanent Washington headquarters, held large annual conventions, and created standing committees on such issues as pure food, civil service reform, public health, and child labor. This structure enabled associations devoted to these causes to partner quickly and effectively with the federation, gaining access to its journals and fund-raising newsletters, as well as to its lobbying, communications, and publicity expertise.

Women's political influence was also aided by their solidarity on the moral high ground. With plenty of political scandals to go around, women could, and did, invoke their long tradition as keepers of virtue in the Republic. Motherhood remained a critical function for the economic and social well-being of the nation. Any political policies that undercut a woman's ability to carry out this sacred (and patriotic) function effectively were portrayed as downright un-American. Alice Birney launched the National Congress of Mothers (NCM) in 1897,[5] in effect arguing for a twentieth-century restatement of the importance of old-fashioned domestic republican motherhood:

> The race which is born of mothers who are harassed, bullied, subordinated, or made the victims of blind passion or power . . .

cannot fail to continue to give the horrible spectacles we have always had of war, of crime, of vice, of trickery, of double dealing, of pretense, of lying, of arrogance, of subserviency, or incompetence, of brutality and, alas of insanity, idiocy and disease added to a fearful and unnecessary mortality. . . .

If you have a daughter who is finer and truer, more capable and noble, more intellectual and able than the rest, she is the one whose education and development as an individual should be carried to the highest reach, not simply because she is to be a writer or speaker or teacher . . . but because it may also be her pleasure and province to be the wife and mother in a real and true and inspiring home life. . . .[6]

Politicians, including Theodore Roosevelt, were quick to align themselves with these traditional values. The popular press, in full swing at the beginning of the twentieth century, proved an excellent ally for the women intent upon pressuring the government to provide more direct support to heroic and fragile American womanhood. Both the GFWC and the NCM established press committees to cultivate working relationships with journalists and editors, and they reported regularly at national and state meetings on their successes in placing stories. In short, the significant shortcomings of elected officials in dealing with social dislocation and change represented a special opportunity for change-oriented women entrepreneurs.

As the federal administrations under Theodore Roosevelt, William Taft, and Woodrow Wilson sought to respond to the pressure to do more for the weakest members of society, and to do it better, no individuals were more influential in creating the relationship between today's social profit sector and the federal government than Julia Lathrop, Mary Bethune, and Frances Perkins. All were experienced social entrepreneurs when they were nominated for federal office. They had been effective creators of social profit in their work on behalf of children, workers, victims of discrimination, and the handicapped for many years. Now they would face a different and more daunting challenge: leading change for the good of their fellow citizens from within the federal governmental bureaucracy.

This effort would necessitate the use of different strategies and skills if they were to succeed in actually making a difference. They faced a new challenge to retain their entrepreneurial imagination and determination while becoming paid policy administrators in a system where male leadership was entirely dominant and taken for granted. They qualify as social entrepreneurs because they proved remarkably creative as administrators. They took government practices that were, in their judgment, "supporting stable but disabling equilibriums" and invented new partnerships with the voluntary sector to keep the American Dream alive.

The business world has a term for individuals with the skills to become value creators from within. They are called "intrapreneurs."[7] Anyone who has worked in a large organization will recognize as least some of the "ten commandments of intrapreneurship" advanced by the term's originator. Among the most powerful: "Do any job needed to make your project work regardless of your job description," "Come to work each day willing to be fired," and "Share credit wisely." It is as if Lathrop, Bethune, and Perkins had read the book seventy years before it was written.

In 1912, President William Taft appointed Julia Lathrop (1858–1932)[8] to head a newly created federal agency, the Children's Bureau. Congress had pondered the wisdom of involving the federal government directly in the well-being of the nation's children for decades. Finally, legislation was passed for a bureau to "investigate and report on all matters pertaining to the welfare of children and child life among all classes of our people."[9]

Similar legislation had been introduced in 1906, soon after Wald and Kelley visited Theodore Roosevelt in Washington to propose the idea, but it had encountered opposition from legislators representing industries such as textiles that made abundant use of child labor. Under enormous pressure from Kelley's National Consumers League, the National Child Labor Committee, the General Federation of Women's Clubs, and many others, the legislation finally reached the president's desk. Julia Lathrop herself proved to be a worthy heir to the idea of Wald and Kelley. With the support of President Woodrow Wilson, who was elected in 1912, she built a foundation for a system that defined standards for American society to meet for the just treatment of children.

Lathrop was a natural choice to become founding director of the bureau. By the time she reached Washington, she had built a distinguished career as a legal thinker and engaged social science researcher in the Chicago tradition. She had made a successful case for the creation of a juvenile justice system in her home state of Illinois, the first of its kind in the nation. She had founded the Immigrants' Protective League and become an outspoken champion of better treatment for the mentally ill. She had even headed the research division of the Chicago School of Civics and Philanthropy for a brief period. There was every reason to believe that she would be a brilliant leader of this new agency. She did not disappoint.

Her work in the field of juvenile justice offers perhaps the most relevant illustration of the entrepreneurial skills she would eventually put to good use in Washington, D.C. Lathrop was born and raised in the thriving town of Rockford, Illinois, in a prosperous, politically active family. Her father was a lawyer who had served a term as a U.S. congressman. She graduated from Vassar in 1880, placing her in the ranks of educated women who were obliged to invent ways to put their educations to work for society and for themselves.

Lathrop found no one who had any expectations of her beyond the traditional role of wife and mother. She returned home after college to await a proposal of marriage and to take up her role as a prominent member of Rockford society. While she waited, she worked as secretary in her father's law office, using her time to study the law and ultimately to take the bar examination in Illinois (although women were not actually allowed to practice law at that time).

One evening in 1890, she and her father attended a lecture by an alumna of the local college, Rockford Female Seminary. Jane Addams had clear ideas about what an educated woman like Lathrop should do, and she could articulate them in compelling fashion. Addams made two points in her presentation that Julia never forgot. She argued that "political democracy," by which she meant the creation of laws through representative government, had made considerable progress in America over the first 100 years of the Republic. The same could not be said for what Addams called "social democracy," the relationship of citizens of all classes to one another. Without a strong social democracy, the system was in danger of failing all citizens. It was up to (educated) women, Addams believed, to fix this problem.

Lathrop heard Addams loud and clear. She soon moved to Chicago and became an active resident of Hull House. Lathrop lived at Hull House for some twenty years, becoming close friends with Addams[10] and with the always energized, fellow law-school graduate, Florence Kelley.

Lathrop was more reserved than Kelley, and she brought a certain scholarly approach to her Hull House work. But Lathrop and Kelley shared a fearless passion for gathering good information.

During the smallpox outbreak that followed the Columbian Expo of 1893, they did what government officials did not do. They went house-to-house looking for victims. They wanted to help sick children hidden by frightened parents and, while attempting to calm the panicky adults, notified health officials about the locations of victims of the epidemic. They also put their basic scientific understanding about infectious disease to work, organizing large-scale efforts to destroy clothing and bedding found in the victims' homes (and to raise contributions to replace them), in order to reduce the spread of the epidemic.

Lathrop also volunteered for the Cook County Board of Visitors and personally inspected each of the municipal asylums and poorhouses in the county. Subsequently, Governor Altgeld (who had appointed Florence Kelley chief factory inspector of the State of Illinois) appointed Lathrop as the first female member of the State Board of Charities. Her job was to document the living and health conditions of children in state facilities. She took her responsibilities seriously, personally visiting all 102 facilities across the state. She got a firsthand view of the poorhouses, which served as combined orphanages, mental institutions, prisons, and general catchalls for those without the ability or means to care for themselves. According to Jane Addams, on one memorable occasion, Lathrop took it upon herself to test a newly installed "fire escape" that she was being shown by the administrator of a residential facility. The escape consisted of a fireman's pole running from the top to the bottom floor of the building. Apparently, Lathrop gathered her voluminous skirts and petticoats and leaped onto the pole on the top floor while the startled bureaucrats looked on.[11]

Lathrop dutifully reported on the failings of these facilities: the poor training of the political appointees in charge and the poor state of the facilities themselves. She also learned that most middle-class taxpayers were unwilling to increase their own taxes to pay for the care of poor children or the mentally ill. While conducting these taxing visits across the state, Lathrop worked with Florence Kelley and the other residents of Hull House to assemble the insights gained through her Cook County visitations, ultimately producing the *Hull House Maps and Papers*, of which Jane Addams was so proud.

Lathrop was a problem solver, although she was an exceptionally talented researcher as well. The social entrepreneur in her wanted to fix the problems she had encountered on her volunteer visits. Lathrop's knowledge of the law caused her to take special interest in the plight of juvenile offenders whom she encountered. The criminal justice system of the late nineteenth century made no provision for juveniles. They were simply treated as adults, no matter their age.[12] She had witnessed the destructive impact of the undifferentiated system on children, from sexual abuse to hard labor. She concluded that the interests of children could hardly be served by the rigid rules of criminal procedure, noting that such procedural approaches seemed to do little to prevent offenses on the part of adults.

She approached the problem, as she would many others, with thorough research and careful preparation. She used her position on the State Board of Charities to organize a conference on the theme of "The Children of the State." In partnership with her friend Lucy Flower, the president of the Chicago Women's Club, Lathrop prepared to make her case during the meeting for a separate juvenile justice system. They had painstakingly researched the exact percentage of juveniles currently in the Illinois justice system. They had pieced together case records that documented the treatment of children as young as eleven years from their first arrest to their prolonged imprisonment among a population of adult men. Flower had even traveled to Boston to learn about the treatment of children in Massachusetts. The women had recruited prominent lawyers and judges to support their concerns. The conference attendees were suitably shocked by what they heard.

The timing of Lathrop and Flower was superb. The original idea for juvenile justice had been introduced in the legislature in 1890, but there had been no catalyst for action until Lathrop shocked the leadership with her case studies. "An Act to Regulate the Treatment and Control of Neglected, Dependent and Delinquent Children" passed one year after the conference. The legislation created a juvenile justice system as part of the existing criminal justice system, but with separate facilities, judges, and, most important, the involvement of parole officers with expertise in child development.

The passage of the world's first juvenile justice law committed the state to responsibility for both dependent and delinquent children, combining for the first time systems for child welfare and crime control. Unfortunately, the legislature failed to fund the act, so it initially had little meaning. Undaunted, Lathrop enlisted her network of philanthropic volunteers, many from the Chicago Women's Club, to raise the money to hire a judge and a probation officer to get the Juvenile Court up and running. When the act was ultimately funded in the next session, this grassroots support group morphed into the Juvenile Protection Association, whose volunteers funded free legal counsel for juveniles in subsequent years.

This brief example demonstrates the potential for social profit production through collaboration with elected officials. It also testifies to the effectiveness of Julia Lathrop as a talented social entrepreneur able to work across boundaries between the legislative, judicial, and executive branches of government. Her ability to make her case through careful research and documentation, coupled with her coalition-building skills, created political and financial leverage to put good ideas into practice.

The second problem that Lathrop addressed was the lack of trained administrators for social services organizations. This deficiency seemed most obvious in state-administered facilities, but it also occurred in organizations supported by churches and civic groups. She reached out to Graham Taylor at the Chicago School of Civics and Philanthropy. Her idea was to provide adult education classes in applied social science to those who were working or volunteering in the field. These programs proved widely popular, and the tuition kept the shaky school afloat. She then agreed to Taylor's request to become the research director of the school and in this capacity sought and won the support of the Russell Sage Foundation for the school's work.[13] Sage funding underwrote the Chicago School for a critical five-year period before it became a school of the University of Chicago. Lathrop proposed the multitalented Sophonisba Breckinridge as her successor, a move that brought a young, brilliant University of Chicago PhD in political economy to the school as well as an end to Taylor's single-handed control of the Chicago School.

Lathrop also took up the cause of the mentally ill, whom she had encountered with great regularity in her criminal justice work. The mentally ill were generally treated as criminals or moral defectives and locked up in asylums. She traveled to Europe on two occasions to explore ideas for extramural care of the insane and recorded her ideas in a guidebook for well-intentioned citizens, *Suggestions for Visitors to County Poorhouses*. She traveled to Connecticut to meet the pioneering child psychologist Clifford Beers,[14] and then joined the board of directors of the National Committee on Mental Hygiene in 1909, a newly formed volunteer group calling for medical treatment rather than incarceration of the mentally ill. It was testimony to her intellectual standing that Lathrop was invited to join the distinguished group of scientists to advocate for this unfortunate population of citizens. In her biography of Lathrop, Jane Addams recalls many occasions when Lathrop would leave Hull House, often at night, to assist police officers confronted with psychotic "criminals."

Lathrop's career to this point exemplified the rationality and devotion to evidence of an effective lawyer. It also reflected the empathy and social activism of the first generation of trained social scientists. It may seem perfectly natural that such a brilliant and accomplished champion of justice for all would be chosen to head the federal Children's Bureau. But her presidential appointment was a genuine milestone, marking the first crossover for a female entrepreneur from social enterprise to leadership responsibility within the federal government. It took plenty of political lobbying from Lathrop's well-connected friends in the Republican Party to assure the nomination.

Would Lathrop's extensive knowledge and compassion enable her to lead a federal bureau? She had one advantage at the outset. There was no bureaucracy! Her budget was $25,600, and she could hire fifteen staff in addition to herself. President Taft noted that the government was already spending some $15 million per year studying animal husbandry and boll weevils through the Department of Agriculture, so a small investment in studying how to provide the best care for infants, mothers, child workers, child criminals, orphans, disease victims, and the like seemed reasonable enough.

Lathrop's mandate for the Children's Bureau was research. People had guessed that some 2.5 million babies had been born in 1911, and that about 300,000 had died before attaining one year of age. No one knew for certain, and certainly no one knew why America had such a high infant mortality rate.[15] Whatever the politicians thought, Julia believed that her work would be meaningful only if it led to improvements in the welfare of children in America.

Lathrop put her well-developed networking skills to work in her new position. She assembled an advisory board of distinguished thinkers and steered them toward an ambitious agenda of research projects that could form the basis for a campaign to educate citizens, especially parents, about what is best for children. She also wanted to design research that could provide a factual foundation for use in drafting legislation on behalf of the needs of children. The resulting effort was the first-ever national comprehensive study of infant mortality in the nation (and perhaps the world). The findings were revolutionary: Death rates went down when fathers' wages went up; breast-fed children survived better than bottle-fed infants; a mother at home increased infant survival; home sanitation was a significant factor; and on and on. A follow-up study on maternal deaths in childbirth uncovered more correlations between poverty and health.

The findings were widely published in newspapers, and a number of grassroots initiatives sprang up that benefited mothers and babies. Lathrop's work, coupled with the Sage Foundation research described previously, generated a citizen campaign for consistent pasteurization of cow's milk. Lathrop's work also revealed a significant data deficiency. The United States lacked a system to register births, and thus no one even knew how many births were occurring each year, or when or where they occurred. Lathrop reached out to her allies at the General Federation of Women's Clubs, who began the process of counting births in their local communities. It would be another twenty years before a complete national birth registry was in place, but such remarkable progress, achieved on a miniscule budget, testifies to Lathrop's ability to engage and direct the energy of volunteer labor on behalf of the well-being of children and the nation.

Her research-based approach established a new framework for protecting the lives of children. The visibility and popularity of her work led Congress to approve a sixfold increase in her bureau's budget in the following legislative session (although a sixfold increase of $25,000 still did not amount to much of a budget for a federal agency, even in 1914). She quickly won over Woodrow Wilson, the new Democratic president, with her focus on bureaucratic competence in her department. An annoyed congressman complained to the president that Lathrop, appointed by Republican William Taft, had been unwilling to hire the Democratic congressman's friend for a post in the Children's Bureau. "Mr. President," he asked, "are we to understand that it is your policy to retain Republicans and let good Democrats starve?" Wilson is said to have responded: "You may understand, Mr. Senator, that it is my policy to retain Miss Lathrop!"

The bureau next took up another of Lathrop's data-driven educational efforts. The staff drafted and published a small pamphlet entitled *Prenatal Care*, followed the next year by *Infant Care*. While dexterously avoiding the toes of the medical establishment, the brochures spoke directly to mothers in lay terms, encouraging loving, gentle care for babies, exposure to fresh air and clean water, and warning against harsh physical punishment. They proved so popular that Lathrop was besieged by congressmen asking for copies to distribute in their districts. She once again called upon her network of volunteer women advocates. She committed the agency to responding individually to the tens of thousands of inquiries from mothers across the nation who had discovered a source of useful information for their needs. To do so with her limited staff and financial resources, she deputized thousands of volunteers to respond to these inquiries, providing basic information on the care and handling of infants and on additional local sources of help. The bureau commanded an excep-

tionally loyal and active block of engaged citizens. As the Social
Security Administration notes, *Infant Care* is the U.S. government's number one publication of all time, with distribution of
34,617,841 copies between 1914 and 1955.[16] Lathrop established
a system of dependable, research-based information transfer to
families with children. The result was nothing less than a healthier America.

Lathrop was not content with such successes. She rapidly developed a more ambitious agenda for her research and pursued
the political strategies to put this agenda into practice. She could
see the possibility of legislation that would support mothers and
children, despite the engagement of the nation in World War I.
In fact, she tied her work to the war effort, studying the needs of
mothers and children deprived of fathers or husbands by the
bloody conflict. Because many young men summoned for con-
scription failed their physical examinations, she asserted that the
health of children was an important national priority for future
war efforts. In 1918, the year she engineered the presidential declaration of "The Year of the Child," Lathrop again mobilized millions of volunteer women (11 million, according to Jane Addams)
to organize a nationwide campaign to weigh and measure growing
children, and not, coincidently, to inform their elected representatives (even though the women could not yet vote directly)
of the importance of support for children's well-being. In 1919,
she addressed the National Education Association: "We cannot
help the world toward democracy if we despise democracy at
home; and it is despised when mother or child dies needlessly."[17]

She kept the issue in the public eye by sponsoring White House
conferences on child welfare, conferences that offered legislators
the opportunity to align themselves with this popular cause. Her
work culminated in the Maternity and Infancy Act of 1921. The
Sheppard Towner Act, as it was named, provided some $500,000

annually in federal support to states for the purpose of "supporting the welfare and hygiene of maternity and infancy." This landmark legislation established a formal role for the federal government in the protection of children.

This bill represented the achievement of Lathrop's audacious goal: a fundamental change in the role of government with respect to children's rights and needs. She reached her goal inside a political bureaucracy with a small staff, a tiny budget, and a very large, active constituency of engaged volunteers. She produced unassailable research as a foundation for change. She developed a new consensus about the value of investment in the well-being of children, and as a result, America became the first country in the world to build a formal system of child protection.

William Chenery, a journalist and former Hull House resident himself, describes Lathrop's accomplishments as follows:

> The Children's Bureau was an organization which, measured by farsighted purpose, instinctive loyalty to democracy, and capacity to achieve, was almost without precedent in Washington . . . public officials who are wise leaders of the people and at the same time shining examples of effectual administration are all too few.[18]

Lathrop's work embodied "a marvelous combination of the long benevolent/reform tradition and a new faith in social science."[19] Her skilled leadership established a constructive partnership between the federal government and engaged citizens.

The struggle for civil rights for blacks began with the Emancipation Proclamation. It has played across the efforts of many of the women social entrepreneurs we have highlighted in the post–Civil War era, particularly in the investments made by Caroline Phelps Stokes. But no social entrepreneur produced more social profit on behalf of blacks during this period than a woman who began life in a cotton field and ended as a friend and adviser to presidents.

> What then does the Negro want? His answer is very simple. He wants only what all other Americans want. He wants opportunity to make real what the Declaration of Independence and the Constitution and Bill of Rights say.[20]

These powerful words define the challenge that has motivated social entrepreneurs since the founding of the Union. They are timeless and particularly poignant, coming as they do from a black woman who lived through the most racist, violent chapter in American history. Just as Maria Chapman had called on the federal government to exercise its moral authority in the cause of abolition in the early nineteenth century, so almost 100 years later, Mary McLeod Bethune (1875–1955) continued the challenge to the nation's citizens to live up to the ideals of the Declaration.[21] Creative, optimistic, indefatigable, Bethune incarnates the combination of idealism with entrepreneurial pragmatism that characterizes the women who built our social profit sector. Over the course of a long life, she initiated and executed one entrepreneurial project after the other. But her diverse ventures shared a single audacious goal. She wanted African Americans to enjoy the promises and accept the responsibilities guaranteed to all citizens of the United States by the Declaration of Independence. She was prepared to work hard for this opportunity. In turn, she held high expectations that her fellow citizens, especially those entrusted with representing the citizenry in government, would also work hard for racial justice. In the era following the Civil War, this was a courageous and daunting commitment to pursue.

Slavery created a far more disfiguring stain on American ideals than poorly kept cities, and it was harder to remove. The social entrepreneurs who had taken on the cause of abolition in the first half of the nineteenth century had won a great victory, but as late as 1944, Mary McLeod Bethune, who lived this reality from her birth in 1875 to her death in 1955 and had just completed a decade of service in the Roosevelt administration, itemized for the president what black Americans still needed from the federal government.[22] Among the nine items are the following:

1. Democracy in the Armed Forces
2. The protection of his [the Negro's] civil rights and an end to lynching
3. The free ballot
4. Equal access to employment opportunities and an elimination of racial barriers in labor unions.

The second and third items on Bethune's list reach directly back to the days immediately following the emancipation of enslaved blacks. The federal government instituted a program of "reconstruction" in the South that included a series of protections for the civil rights of the freedmen. Two civil rights acts were passed by Congress (in 1866 and 1875) and the Fourteenth and Fifteenth Amendments to our Constitution were enacted as well.[23]

These legislative efforts were largely ineffective. The 1875 civil rights act was declared unconstitutional by the Supreme Court in 1883. The act held "that all persons . . . shall be entitled to full and equal enjoyment of the accommodations, advantages, facilities, and privileges of inns, public conveyances on land or water, theaters, and other places of public amusement." The Court reviewed five separate complaints involving acts of discrimination on a railroad and in public sites, including a theater in San Francisco and the Grand Opera House in New York. In declaring the federal law unconstitutional, Chief Justice Joseph Bradley and the majority held that the Fourteenth Amendment did not protect black people from discrimination by private businesses and individuals, but only from discrimination by states.

The ruling opened the door to an era often referred to as the Jim Crow period. States passed countless laws that made it illegal for blacks to use the very facilities that the 1875 act had intended to make accessible. When blacks responded by testing the constitutionality of specific prohibitions, such as riding in "white" railroad cars, the Supreme Court, in the case of *Plessy v. Ferguson*, held that the law was indeed constitutional, as long as a separate car for blacks was provided, and so the doctrine of "separate but equal" was legitimized. Many states piled on with so-called miscegenation laws, making interracial marriage a crime. When applied to educational facilities, the law produced a two-tiered educational system.

Meanwhile, few blacks were willing to risk testing any of the local laws. Whites took it upon themselves in many communities to police the actions and whereabouts of blacks, and violence flourished. The membership of the Ku Klux Klan and the Knights of the White Camellia numbered in the thousands and operated openly as judge and jury for blacks deemed to have stepped out of line. It is difficult to imagine that in 1944, Bethune felt it necessary to ask President Roosevelt for a federal law against lynching. But there had never been one, despite the ghastly tradition of vigilante justice that arose across the South during the 1880s and 1890s and clearly continued well into the twentieth century. Numbers are difficult to come by, but scholars have documented in excess of 3,700 such events between 1889 and 1930 alone. By many accounts, lynchings were often publicized in advance and attracted enthusiastic crowds of men, women, and children as well as a ghoulish trade in body-part souvenirs.

The seemingly bulletproof wording of the Fifteenth Amendment with respect to voting rights still left to the individual states the ability to determine voting qualifications, as long as these did not violate the amendment. Southern states responded with a deluge of requirements, most of which were aimed at preventing black men from voting. Bethune refers to such requirements in item three of her list. She names the "poll tax," a requirement to pay a tax in order to vote that disproportionately affected poor blacks, although some poor whites were caught up in the requirement as well. She also identifies the "white primary," a scheme based on a rule that only political party members can vote for the party's candidates in primary elections. Because political parties were ruled to be private organizations, and could therefore legally exclude blacks, blacks were unable to vote in such elections. A third favored strategy was the literacy test, requiring aspiring voters to be able to read and write at a time when the literacy rate among black men ran between 5 and 30 percent at best. On-the-spot decision-making by poll workers enabled them to bend the rules as needed to ensure that these requirements did not unnecessarily impede white voters.

Finally, it is not difficult to imagine that Bethune would be calling for equal opportunity for blacks in employment and for access to labor unions. Because they were considered private enterprises, businesses and unions were not covered by the Fifteenth Amendment, even at this late date. It is perhaps more disappointing that Bethune had to remind the president, in a separate request, that America's armed forces were rife with racism and segregation, and that the Negro who had fought and died with honor during both world wars deserved better treatment in exchange for fulfilling the duties of citizenship.

This brief overview is essential to appreciate the work of Mary Bethune. To support her ambitious goals, she developed and deployed the familiar skills of the social entrepreneur. She wrote, she spoke, she raised funds, she recruited friends of all races; she lobbied and cajoled; she invested and invested again. Through her leadership in secondary education, higher education, national lobbying associations, federal governmental policy, international relations, and private economic development, she demonstrated to all why it was important for the nation to give the Negro access to opportunity.

Mary McLeod Bethune shared many characteristics with Maria Chapman, even though her background could not have been more different. She lacked all of Chapman's obvious advantages: money, social standing, and a supportive spouse. As she complained herself, Mary Bethune also lacked any measure of traditional feminine attractiveness. But despite being the fifteenth of seventeen children born to her formerly enslaved parents in rural South Carolina, she did have "privileges." Foremost among these were caring and diligent parents who, upon obtaining their freedom, regathered their children from the many separate owners to whom they had been sold. The parents purchased land and began a small family farm. Bethune writes in her biography that people seemed to look up to her for as long as she could remember. As a girl of ten, she was the one the foreman counted on to keep track of the cotton picked by the field hands. Her parents noted her brightness and allowed her to attend the local free "mission school," run by a black missionary from the northern Presbyterian Church. Emma Wilson was so impressed by young

Mary McLeod that she sought a gift from a Northern "church lady" (in Denver) to enable Mary to continue her education at the Scotia Seminary in Concord, North Carolina.

At age twelve, Mary took her first train ride, saw her first brick building, and climbed her first flight of stairs at the Scotia Seminary. Scotia was an exceptional institution at the time, with an integrated faculty and student body. Remarkably, Mary became the peer counselor and club organizer for all the girls. She felt called, as she put it, to do great things. At a time when 95 percent of all blacks in the South were illiterate,[24] she took her educational opportunities with utmost seriousness. She often told the story of playing with the child of her parents' former owners when she was a little girl and being given a "picture book" because, as her playmate noted, "Negroes can't read."

Upon graduation from Scotia, Mary again received financial support to attend the Bible Institute for Home and Foreign Missions in Chicago, created by Dwight Moody, the evangelist friend of the Dodge family. She set her sights on missionary work upon graduation in 1895, wanting to reach out to Africans. But her wish to go to Africa was denied by the Presbyterian Church: It seemed that there were no posts available for Negro missionaries. Bethune returned instead to her hometown in South Carolina and took up teaching at the very mission school she had attended as a little girl. Subsequently, she taught in Augusta, Georgia, and at the Kindell Institute in Sumter, South Carolina, where, in 1898, she married a men's clothing salesman, Albertus Bethune, and bore her only child, Albertus Jr. Inspired by her teaching experience, Mary wanted to start a school herself, ideally a school for black girls whose educational options were so severely limited. So she accepted the invitation of a Presbyterian minister and the family moved to Palatka, Florida, where she launched a mission school that attracted mostly boys. Over the next five years, she directed the school, found time to work with local incarcerated men, and sold life insurance to support the family, an area in which Albertus proved to be a disappointment.[25]

But her dream of a girls' school was still unfulfilled, and in 1904, she made her move to Daytona, spending the only money she had on transportation to this lively city. Daytona was a city with considerable wealth, the summer home of some of the nation's business magnates, including James Gamble of Procter & Gamble fame, and Thomas White of the White Sewing Machine Company. Daytona had plenty of poor black citizens as well, the fortunate ones laboring on building the Florida East Coast Railway at the time, and the less fortunate working in turpentine camps in the surrounding pine forests. The black community pitched in to help Mary launch her school in a rented house, furnished according to legend with furniture scavenged from the local dump. Food, money, and supplies were gathered (the children famously using charcoal lumps and ink made with elderberries), and the school, the Daytona Educational and Industrial Training School for Negro Girls, opened with six students (five girls and Mary's son) in 1904.

The school curriculum focused on religious training and "industrial arts" and proved a remarkable early success. Enrollments grew rapidly to some 250 by the end of the second year. Bethune's strategy for building her institution did not include asking white people for charity. She relied on an important economic argument that she would use on many occasions to build support for equal opportunities for her race. She went to great pains to explain that it was in the interest of the City of Daytona to support the education of black girls. She invited the mayor and city council members to inspect the facility and learn firsthand about the work being done. The curriculum was built to support this argument and to reflect the controversial educational philosophy of Booker T. Washington, one of Mary's early heroes. Courses included Bible Studies, Vocational Studies (the domestic arts of cooking, cleaning, and ironing for girls), and English designed to teach reading and writing to prepare the next generation of teachers for the Negro community. A nurses' training program and "elder care" facility for blacks were added as the institution grew. Who could argue with the merits of such efforts and the economic benefits that self-sufficient black women would bring to the community? The town fathers' support would certainly demonstrate "self-interest, rightly understood." Bethune did not miss the opportunity to write a lengthy open letter to the editor of the *Daytona Morning Journal,* thanking the public officials for their visit and their wise suggestions.

As the school grew, Mary and the students baked sweet potato pies and made ice cream, finding an enthusiastic audience for their products among the railroad laborers. Bethune also sought and received the support of the "summer visitors," through a strategy that all present-day educators will recognize. She invited James Gamble to join the board of trustees and to provide guidance to her humble enterprise. He accepted and served for decades as chair of the board. She also approached the ladies of the Palmetto Club, who included many spouses of the moguls, and enlisted their support for the school. These efforts were, in general, successful; and as for the school, within five years it had over 100 boarding students. Land was purchased in 1909 for the first permanent building, and a hospital facility was added in 1911 (when the students were refused treatment at the local hospital). In keeping with her community commitments, Mary also offered outreach classes to the turpentine workers.

Bethune was not satisfied, however, to cultivate support among the local community leaders. She sought support from "national" sources as well, including the General Education Board (GEB), created with an initial gift of $50 million by John D. Rockefeller and from Julius Rosenwald, the president of Sears, Roebuck. Rockefeller's fund was designed to support the education of the newly freed blacks, and Rosenwald invested millions of his personal fortune in building secondary schools in partnership with Southern black communities. Mary Bethune wrote an open letter to the *New York Times* in 1920 advertising her need for $50,000 to expand the physical plant of Daytona School for Negro Girls. She listed the many practical and civic benefits of educating the girls and invited contributions to be sent to her attention, yet she never heard back from Rosenwald and she would wait fifteen years before the GEB provided support to her efforts. When a $62,000 grant did arrive, it was awarded to Bethune-Cookman College, the institution created by the merger of Mary's girls' school with Cookman Institute, a school for Negro boys, in 1923.

Bethune agreed to this merger plan in the vain hope that the Methodist Episcopal Church, which brokered the arrangement, would become a stable source of funding for the merged institutions. Such was not to be the case, and Bethune, the nation's first black female college president, devoted much effort in subsequent years to fund-raising for the new institution. Nevertheless, it was a remarkable accomplishment to shepherd the development of a one-room girls' school into a coeducational junior college accredited by the Southern Education Board in 1931 (a four-year degree was in place by 1941). Bethune led Bethune-Cookman for over twenty years, although she considered her leadership to have begun in 1904, the year she founded the Daytona Girls School.

Bethune's college presidency, and her outgoing ways, provided a natural platform for her broader leadership in education. Her always-visible commitment to the importance of female education made her a natural advocate for all issues affecting women. She was also an effective coalition builder whose natural instincts were to bring interested parties together to make common cause. Years of "selling" her ideas on the economic and social value of education had honed her public-speaking skills. She put all these abilities to work aligning interested parties on behalf of her ideal: a nation that treated all citizens, including blacks, with respect and dignity.

Mary was asked to assume the presidency of the National Association of Teachers in Colored Schools, representing black educators at both the secondary and post-secondary levels. She eventually headed the National Association of Colored Women (NACW), the organization founded in 1896 to "furnish evidence of the moral, mental and material progress made by people of color." The NACW boasted over 10,000 members when she became president in 1924. In her earlier work with the Florida chapter of the NACW, she had championed involvement of the group in two national issues, entry into World War I and the women's suffrage movement.

She immediately sought a similar vision for the larger organization: "This organization must assume an attitude toward all big questions involving the welfare of the nation . . . especially the present and future of our race." As if to symbolize the presence of Negro women as part of the nation's democratic fiber, Bethune oversaw the acquisition of an imposing building in Washington, D.C., to serve as the national headquarters of the NACW.

Ultimately, Bethune's vision proved too large for the NACW, and she chose to found a new organization, the National Council for Negro Women. The council promoted engaged citizenship, interracial cooperation, and international collaboration. Mary's efforts culminated in her receipt of the Spingarn Medal from the National Association for the Advancement of Colored People

(NAACP) in 1935, awarded annually to the individual "who has done the most for the colored race."

Patriotism had always been at the forefront of Mary's agenda. She called on her fellow blacks to transcend the slights and injustices and never to compromise their own integrity in response to unjust treatment. She believed the promises of the Declaration and the Constitution and saw her responsibility as an engaged citizen to fulfill these promises. Such positions undoubtedly contributed to her attractiveness as a minority member of various initiatives sponsored by the administrations of Presidents Calvin Coolidge (Child Welfare Conference in 1928) and Herbert Hoover (Child Health Conference in 1930). The most important opportunity, however, was her highly visible role in President Franklin Roosevelt's administration as the highest-ranking black woman in the federal government. Her leadership among black educators and black women and her acquaintance with First Lady Eleanor Roosevelt made her a natural choice to join the board of the National Youth Administration (NYA) in 1936. The NYA was a New Deal agency created to manage funding for job training, employment development, and education in the basics of democracy for the nation's young people. In a short time, Mary had moved from her advisory board position into a full-time, paid role as director of the Negro Affairs division of the NYA. As the NYA was primarily state-based, and all the state-level directors were white, she faced an obvious challenge in attempting to ensure that the "Negroes" received a fair share of the $685 million allocated to the NYA over its five-year life span.[26]

She embraced the challenge and traveled extensively from state to state to make the case, as only she could, that funds allocated to training and education for blacks were indeed a good investment for the nation. Despite what must have been tedious and dispiriting battles over the failures of states to appoint any black representatives to their local oversight boards or to allow the creation of separate black and white boards on an experimental basis, she won praise from at least some white colleagues. The director of the Oklahoma NYA spoke positively:

> Her visit was an inspiration to me personally, to all of my people who came in contact with her, and needless to say she showed great leadership and great ability to stimulate, to lead her own people. . . .[27]

Bethune's work did lead to significant increases in college enrollments by blacks during these years. When the NYA was given responsibility for a program called Civilian Pilot Training, Mary ensured that black institutions received a portion of the funding. Her work ultimately led to the birth of the famous Tuskegee Airmen squadron of fighter pilots that distinguished itself during World War II.

Bethune used her NYA position to continue her entrepreneurial work. She did her job well, but her job description served as inspiration, rather than as a "to do" list. Perhaps this is the definition of an "intrapreneur." She convened two national conventions on the state of Negro affairs under the aegis of NYA in 1937 and 1939, and she summarized the concerns expressed in these conventions in her imposing document entitled "What the Negro Wants." These documents were shared with the president and with Eleanor Roosevelt, effectively creating a blueprint for the future civil rights movement.

Bethune also convened the group that came to be known as the "Black Cabinet" of FDR's administration. The Federal Council on Negro Affairs, as Mary called the unofficial leadership group she hosted in her living room in 1936,[28] achieved significant progress on Mary's agenda. The group counted as its greatest accomplishment the mobilization of support for the landmark Executive Order 8802. Signed by FDR in 1941, the order banned racial discrimination in employment practices in the defense industry. Bethune rejoiced at this presidential order, noting that it was the first order to issue from the Oval Office since the Emancipation Proclamation in 1863 that clarified the rights of "colored" people to equal treatment under the law.

As modest as these achievements may seem in the light of the present day, their significance should not be underestimated. Mary was rightly proud of her role in increasing opportunities for black Americans in the workplace, in military service, and in access to education. Amid continuing crises, first the Great Depression and then World War II, Bethune found a way to represent the interests of "her people" while serving the interests of all Americans as an official of the federal government. She invented and improvised, treating her position as an invitation to strengthen the nation rather than as a job description to be fulfilled. In her mind, the interests of the nation and the interests of blacks were indivisible.

At the end of the war, Bethune was well into her seventies and Washington changed administrations. Not ready to simply retire, she lobbied hard for one final official opportunity to influence the future. She had always been interested in international affairs, beginning with her missionary dream and fueled by a trip to Europe as a college president that included an impressive meeting with Pope Pius XI. She persuaded the Truman administration to include her as an official representative to the United Nations Conference on International Organization in 1945, thus becoming the only official black female representative at the conference that established the United Nations. In so doing, she again achieved a pioneering place at the table as a black female American.

She returned to Florida in the 1950s in time to initiate one final entrepreneurial effort, an economic development project involving what came to be known as Bethune Volusia Beach. Mary and other investors had purchased a large tract of ocean-front land south of Daytona in the 1940s, and they now set about developing the property, with the goal of enabling access for blacks to the beaches of the Atlantic Ocean. She also found time to write her last will and testament, published in *Ebony* magazine, in which she bequeathed to all citizens, but especially to her black brothers and sisters, the values that she believed constituted her most valuable legacy. Mary Bethune passed on love, hope, the challenge of developing confidence in one another; a thirst for education, respect for the uses of power, faith, racial dignity, a desire to live harmoniously with your fellow man, and as always in her life, a responsibility to young people. She embraced these same ideals and never stopped calling on all Americans to practice the virtues of engaged citizenship.

Mary Bethune was the most senior black woman to serve in the federal government in her era. But the most senior woman of all, and the first woman to serve in the cabinet, as secretary of labor, was Frances Perkins. She created a legal framework that protected workers from both exploitative employers and self-serving union leadership. In so doing, she ensured that "the fundamental purpose of labor legislation is the conservation of the human resources of the nation."[29]

As late as the 1930s, male unions did not admit women as members. Moreover, when social entrepreneurs went to bat to seek federal protections for child workers and for minimum wages for working women, labor unions openly opposed their efforts. (In fairness, some state chapters supported state-based efforts in these areas.) It took a shopkeeper's daughter from Worcester, Massachusetts, to build a working relationship among the highly fragmented and volatile leadership of America's organized labor movement, the nation's large employers, the voluntary sector, and state and federal government.

The career of Frances Perkins parallels the path created by Julia Lathrop and Mary Bethune. She, too, was a successful citizen social entrepreneur before moving to the halls of government. Once she made the transition, she used her government position to further the same objectives—to invent more opportunities for greater numbers of her fellow citizens, in part through legislation, but also through information dissemination and education. Her record of accomplishment as a female public servant remains unsurpassed to this day.

The opportunity for value creation was enormous. The growth of capitalism and the resulting increase in the number of hourly paid workers changed the economic and social fabric of the late nineteenth century. Despite this radical change, state and federal governments (backed by the courts) maintained a "hands-off" policy when it came to employer-employee relations. The parties were free to strike a private bargain for labor and payment.

The free market for labor, however, was hardly in balance. The combination of immigration and urbanization had produced an oversupply of workers for unskilled or semiskilled jobs, and individual workers thus had little leverage to demand safer working conditions, wages, insurance, or pensions. Social entrepreneurs, as we have seen, sought to intervene in these labor markets. The entire settlement house movement could be said to represent a volunteer effort to correct this imbalance, through the voluntary provision of services such as job training, employment bureaus, child care, and the like, until the scale of the problem demanded that elected officials take action using the resources of government to "level the playing field" on behalf of workers.

Perkins provides a fitting conclusion to the story of the creation of America's social profit sector because she expanded the foundation partnership through which the sector continues to operate today. In her government role, Perkins benefited from 100 years of work by social entrepreneurs, identifying gaps in the social fabric and inventing small-scale local solutions for the growing nation. She understood this tradition well. She also understood from her own entrepreneurial successes that moments of crisis provide opportunities. The stock market crash of 1929 and the ensuing Great Depression offered just such an opportunity. She led the nation in forging a new partnership between the private sector, the federal government, and the social profit sector that addressed the dominance of large-scale capitalism across the private sector.

We generally associate this period in American history with the rise of organized labor. Indeed, across Europe as well as in America, organizers called on working men (and women) to join together and to bargain collectively rather than individually with employers. This strategy, they argued, would increase the power of working people to obtain a fairer contract with their employers. The American labor movement produced its share of fiery leaders, large-scale rallies, and violent confrontations between workers and employers. The government most often played the role of peacekeeper in these conflicts, and both employers and union organizers seemed more or less satisfied with this arrangement. Neither group wanted to invite the government directly into their business.

American organizers faced many challenges in achieving solidarity in the many diverse labor markets, with abundant workers, ethnic rivalries, and few precedents to learn from. But unlike European leaders, union leaders felt that they could and should achieve benefits for their members through the direct bargaining process with employers, not by campaigning for labor laws from Washington. They showed little interest in workers who were not members of their organizations. In typically American fashion, a voluntary citizen group emerged around 1906 to address the question of the role of the state in the ever-growing labor market. The group called itself the American Association for Labor Legislation (AALL). It was composed of senior officials from the social service, business, labor, government, and academic sectors, and its goal was to produce disinterested policy recommendations—ideas that focused on the "greatest good for the largest number of citizens."

Over the period from 1906 to 1920, the participants, led by General Secretary John Andrews, researched health insurance, unemployment insurance, pensions, and other large issues. They established state-level affiliates and held annual conventions to discuss their findings. Perhaps their most fully developed proposal emerged in 1916. They advanced a model legislative package that would provide health care for all workers earning less than $1,200 per year. It also included replacement wages for those with extended illnesses, as well as maternity and death benefits. Costs would be divided among employers (40 percent), employees (40 percent), and general government contributions (20 percent). Despite the optimism of the authors of this carefully thought-out initiative, it went nowhere. Remarkably, Samuel Gompers and the American Federation of Labor (AFL), the American Medical Association, and the business community all united in fierce opposition. The only government component that gained any traction was a small program that provided benefits to workers injured on the job, a tiny fraction compared to those who fell victim to illness.[30]

The organized labor movement that was so energized in the earliest days of the twentieth century gradually ran out of steam following World War I. The American Federation of Labor (AFL) claimed some 4 million members in 1918. This number was halved by 1933. The leader of the AFL who followed Gompers in 1924 was John Green, a man seemingly disliked by all constituencies. Frances Perkins became America's first female cabinet secretary in 1932, when Franklin Roosevelt named her the U.S. secretary of labor.[31] Perkins presided over a rebirth of organized labor that despite continuing factionalism and mismanagement built membership back to over 6 million members by 1937, representing roughly 35 percent of all workers at the time. Perkins proved adept at the delicate dance of self-assertion, personal risk-taking, networking, and teamwork that distinguishes the effective intrapreneur. She moved fearlessly (if not always comfortably) between the highest and lowest levels of American society. Trusted by both sectors, she could build bridges, broker accords, and create assets for her fellow citizens in government and in the volunteer sector. She was a citizen who lived her life "in the nation's service."

Biographer Kirstin Downey argues that it was Perkins's personal experience with the Triangle Shirtwaist Factory fire that shaped her commitment to justice for working people for the duration of her life. On a Saturday afternoon in March 1911, Perkins was having tea at an elegant townhouse on Washington Square in New York City. She was completing her graduate studies in political science at Columbia University and enjoying the intellectual ferment of Greenwich Village life. Teatime was interrupted by sirens and shouts from the south side of the square. Perkins ran outside to discover a gruesome scene. A garment factory was ablaze and countless workers were trapped on the upper floors. One by one they jumped to their deaths before her eyes and those of thousands of other spectators. By the time the conflagration was over, 176 women, mostly Jewish and Italian immigrants, had perished.

The event affected Frances deeply. She knew that these New York women, along with thousands of their co-workers from other garment factories, had protested their unsafe working conditions in public demonstrations just a couple of years earlier, only to see their leaders jailed. Soon after the fire, Frances attended a public meeting to hear Rose Schneiderman, a garment worker herself, condemn the public officials for their indifference and call on her fellow citizens to change the laws that governed working conditions. A friend of Perkins, journalist Will Irvin, noted that "what Frances Perkins saw that day started her on her career."[32]

And what a career it turned out to be: New York head of the National Consumers League; founding head of the Maternity Center Association; member of the New York Industrial Commission, head of the New York State Industrial Department; U.S. secretary of labor; university professor, wife, and mother; friend and confidante of FDR and of his wife, Eleanor; personal friend of Sinclair Lewis, Winston Churchill, Al Smith, Henry Wallace, Mary Harriman Rumsey, and Robert Moses; and mentor to a subsequent generation of leaders including John F. Kennedy, Alan Bloom, and Paul Wolfowitz.

Perkins did not begin life in elite circles. Her family had once owned a prosperous brickmaking operation in Maine, but the business had been lost. All that remained was an old house and some acreage on the Damariscotta River. These remnants of better times provided a sanctuary for Frances, where she returned almost every year of her adult life. When Fannie Perkins was born (she changed her name after college), her father and a partner were running a stationery store in Worcester, Massachusetts, fifty miles west of Boston. Theirs was a conservative family, church-going Congregationalists. Fannie had one younger sister, Ethel. She also had a supportive, intellectually inclined father who appreciated her intelligence and enabled her to attend the Worcester Classical High School, as one of only three female students. Her exceptional educational opportunities continued when she was admitted to Mount Holyoke College in nearby South Hadley, Massachusetts. Perkins chose to major in chemistry, perhaps the most challenging curricular choice at the college. In later life, she remembered most vividly a visit to campus by a compelling lecturer named Florence Kelley, who tried to interest the bright young women in careers of service to others.

Perkins's aspirations as a college graduate in 1902 reflected her family and her academic experiences. She wanted to marry and raise a family, as well as save the world. Brimming with confidence and determination, she obtained an interview with the head of the New York Charity Organizations Society (COS), Edward Devine. Her outspoken naïveté did not sit well with Devine, however, and she was forced to contemplate a return to Worcester to await a marriage proposal. To avoid this uncertain fate, and the possibility of failure as she considered herself quite homely, she applied to teach at a (wealthy) girls' finishing school outside Chicago. She was employed sight unseen. In Chicago, she met many prominent families through the school, but the most influential family was the Hull House settlement community. Remembering the unforgettable Florence Kelley, Perkins found her way to Chicago's West Side, where she met Kelley, Jane Addams, and an impressive array of Hull House residents, ranging from Benny Goodman, the jazz musician, to Gerard Swope, the future CEO of General Electric. Between weekends at Hull House delivering baskets of food to poor families and campus life with debutante balls and a trip to Europe, Perkins found time to change her name to Frances and her religion from Congregationalist to high-church Episcopalian. A life that bridged a wide set of economic and class boundaries would soon become a trademark of Perkins's career.

By 1907, the Hull House philosophy of service had won her over. At Kelley's urging, she accepted a low-paying post as general secretary of the newly formed Philadelphia Research and Protective Association, launched by another Hull House alumna, Frances Kellor. Perkins's job was to research the conditions of single women living in boardinghouses. With her trademark gusto, she waded into the seamy world of pimps, human traffickers, and unscrupulous "employment agencies" preying on immigrants and Southern blacks, even posing as a job seeker to test the honesty of the agencies she visited. There was plenty of exploitation of female workers to find, even in legitimate workplaces.

She soon determined to add some additional book learning to this real-life experience. She enrolled at the Wharton School of the University of Pennsylvania, presumably to extend her economic knowledge and perhaps to test the Socialist views of many of her colleagues in the social service arena. After two years and a friendship with one of those Socialists that did not lead to romance as perhaps she hoped it might, Frances elected to move on. With the support of a Wharton faculty member, she obtained a fellowship at Columbia University in New York City to complete her graduate studies in political science. It was during this period of her life, living in Greenwich Village, that she attracted the attention of the writer Upton Sinclair. Sinclair, who went on to win the Pulitzer Prize for Fiction, remained devoted to her throughout his life, although she apparently considered him too unstable to embrace as spousal material. It was also the time when she witnessed the tragic fire in Washington Square.

Her career moved forward rapidly when she was invited to lead the New York City office of the National Consumers League, headed nationally by Florence Kelley. The post was an ideal fit for Frances, who enjoyed the enthusiastic support of Kelley herself. Frances learned to appreciate Kelley's fanatical devotion to facts and figures before advocating any policy positions on labor issues. She also noted Kelley's preferred operating method of convening direct conversations between employers and workers in order to resolve workplace disputes. She set to work advocating for the league's "white label" program across the city, discovering that the favorite shopping destinations among the "smart set" such as Bloomingdale's and Altman's continued to underpay their sales staffs and refused to participate in the program. As part of her job, Perkins was expected to support state-based legislation on limited work hours, the federal courts having consistently rejected such limits as unconstitutional infringements on the personal freedom of workers. Despite her novice status as a lobbyist, Frances was soon engaged in the heat of the battle.

Over a period of months, she spearheaded a lobbying campaign in support of a law that would establish a fifty-hour maximum (!) workweek for female workers in the state of New York. She traveled regularly to Albany, observing the legislative process (most decisions seemed to be made elsewhere than in public hearings), meeting the Tammany Hall power brokers (the Democratic political machine in control at the time), and learning "the art of the deal." She was a quick study: On one occasion Frances had been assured that the proposed law to limit women's legal workweek to fifty hours would be approved in the final session of the legislature. Without her knowledge, however, the bill was amended at the last minute. The amendment excluded women workers in the canning industry. This move was clearly a ploy by opponents to render the entire bill unacceptable to its supporters who were pledged to an all-inclusive law.

Though only twenty-nine years old, Frances refused to be out-maneuvered. On the spot, she made the tough call. Rather than go home empty-handed, she notified her supporters to accept the measure as written, even calling the captain of a ship about to depart from Albany to New York City with legislators on board to hold his ship and allow the legislators to return to the chamber for the vote. The bill passed as amended, and although she won bitter criticism from many "purist" allies for selling out, she had managed to win legal work-hour protection for the first time for 400,000 working women across the state. Florence Kelley was delighted.

Frances Perkins married Paul Wilson the following year (1913) after a courtship of some two years. Wilson was a handsome and well-to-do University of Chicago graduate who worked for the Bureau of Municipal Research, a nonprofit watchdog agency that tried to keep the Tammany Hall patronage machine honest. He shared her interest in progressive politics, and she believed she had found the perfect mate. Sadly, the couple's promising start quickly turned sour. After only two years, Frances was apparently ready to call it quits with the (unfaithful) Paul, only to discover that she was pregnant. She miscarried the baby, but she and Paul refound at least a bit of their earlier happiness. Soon she was pregnant again, only to suffer preeclampsia and ultimately toxemia. Although she carried to term, surviving in an era without anti-biotics, their child, a son, was stillborn. Against her doctor's orders, Perkins became pregnant a third time, and this time she gave birth to a daughter, Susanna.

Susanna's early childhood was a time of great happiness. Both Frances and Paul doted on their beautiful daughter while they lived in a fine town house with a German couple in domestic service. Frances, ever the energetic fixer, took advantage of the hiatus in her professional life to put her prodigious organizing skills to work as a private citizen. She acted, as she would many times in the future, to turn a problem into an opportunity. Amid her extended pregnancy travails, she had noted the lack of maternity care for poor women, so she launched the Maternity Center Association in 1918. Her goal was to bring obstetric and prenatal care to poor women throughout New York City. She called it "her most successful piece of social work."[33]

Perkins raised funds among her wealthy friends, recruited prominent women to serve on the association's board of directors (including the mother of her future son-in-law), and selected two talented public health nurses (a new profession established through the work of Lillian Wald) to establish a network of outreach workers who would find and assist poor pregnant women. In her role as executive secretary, Frances engaged the New York chapters of the Women's City Club, the settlement house movement, the YWCA, the American Red Cross, and the Council of Jewish Women in the effort. After one year, the association grew to employ twenty-six nurses and operated sixteen clinics. These numbers were five times greater by 1921, and soon the Maternity Center Association was training doctors and public health workers in obstetrics and well-baby care. Her work was the perfect complement to the efforts of Lillian Wald and Julia Lathrop. The Maternity Center gradually changed the system of health care available to poor women in New York City and eventually throughout the country by mobilizing the best scientific and medical knowledge for the good of all citizens.[34]

Perkins was unable to sustain her full-time commitment to the Maternity Center Association because she suddenly needed to earn money. Paul had lost his job working in the mayor's office in a change of administrations, had lost his inheritance in a series of misguided speculations, and had fallen into a deep depression.

The family needed a breadwinner, a role that Frances was obliged to fulfill for the rest of her life, as Paul would never work again. This turn of events led her into government service for the first time. She (and Paul) had actively supported Al Smith in his successful campaign for the governorship of New York State in 1918, and Frances was offered a seat on the State Industrial Commission, a paid post with responsibility for monitoring workplace compliance and labor relations across the state.[35] The position made her the highest-paid woman in state government ($8,000 per year). It offered her the opportunity to develop her intrapreneuring skills within the complex executive-legislative-judicial matrix of government.[36]

Being a woman on the inside of government proved every bit as difficult as being a female lobbyist. Perkins was frequently ignored and resented by her government colleagues. In response, she took advantage of her gender to befriend the wives and often the mothers of these officials. She learned much about their values and skills, as well as their strengths and weaknesses, in the process. She also concluded, based on the willingness of some legislators to discuss their personal feelings with her, that she must somehow come off as slightly maternal. She consciously set about building such an image, adopting ever more dowdy clothing and hair styling at the ripe old age of thirty-three.

Her listening skills won her many friends among both the powerful and the "little people" she was committed to helping. She shared this strategy with her fellow industrial commissioners, often dragging them out of their offices and into the field to meet both employers and workers. By holding "hearings" on the spot in settings where labor unrest was brewing, she was able to defuse potentially violent confrontations and demonstrate a visible and engaged face of government. Downey recounts a high-stakes confrontation in Rome, New York, in 1919 between the owner of a copper-wire manufacturing plant, James Spargo, and his work-force, primarily southern Italian immigrants, who were insisting on an eight-hour workday. When confronted by the workers in his office, Spargo responded by literally kicking several of them down the stairs. Chaos, a shooting, and escalating threats ensued; the workers stockpiled dynamite as a group of employers allied with Spargo asked the governor to send in the state police to re-store order. Perkins took a train to Rome to investigate personally, arriving at the scene in a taxi. She waded into the agitated crowd and introduced herself as an industrial commissioner. She prom-ised to mobilize the entire commission to hold hearings in Rome to hear the full story from both sides. She appealed to Governor Al Smith by phone to call off the state police, noting the potential for violence should they arrive with their own weapons. She got the reluctant commission chairman, John Mitchell, to show up for a preliminary hearing, to buy time until the rest of their fel-low commissioners could arrive.[37] When the actual hearing was convened, it made little progress, with both parties refusing to en-gage in any real negotiation. But Perkins found a point of leverage in a letter filled with scatological references that Spargo had writ-ten to his employees. She obtained a copy and asked Mitchell to read it aloud during the hearing. She smiled sweetly during the litany of vulgarities while the men squirmed in their chairs. None of Spargo's employer allies were willing to be publicly associated with such language directed at employees, and the employers soon expressed a willingness to discuss the workers' demands in a more constructive spirit. The conflict was eventually resolved peacefully, and Governor Smith expressed both gratitude and admiration for Perkins's successful management of the crisis.

Frances recognized that accurate information was often in short supply, or readily ignored, in the political fray. She had studied the data-driven methods of the Sage Foundation's Pittsburgh study while in graduate school. She was married to a statistician. As a commissioner, and later as chief executive of the New York State Industrial Department, she made it her business to collect accurate information on the topics that fell under her jurisdiction, and she was not afraid to use this information against her opponents. Such data proved essential in one of her most influential moments as a public servant.

When the stock market crashed in 1929, Perkins was serving in the administration of Franklin Roosevelt, who had been elected governor of New York in 1928, the year that Frances's former boss, Governor Al Smith, was losing the presidential election to Herbert Hoover. She enjoyed the confidence of FDR and had a good working relationship with him. As the financial crisis of the Great Depression deepened around Hoover and the White House struggled to find an appropriate response, Perkins studied her data and reached some insightful conclusions.

She came to believe that unemployment was a critical factor in the economic downturn, not simply the price of stocks. She grasped the implications of the collapse of housing prices and the consequences of those changes for the banking industry. She also believed that because the crisis was so broad based, affecting both the wealthy and the poor, it offered a unique opportunity to bring people together for the greater good. She acted on these insights by proposing to FDR a series of innovative programs for the state, including the creation of a state-run employment agency, and the creation of a regional unemployment insurance program encompassing New Jersey and Connecticut. She persuaded him to speak out on unemployment and to announce specific programs designed to combat this root cause of the economic crisis through infrastructure investment and the like.

Perkins even took on the president of the United States. When Hoover announced in December 1930 that unemployment had increased only 4 percent month over month, Frances called the news services to dispute his numbers. She knew better and explained why the president was wrong. In her enthusiasm, she had forgotten to check with her boss, the governor, in advance. But she proved to be correct and instantly became the "go to" authority on the issue of unemployment for a wide range of officials, thus illustrating another intrapreneurial truism—it is often easier to ask for forgiveness than for permission.

Perkins's visibility and competence only reflected positively on her boss in the governor's mansion, and Roosevelt was delighted with her accomplishments. Her leadership on the economic front provided excellent impetus to FDR for his own presidential bid in 1932. And it is not difficult to see why, after his election, he chose this hardworking, competent, uncomplaining, and loyal woman to be his secretary of labor, the nation's first female cabinet secretary. Although he did not always do as she wished, and on more than one occasion sacrificed her interests for politically expedient ends, he remained loyal to her over his entire presidency, including the devastating (to her) effort by Congress to impeach her when she refused to deport a labor leader accused of Communist sympathies. She in turn spearheaded some of the greatest changes in the history of American social policy.

As the Great Depression deepened, only 450,000 persons out of 6.5 million over the age of sixty-five had pensions. The rest were on their own, or relied on their families and friends. The Depression intensified this problem immensely. It was clear to Frances that a new system of post-work life support was needed.

She knew of systems in other countries where people paid in while they worked and then cashed in when they no longer did so. She believed that this approach would calm those who objected to the idea that the government should somehow "give" something to citizens. In this plan, people would put away their own money and get it back. The key term was "economic security." Frances persuaded FDR to create a cabinet-level economic security committee charged with developing a bill that could pass the House and the Senate and not be overturned by the courts.

Perkins believed that any committee recommendations would require unanimous cabinet (and presidential) support to have a chance in Congress. Having carefully engaged each one of her commission colleagues ahead of time, she asked each member to pledge openly in front of the others their willingness to support economic security for all citizens. She pulled this off at a meeting that the president himself attended, and Roosevelt ultimately unveiled his administration's plans on June 8, 1934, in a program that he announced would offer "security against the hazards and vicissitudes of life."[38]

FDR did not get the clear positive reaction he was looking for from the announcement, and he was reluctant to fund additional committee work. But money was required for the research, travel, and staff support to develop a strong bill. So Perkins, undeterred, was obliged to beg contributions from agency and cabinet colleagues. The Federal Emergency Relief Administration came through because its director, Harry Hopkins, was one of her oldest friends from New York politics. Two Supreme Court justices whom Frances knew socially offered informal advice on the structure of the legislation that was being drafted, ensuring that the Court would be less likely to overturn the legislation. Perkins attended all the meetings herself and figured out how to integrate the complicated elements of state and federal responsibilities in the administration and funding of the legislation. Ten months later, after several more solid agreements and last-minute collapses, the president presented the economic security legislation and urged Congress to pass it.

Frances stepped back to watch as the Senate and House engaged in the democratic process of debating her bill, over and over again. Hostility and enthusiasm, condemnation and collusion. Attackers called it "the ultimate socialistic control of life and industry,"[39] and allies refused support because their favorite provision had been dropped in negotiations. At the last moment, Frances was inspired to collect the signatures of fifty prominent Americans on a letter encouraging congressmen to sign the bill for the good of the nation.

Compromises evolved. Unemployment insurance was established as a state-federal program and old-age retirement coverage passed. Health insurance did not. But the core of Perkins's legislation survived. On August 14, 1935, the president signed the measure into law, and the Social Security Act became effective immediately. The "New Deal's Most Important Act," proclaimed the *Washington Post* that day. "Its importance cannot be exaggerated . . . because this legislation eventually will affect the lives of every man, woman and child in the country."[40]

The essential contribution of Perkins to the process was widely acknowledged. "The one person, in my opinion, above all others who was responsible for there being a Social Security program in the early '30's was Frances Perkins," said Maurine Mulliner, a senatorial assistant who left office to join the Social Security Board. She continued: "I don't think that President Roosevelt had the remotest interest in a Social Security bill or program. He was simply pacifying Frances."[41]

"By 1936, Frances could report that nearly 1 million people were receiving benefits. Nearly three-quarters of a million were old people, 184,000 were dependent children and nearly eighteen thousand were blind."[42] In addition, all states were enacting unemployment compensation laws. Even health insurance for working people, a dream that Frances pursued without success during her tenure, came to pass in a roundabout way, as employers began to offer such a benefit to workers during a period of wage and price controls when they were unable to raise wages.

Perkins's leadership would yield additional gains for working Americans as well. She won the right for workers to vote on union membership and oversaw the passage of the landmark 1938 Fair Labor Standards Act, the culmination of decades of work to set limits on the workday and to create a minimum wage. The act was not what its most ardent supporters might have wished, but Perkins was well versed in the art of compromise. It set the initial minimum wage at 25 cents per hour, well below what most industries had voluntarily imposed on themselves. It set the work-week at forty-four hours. However, it did establish a requirement for overtime pay (time and a half when over the forty-four-hour limit), and more important from Perkins's perspective, it passed muster with the Supreme Court and established a framework for the federal government to provide minimum protections for working Americans.

From even this brief retelling, Frances Perkins emerges as a remarkably successful intrapreneur. Few individuals, men or women, can be said to have done so much to help their fellow citizens gain access to life, liberty, and the pursuit of happiness. Convinced that neither labor organizers nor the partisan political machines could be counted on to work dependably for the best interests of workers in the highly industrialized economy, Perkins took her idealism into the political fray in an effort to create protections in law—the surest safety net for those without great fortunes or influence.

Perkins's story is notable for another reason. Social entrepreneurs must be prepared to be risk takers, willing to upset the status quo in pursuit of audacious goals. Such risks can be easily over-looked in a story of many accomplishments. Frances Perkins took many risks, and on one occasion, paid a very high price.

In 1939, the House of Representatives held hearings with the intent of impeaching Frances Perkins. She was accused of failing to carry out the law of the land to protect the country from the threat of communism. The Labor Department, over which she presided, was responsible for the Immigration Service. Harry Bridges, an Australian longshoreman who had successfully led a general strike in Oakland, California, in 1934, was accused of being a Communist. Americans could declare themselves Com-munists, but an alien sympathizing with any organization pledged to the overthrow of capitalism was subject to deportation.

After reviewing his case in detail, Perkins remained uncon-vinced that Bridges was a Communist. He denied the charge under oath. She studied other deportation cases involving labor activists and concluded that these proceedings had often been politically motivated. She even visited San Francisco to interview Bridges' acquaintances, including the city's archbishop, who con-firmed that Bridges was a devout practitioner who was generous to the church and sent his daughter to parochial school. FBI records documented Bridges' extramarital affair with the wife of a fellow labor organizer, but much of the evidence about him was being supplied by rival union officials and others who seemed to Frances to have much to gain from his deportation.

Perkins was not persuaded that the evidence merited depor-tation. During her investigations, a federal appeals court overruled a deportation order for another alien accused of Communist Party membership, remanding the decision to a lower court. Frances followed the advice of her counsel to delay action until the Supreme Court could issue a ruling on a set of these cases, in-cluding the Bridges case. For her efforts, she became a punching bag on Capitol Hill, with a variety of legislators accusing her of being a Communist sympathizer, even a Communist herself. Others wrote that she was simply a dupe, a soft-headed lady whom the Stalinists were exploiting. As Immigration Department records revealed an increase in immigrants arriving from Europe from 1938 to 1939 (most of whom of course were fleeing Hitler's growing war machine), Perkins was said to be "soft on aliens." Soon the smear campaign was in high gear, with rumors circulating that she and Bridges were lovers, if not husband and wife, that she was in reality a Russian Jewess named Mathilda Watsky, masquerading as Frances Perkins. While the clamor got louder and more outrageous, the White House remained silent. Ultimately, Perkins was able to appear before her accusers in a committee hearing to defend herself and her reasoning. She kept her cool under an onslaught of provocative accusations and in the end the majority of committee members declined to bring formal impeachment charges.

The fallout from the episode continued. In 1939, the Supreme Court ruled that new standards were required in deportation cases for determining Communist affiliation and the risks to U.S. security, effectively upholding the appeals court ruling. The Immigration Department was obliged to proceed with the case against Bridges, and Perkins asked James Landis, dean of the Harvard Law School, to serve as a special hearing officer in order to ensure objectivity in the volatile case. Landis found for Bridges, allowing him to remain in the United States, although the action proved costly to Landis's own professional career. Over the years, subsequent appeals by the federal government of the Landis decision made their way to the U.S. Supreme Court. None was successful, and the Australian eventually became a U.S. citizen. Many years later, after the fall of communism, Kremlin records revealed that Harry Bridges had indeed been a Communist agent, code named "Rossi."

The fallout for Frances Perkins at the time of the original congressional hearings was deeply personal as well as professional. She was wounded by the lack of support from the president. The hurt only deepened when Roosevelt endorsed a plan in 1940 to move the Immigration Department out from under her supervision to the Department of Justice. Her enemies rejoiced at this humiliation, even though in private Perkins agreed that immigration was a poor fit in the Labor Department.

During such difficult times, Perkins had frequently taken refuge in a convent in Maryland, spending weekends in meditation and prayer, seeking the spiritual strength to endure the unending difficulties she faced. She gained some solace from the happy state of her daughter, Susanna, who had married a successful photographer, traveled in Europe, and now resided in Connecticut. But this happiness ended when Susanna's husband fell in love with another woman and divorced Susanna, leaving her in a state of depression and alcohol dependence that bore a frightening resemblance to her father's condition.[43]

There would be subsequent moments of happiness and normalcy for Susanna, who eventually remarried and bore Frances a grandson, but she battled her addictions and her mental illness for the rest of her life, losing her money and becoming ever more estranged from her aging mother, whom she chose to blame frequently for her own failings.

Frances continued in Roosevelt's cabinet throughout World War II, becoming the longest-serving cabinet member in history. Despite her resolve to resign and join the private sector in 1940, she chose to stay on when the president asked her to. Her political career was far from over. Following Roosevelt's death, she left the cabinet but was appointed to the Civil Service Commission by President Harry Truman. She ultimately left public life in 1952, when the Republicans and Dwight Eisenhower won the White

House. Needing to work to support herself, she took a number of teaching jobs and ultimately landed a full-time appointment at Cornell, where she continued to teach in the School of Industrial and Labor Relations until her death in 1965. With Paul's death in 1952, and her estrangement from Susanna, Frances did not have the good fortune to enjoy a loving family context in her old age. She persevered alone, as she had learned to do on many occasions, and built relationships with her students, including John F. Kennedy and Paul Wolfowitz, who provided at least a bit of the respect and admiration she deserved.

The development of America's social profit sector does not end with Julia Lathrop, Mary Bethune, or Frances Perkins. Neither does the tradition of women social entrepreneurs taking responsibility for preserving the ideals of the Declaration of Independence. Since the era of FDR, there have been generations of creative women who have added to the legacy. But the work of these three women reaches a vital milestone. They had brought the values and the skills of women social entrepreneurs to the heart of the nation's political process.

THIRTEEN

Conclusion: Cooperative Individualism

You and I must fight as never before to make our government
realize the ideals upon which it was founded. . . . We must help
save the soul of our own nation . . . so we can really save the world.
—Mary Bethune, "Americans All, Which Way America?"

American optimism and idealism reached a high watermark
in 1938. Despite the hangover from the Great Depression,
and the looming prospect of a second world war, Henry Luce felt
justified in proclaiming the dawning of "the American Century,"
a period when the core values of the United States would set the
standard for the world. He described these values as follows:

a love of freedom, a feeling for the equality of opportunity,
a tradition of self-reliance and independence, and also of
cooperation. . . . We are the inheritors of all the great principles
of Western civilization—above all Justice, the love of Truth, the
ideal of charity. . . . It now becomes our time to be the power-
house from which the ideals spread throughout the world and
do their mysterious work of lifting the life of mankind from the
level of the beasts to what the Psalmist called a little lower than
the angels.[1]

America's continuing commitments to Justice and Truth that Luce was prepared to celebrate had not endured by chance. They were the product of hard work by millions of citizens striving to maintain a productive balance between what Luce calls "independence and cooperation," between "freedom and equality of opportunity." The Founders identified the need to balance personal enterprise with a sense of responsibility for the well-being of others in creating a new republic. Women social entrepreneurs figured out how to turn this abstract concern into citizen actions that have built our successful democracy.

Two landmark pieces of federal legislation addressed this question of balance during the 1930s. The Social Security Act of 1935 provided a mechanism through which working individuals, their employers, and the federal government could share the risks of growing old, providing a means of support to people too old to work. The Social Security Act also contained a provision called Aid to Dependent Children, which offered protection to single and widowed women and children. Three years later, the Fair Labor Standards Act outlawed the employment of children under the age of eighteen in dangerous positions, established a minimum hourly wage, mandated overtime pay for most workers, and set standards for the education of children employed in agricultural activities. It had taken eighty years of work by generations of social entrepreneurs to win basic protections for children, single women, and working-class members of society, through a partnership that involved the private sector, citizen volunteers, and the government.

The hard work of building and strengthening partnerships between the sectors did not end in 1938. But an important chapter in the history of the social profit sector had been written. A national consensus that our federal government and the private sector must stand for fairness, must recognize the needs of citizens at risk, and must play a role in maintaining the delicate balance between free enterprise and the well-being of all citizens had been achieved. Although it is tempting to press forward with the ongoing story of the social profit sector—for instance, 1938 also marks the launch of the National Foundation for Infantile Paralysis, popularly known as the Mothers' March of Dimes, one of the greatest social profit campaigns of all time—the greater accomplishment is the fact that the sector had achieved a level of influence by the 1930s that made it a recognized component of American life.

The Founders hoped to engage the best of human nature to work for prosperity for self and others, while moderating the natural forces of greed and avarice that could overwhelm fairness and doom the Republic. Thanks to social entrepreneurs, the ideal of optimizing both ingenuity and integrity within the culture had become a hallmark of American society. Americans draw their freedom and security from the commitment of fellow citizens to assure that the words of the Declaration of Independence become a reality for every citizen. The balance that this commitment entails is, of course, an ideal that always remains in flux. Citizen commitment to mutuality, for instance, had to increase to balance the force of successful commercial profit during the nation's first 150 years. What de Tocqueville called "self-interest, rightly understood" in the 1830s, a reviewer of Lillian Wald's *House on Henry Street* called "cooperative individualism"[2] almost a century later. The female social entrepreneurs recognized the need to constantly renegotiate this delicate balance through democratic discussion. The social profit sector they invented provided just such a space to ensure that this optimistic ideal did not simply wither away as the nation matured. The negotiated balance between wealth-building enterprise and opportunity-expanding mutuality is what enabled the Republic to thrive.

The Declaration of Independence could have become a set of platitudes, like so many mission statements and mottoes: many high-minded words signifying nothing and forgotten in the quotidian life of the organizations that claim them. It did not. Women social entrepreneurs imagined and built a social profit sector to keep the Declaration alive for an ever-wider proportion of society. They animated the aspirations of the Declaration in communities all over the nation. The nation's women engaged this work voluntarily, on behalf of the greater good, initially through small societies and then through larger institutions with a national span, and through hundreds, then thousands, of local sites. These collective efforts produced the growth of aspirations for equality and justice among their fellow citizens. Social profit emerged from successful efforts to help more Americans achieve access to the full measure of life, liberty, and the pursuit of happiness in the Republic. Cynicism was restrained; optimism was enhanced; and more citizens came to participate in the Founders' intent, as documented in the Declaration.

Abigail Adams would be proud of what her American sisters had achieved by 1938. Her worries that "all men would be tyrants if they could" might well have proven true, had it not been for the imagination and courage of America's women. They instinctively understood the need for self-discipline and mutuality, and they set about, with very little formal encouragement, ensuring the teaching of these values in the new nation. What might well have remained a domestic responsibility became a larger calling because women saw the need and dedicated themselves to the challenge of teaching republican virtues to larger, tougher audiences beyond their own families. The democratic Republic needed to sustain justice and compassion, as well as provide economic opportunities for all citizens. Communities, as well as households, needed to practice these values if the economy was to thrive.

Women changed the value calculus around slavery over decades, local fair by local fair, pen wiper and potholder by pen wiper and potholder, speech by speech, and text by text. They led similar changes in the collective attitude of Americans about the value of education for poor and black children, about the value of regulating the consumption of alcohol, the value of safety standards in the workplace, and the value of welcoming immigrants into the American workforce.

By the end of the nineteenth century, women had demonstrated that they could bring an impressive combination of compassion, common sense, and determination to the leadership of mutuality in the nation. They had proven remarkably adept at utilizing the tools of influence and public opinion—petitions, lobbying efforts, fund-raising, media campaigns, consumer boycotts, civil disobedience, muckraking, coalition building, appeals to patriotism and to the love of God—in their pursuit of social profit.

The system that they invented in pursuit of social profit is remarkably creative, given the social and financial constraints faced by women in the period. They borrowed techniques that were working well to benefit private enterprise, and they invented new ones suited to their patriotic objectives. They developed multiple solutions to multiple social inequities. They brought information and ideas forward for all citizens to see. They established goals, set out strategies, and created budgets. And they went to work, as all sellers do, to make the case that a particular idea offered an excellent chance to realize a (social) profit. Katy Ferguson, Mother Seton, and Elizabeth Stott each made the case for her "product" (a system to educate poor children, an institution to care for orphans, a mechanism to produce self-reliant decayed gentlewomen). They sought investors among friends and family, venture investors (wealthy philanthropists), and giving circle-level investors (a ladies auxiliary, for instance), and on occasion, town fathers and state-level officials.

The women brokered their own assets to advance "sales." Successful outcomes, properly brought to public attention, had the power to change minds. Poor children's potential became more visible to others. Had the education of these children not ultimately proved valuable, both socially and economically, the schools and orphanages would have failed, religious orders would have closed, and funders would have abandoned this work.

Instead, the good ideas they brokered in the public marketplace improved and stimulated others to believe that their good ideas could also thrive. After the Civil War, social entrepreneurs expanded and improved the marketplace for social profit investment. They assumed more visible leadership in the fast-changing, modernizing world around them. They embraced the leverage that technology (from the telegraph to the railroad to the rotogravure) gave them to enlist more women in their campaigns to improve justice, equity, and opportunity of all kinds. As the nation grew, economic and demographic shifts brought new injustices that too few people noticed. But women entrepreneurs maintained an optimistic, even idealistic faith in their fellow citizens' ability to understand and address these problems if they had access to accurate information. Industriousness and self-reliance along with fairness and compassion were qualities that made good families, good neighbors, and, they firmly believed, a good nation.

Women invested in building national organizations with efficient management structures. Their newsletters, magazines, and journals spread their carefully considered viewpoints across large segments of the ever-growing population. *Godey's Lady's*

Book alone had a circulation of 150,000 and a readership of over 1 million in 1853. Articles on slavery and actual proposals to Congress to expand women's education mixed easily with pages of detailed, illustrated patterns for the most fashionable baby booties and evening dresses and recipes for Bavarian creams. All arrived together, in one publication. The entrepreneurs culti- vated a set of values that underscored the commonalities among American women of different classes, races, and income levels. All over the nation, from one local community to another, women engaged with each other in their work of raising their children and raising America.

Women's entrepreneurial work gradually built a productive and diversified network of social profit enterprises. By 1938, vir- tually all communities had Community Chests, Boys and Girls Clubs, YMCAs and YWCAs, Women's Exchanges, and chapters of the NAACP, the SPCA, and the SDA among dozens of such national organizations. Most states, North and South, had affil- iates of the General Federation of Women's Clubs. Likewise, most cities had scholarship opportunities for promising local scholars managed by women's groups. Women's religious orders taught the majority of the children of immigrants. By 1938, some 12,500 social profit organizations were operating in America, and 243 private foundations were up and running in thirty states. With little power and less money, the social entrepreneurs of ear- lier years founded, funded, and established the institutions that would outlast their individual creators and continue to represent the values and the value creation energy that American culture needed to remain true to its ideals.

As the second decade of the twenty-first century begins, Amer- ican citizens have organized almost 2 million nonprofit organi- zations and 70,000 foundations. The sector employs roughly

10 percent of the U.S. workforce.[3] In addition, more than 400 women's religious orders with just under 70,000 dedicated women now serve in the United States. But it is not the numbers that define the social profit sector. It is the shared commitment to engaged citizenship on behalf of American ideals. The sector has designed and built the basic value system of American society. It was, and still is, a culture where Americans feel responsible for the quality of life around them.

The social profit sector designed and built institutions that created value in their own time and continue creating value in the twenty-first century. We also expect the social profit sector to produce and disseminate important new knowledge. The sector has developed and funded research on issues that self-interested parties would have found no reason to support. Maria Chapman collected and published the thoughts on slavery of the greatest minds of her era, in America and in Europe, creating the annual volumes of her coffee-table books, *Liberty Bell*. Investments from Caroline Phelps Stokes enabled a young black scholar to compose the first bibliography on people of African descent. Olivia Sage funded the Pittsburgh study that established the first scientific inquiry into the specific features of poverty. Florence Kelley researched and published the detailed studies of the lives of working children. Julia Lathrop's research brought the inadequacies of the adult justice system for the needs of juveniles to the attention of her state and eventually the nation.

As time has passed, this advancement of knowledge by the sector has increased. Citizens have designed and built permanent institutions to address this issue. They succeed or fail based on how well they address a need and how many citizens recognize the need as worthy of continuing volunteer and financial support. The Russell Sage Foundation became the original think tank on social welfare and public health issues of the day. The Phelps

Stokes Fund researched the learning needs of blacks, Africans, and Native Americans. The research became the basis for count- less social profit initiatives to correct deficiencies in the care of all citizens. The Rockefeller Foundation supported the discovery and delivery of knowledge to eliminate hookworm in the Amer- ican South. With the help of educated citizens, the disease was eliminated from eleven states in less than five years.

Research and development of new knowledge remains a crit- ically important feature of the contemporary social profit sector. In the 1950s, Mary Lasker led a decade-long campaign to gain federal support for the funding of basic scientific research, leading to the present-day National Institutes of Health. Through the Komen Foundation, Nancy Brinker made research on breast can- cer available to millions of citizens and changed the course of that disease over the past thirty years.

As a corollary to our expectations for the creation of new knowledge, we also expect that social profit organizations and institutions will actively share what they learn with all of us. We expect these organizations to teach citizens about justice and equality, about health and opportunity. We don't expect the gov- ernment alone to educate us and shape our knowledge and our thinking. Public education has come from the social profit sector to the benefit of all citizens, and we have come to expect it be- cause it has been provided for 230 years. Women opposed to slavery sponsored readings of slave diaries and speeches by the Grimke sisters and formerly enslaved people. Women opposed to child labor sent Lewis Hine to photograph children and to place the photos and interviews he obtained in local newspapers. The Women's Christian Temperance Union published exhaus- tively about the dangers of alcohol abuse for the drinker, his or her family, and the community. Posters and ads were part of the public education. Alcoholism and, later on, mental illness became diseases rather than moral failings, a change that inspired research and garnered support for even greater changes in perception and treatment of these illnesses.

Today, we rely as never before on the work of social profit organizations to enlighten us about social, scientific, and political issues. Since its founding in 1942, a not-for-commercial-profit organization called the Ad Council has carried out its mission by using commercial marketing techniques to present public service announcements to U.S. audiences. Other social profit organizations such as Human Rights Watch, the Children's Defense Fund, and those dedicated to increasing public awareness about specific diseases all help educate Americans about access to life, liberty, and the pursuit of happiness.

We have also developed American consumer awareness because of educational efforts of the social profit sector. Maria Chapman understood this approach to civic engagement when she had witty mottoes embroidered on household items that would remind users of the horror and injustice of slavery. So did Florence Kelley, whose leadership of the National Consumers League white label program is echoed today in multiple campaigns through which consumers express their social values by their purchases. Colleges and universities, for instance, now use a similar sign to assure those who purchase merchandise in "college colors" that fair working conditions have been met by manufacturers of items in overseas factories. The "RugMark" label offers the same assurances to purchasers of rugs made overseas.

The social profit sector marched forthrightly into the world of shaping markets to reflect more ethical behavior. Women entrepreneurs did so at the height of the Industrial Revolution and laissez-faire economic rules. Ultimately, they have helped our society develop a collective awareness of personal responsibility for making our markets responsive to moral values.[4]

As important as these social assets are, it is the legacy of values, attitudes, and behaviors developed by women's social profit work that matters most to our civic culture today. We value the concept of human potential. All children are understood to be potential assets to themselves and to the nation, and following the lead of Katy Ferguson and Elizabeth Lange, we are prepared to invest in people. Caroline Phelps Stokes anticipated every person, blacks and Native Americans included, as an asset and thus worthy of the best education possible. We all share this responsibility. We also have expectations of those in whom we invest. Female college graduates in the 1880s arrived at settlement houses to apply their knowledge to the nation's needs. We expect the same of Teach for America teachers today, thanks to a modern female social entrepreneur, Wendy Kopp. Perhaps neither Katy Ferguson nor Grace Dodge would approve of our defining their work as human capital development. No matter, their work was, is, and continues to be essential because it improves individual lives and the collective life of the nation. Economists believe that 75 percent of a nation's wealth is in its people,[5] therefore these investments in fellow citizens have made us the richest country in the world.

We can also attribute our civic culture of fairness to the work of women entrepreneurs. We believe, with remarkable idealism, that the rules should apply to everyone. As a result, we have achieved high levels of trust within our society—confidence that fairness will dominate our social and commercial activities and will be reinforced by fair-minded citizens. American culture has made civic virtue, along with rule of law, a competitive advantage. Our culture is oriented to pursue and punish breaches of conflict of interest (from a governor's acceptance of the gift of two $85 football tickets to a hedge fund manager's acceptance of a gift of insider information). Civic culture expects all citizens, the wealthy and powerful and the not so wealthy or powerful, to play by the rules. This does not mean that breaches do not happen or that scoundrels don't get away with damaging society from time to time, but our civic culture makes a point of expecting virtue and personal responsibility. Americans would have no patience with a Silvio Berlusconi. We had none with Bernard Madoff. We have learned, through the exemplary work of women entrepreneurs, that virtue is a competitive advantage.

These are important examples of the influence on American values exerted by social entrepreneurs. But by far the most important legacy from these women is our national commitment to moral ambition. America is unique in the world in having an entire sector of the nation devoted to the encouragement and nurture of moral ambition among its citizens.

We expect that citizen initiative, not government-initiated action, will create the first resources for improving life for fellow citizens. Foundations and social profit organizations bear witness daily to the importance of citizen action to address local inequities. Citizens can move quickly, compassionately, and intelligently to address both problems and opportunities. Across generations, and endless social, political, economic, and technological changes, citizens have recognized that extreme poverty harms both individuals and the greater community, and they have acted to address it as a civic imperative. In similar fashion, citizens acting together have demonstrated again and again the ability to plan, fund, and build a library, museum, or hospital, or to attract a business or a park developer. This work is alive and well through volunteer economic development committees across the nation.

From our founding to the present, regular citizens, not just those who are wealthy or powerful, have succeeded in getting laws passed to advance justice, equality, and opportunity. They have assembled and petitioned and spoken freely, as we all enable each other to do.

The social profit sector has sponsored the design and passage of legislation that drew the public consensus and elected officials closer to the ideas defined in the Declaration. Maria Chapman and thousands of women who followed her work delivered pamphlets making their case to officials throughout the nation. Frances Willard fought for women's suffrage in local elections through petitions that eventually included millions of signatures. A century later, the issues these women pursued are now standard practice in most democracies. Candy Lightner's Mothers Against Drunk Driving (MADD) has succeeded in the past three decades in passing over 3,000 state and federal laws criminalizing drunk driving. Today, social profit law firms fight the death penalty and work to reexamine cold cases where evidence suggests imprisoned people may deserve exoneration. The legacy of our women social entrepreneurs is alive and well.

The partner of moral ambition is the spirit of social entrepreneurship, another of the legacy gifts from America's virtuous women. American culture has a great tradition of individual effort to achieve a goal and to create value in the process. The adapting of this attitude—the spirit of optimism, idealism, and enterprise that characterizes the entrepreneur—to the pursuit of fairness and opportunity is perhaps the greatest gift of all. The social profit organizations imagined and created by American women demonstrate the power of entrepreneurship in everyday life. From their earliest experiences, American children learn how to work together to make things happen. Kids do bake sales, hold car washes, and sell candy to raise money for athletic teams or to assist a seriously ill classmate. In the era of social networking, young people can communicate ideas and build coalitions in a matter of minutes. Many Americans practice social entrepreneurship during the first twenty years of life because it is part of their communities.

From the outset, women social entrepreneurs established justice as a value creator, not just a virtue. Like commercial entrepreneurs, they advance ambitious goals that will create significant value if achieved. Building an ecologically friendly automobile or building a school to teach poor orphans to read would each benefit specific individuals as well as the greater good of the whole society. Both kinds of ventures require considerable risk taking. They also require capital, trial and error, tolerance of failure, and willingness to reorganize and recommit. Each requires optimism and idealism to launch the effort in the first place.

From their earliest efforts, the women entrepreneurs understood that they were engaged in a competitive activity. Most often, they needed to sell their idea, to their peers, to potential funders, and often to the community at large. This was seldom done by sitting down to a cup of tea with a couple of friends. It was not a hobby. This was work that required organization, confidence, and a clear sense that they had the solutions to the problems they were tackling. Value had to be demonstrated to a range of interested parties and continuous funding obtained. Organizations needed to respond rapidly to community needs and also remain forces for change over decades, not simply for a short period. Their value creation needed be visible, efficient, and measurable or they did not survive. That is how the social profit marketplace worked.

The optimism and idealism that has proved so valuable to women social entrepreneurs has been drawn historically from both patriotic and religious sources. The work of the social profit sector reminds the community of the importance of acting on the ideals our nation stands for, as articulated in the Declaration of Independence and the Constitution. These documents belong to each generation only when community members act locally on their literal meaning. People at all income and educational levels say "Only in America" as a way of expressing how good life is in the United States when our actions are guided by these ideals. Social entrepreneurs have also honored industriousness as forcefully as they have honored compassion and generosity. From the early Houses of Industry for penniless widows with children to the elaborate Women's Exchanges, ambition has been recognized and rewarded, both economically and morally.

Optimism and idealism are also grounded in the Judeo-Christian tradition. The early social entrepreneurs shared a set of texts and beliefs that shaped a narrative of how human life was meant to be. That commonality gave them a sense of purpose. Their work had importance and meaning beyond its day-to-day impact, just as a mother's does. Maria Chapman linked abolition to the biblical teachings of God's love for each and every living soul. Frances Willard tied her campaign to prohibit the consumption of alcohol to a single set of ideas. She expressed her faith that the ideals of Christianity, of the United States, and of a secure, loving home comprised a single set of shared values in her motto: "For God, For Home, For Native Land." Mary Bethune was perhaps most outspoken of all about the inspiration she drew from her religious faith and its importance to her ability to articulate the case for justice and equal opportunity. She wrote: "Faith and love have been the most glorious and victorious defense in this warfare of life, and it has been my privilege to use them, and make them substantial advocates of my cause, as I press toward my goals whether they be spiritual or material ones."[6]

The first American women's movement seems to have shaped society as profoundly as the men shaped the economy in the highly gendered nineteenth century. Only modest attention has been paid to this phenomenon. America's women have not historically concentrated on their own needs as much as they have focused on the fullness of democracy's abundance in the society around them. Their work created such a strong civic culture that it has seemed a natural evolution. Perhaps like the work of successful parents, their efforts have impacted society only decades after the fact. The more selfless the women's entrepreneurship appeared, the more support it gained. The social profit organizations that focused solely on women's suffrage had less success expanding their influence over the nineteenth and early twentieth centuries than did those with a wider, more inclusive mission. Often, these latter organizations included suffrage as a means to solving an important social problem rather than as an end in itself.

Peter Drucker maintained that the twenty-first century would be the age of the nonprofit sector in America.[7] We believe that he grasped the impact of the first women's movement before the rest of us. The longevity of the Republic was predicated on the selection of self-disciplined leaders surrounded by fellow citizens raised to live the virtues that would perpetuate the Republic. They would have to be able to build personal and community prosperity without losing their integrity, generosity, or self-discipline. The Founders believed that limited government would work under these circumstances. The record shows that many retained considerable doubts. The work of mothers seemed to ease their worries and give them hope. From Esther Reed's "The Sentiments of an American Woman" in 1778 to Frances Perkins's assembling the forces to pass Social Security and the Fair Labor Standards Act in 1938 and on to Mothers Against Drunk Driving and Teach for America, women identified opportunities to model these virtues so that the prosperity-mutuality balance required for the American idea would thrive in the Republic. And so it has.

The proof is that Americans are not cynical. Most citizens take the founding documents seriously, just as the women entrepreneurs did. For the most part, our history does not show evidence of intraclass hatreds or jealousies. This may always change, especially depending on how well the culture recovers from the economic crises of 2007–2008, but our past shows that people anticipate that their children will succeed even where they, the parents, may have missed a step.

The idea of America grew to global leadership because our economic and social sectors have complimented each other since the Declaration was signed. Upward mobility became synonymous with the American Dream in large part because of the social profit sector. The sector grew because it worked for Americans and for America. That is how marketplaces work.

Women did share the responsibility to raise generations of Americans whose personal character would sustain a democratic republic over centuries. They succeeded. As mothers, or surrogate mothers, women made coalitions of all kinds to achieve the well-being of their families. They did this for their nation as well. Women were accustomed to remaining engaged in their personal commitments to their families over extended periods of time. Many of the entrepreneurs we met spent lifetimes on their social profit work. They imagined a better nation and set to work to make it be. Jane Addams spoke of the work products of Hull House as "her children." She and her fellow entrepreneurs hoped that all children—including the young nation— would enjoy a better future, and they devoted themselves to making it happen.

Conclusions such as these bring to mind an unmodern term: maternalism. This word has collected considerable scholarship around it, particularly in the last decade. The term has become highly politicized by issues of gender and biological identity. Nevertheless, we find that the history of women's entrepreneurial work from 1778 to 1938 often reflected maternal values— attitudes that resembled those of well-meaning mothers raising children for whom they have great hopes. Raising them well meant teaching and modeling self-discipline, generosity, and industriousness, and then carefully watching over their environment, ready to counter any forces that threaten to throw children off course from their virtuous, productive lives ahead. Certain exceptional women saw this work in an expansive, patriotic context and rose to it with particular clarity and energy. They shaped the fundamental characteristics of their nation's culture day by day, village by village, and issue by issue. We see no reason to apologize for this metaphor. As history has suggested from Lysistrata to Liberia, women can sometimes exert unique forces for good in the societies to which they apply their feminine collective force.

Indeed, it has worked so well that today in America we live in a less gendered culture at all levels of society. In the contemporary social profit world, men and women work together in more balanced numbers than in any other sector. Men and women raise children in more balanced arrangements than this nation has seen in its history. Many couples involve their children in philanthropy earlier than older generations typically did. Ideas of human rights, justice, and equality are widely shared across our population. Men and women pursue higher education and professions in a closer male-female balance than ever. Men and women start new social profits all through their lives. No longer is this sector the sole province of imaginative entrepreneurial women and men of the cloth. Maternalism is widely shared. The women we have studied remind Americans, of both genders, that the work of social profit was developed as carefully, imaginatively, and productively as the market economy. The Founding Fathers and the republican mothers would be justifiably proud of their progeny, the daughters who created the sector that has become the distinguishing feature of American society.

ACKNOWLEDGMENTS

In writing *Daughters of the Declaration*, we relied on the work of many scholars of women's history, most of it created after 1970. These researchers did the hard work of recovering—through diaries, meeting minutes, and other archival materials—the lives and accomplishments of women who built our nation according to the ideals of the Founders. In the process, they became academic pioneers in their fields, and without them, *Daughters* would not have been possible.

We are also indebted to the many audiences that listened to Claire discuss the ideas in the book while it was a work in progress over the past five years. Giving circles, community foundations, professional fund-raisers, and even bankers and money managers consistently asked great questions and expressed eagerness to hear more stories about America's first social entrepreneurs. No group was more helpful than the graduate students at New York University who engaged enthusiastically in the history of American philanthropy and its impact on the success of our democracy. We are particularly grateful for the research assistance of Paul Sager along the way.

Sincere thanks to Tina Bennett of Janklow and Nesbit for her efforts on our behalf and for her introduction to Clive Priddle of PublicAffairs. Clive encouraged us to refine both the scope and focus of our original manuscript. The final product, mistakes and all, is, of course, our own, and we thank Clive and his robust team at PublicAffairs for all their efforts to bring *Daughters* to life.

Finally, we are grateful to our families. Our mothers are each benevolent and patriotic women, and we are fortunate to have their insights in our lives on a daily basis. Our maternal grandmothers were active participants in the work described in *Daughters*. David's grandmother, Annie Graham, was widowed with four children to care for, and as we mentioned, she supported her family by providing catering services through the Detroit Women's Exchange. Claire's grandmother, Rosa Rossano, sold War Bonds during World War I, while her physician-husband served as a captain in the U.S. Army. When her husband's immigrant patients in East Harlem, New York, paid for their health care with fresh produce or a basket of fish, she turned her kitchen into a food distribution center for families in need in the neighborhood. We appreciate that we were both raised in homes where faith and patriotism made generosity a part of daily life, and we have made an effort to carry on these values in our own home over the past forty-three years.

A word of thanks to our children and their spouses. Our son, Graham Burnett, and his wife, Christina Duffy Burnett, are the professional historians in the family. It seems certain that they had some misgivings about our efforts to blend complex historical crosscurrents into a story about the idealism and determination of a set of American women. But they valiantly guided us toward reliable and important sources and kept severe critiques to themselves.

Our daughter, Maria Burnett, and her husband, Ledio Cakaj, are the "doers" in the family. Both have worked for years as human rights researchers and advocates in East Africa. They take daily risks on behalf of the "greater good," just as many of the women in *Daughters* did during their lifetimes. Maria and Ledio are also able to witness firsthand the courage and entrepreneur-ship of exceptional women in the developing world.

We appreciate the patience of Francesca, Alexander, and Consuelo on the many days when Nonna and Grandpa were too busy to come out to play. And happily, we appreciate each other most of all.

NOTES

Introduction

1. These are organizations often referred to by the part of the IRS tax code that governs them—501c3 organizations. The categories can sometimes be confusing as some hospitals such as community hospitals are 501c3 organizations whereas others are for-profit businesses.

2. Somehow, we got started calling this the "nonprofit" or "not-for-profit" sector. This inept terminology has recently come under attack, thank goodness. Bill Drayton, for instance, has proposed "social benefit" sector, although we prefer "social profit" because all investors are rightly interested in "profit." See Claire Gaudiani, "Opinion," *Chronicle of Philanthropy*, July 26, 2007.

3. Alexis de Tocqueville, *Democracy in America*, trans. Francis Bowen (Cambridge, MA: Sever and Francis, 1868), p. 148.

4. We recognize, of course, that exceptional men also organized and led citizens in the building of American democracy and social profit. We do not intend to diminish their accomplishments in support of abolition, education, scientific research, the arts, and religion, particularly through philanthropy. Our intention is to describe the unique leadership of women in the creation of citizen-based commitments to the ideals of the Founders in the formative years of the nation.

Chapter One

1. Richard M. Gummere, "Some Classical Side Lights on Colonial Education," *Classical Journal* 55 (5) (February 1960): 225.

2. Ibid., p. 228.

3. Aristotle, *The Politics*, trans. B. Jowett (New York: Cosimo Books, 2008), p. 22.

4. Peter Gay, *The Science of Freedom*, Vol. 2 of *The Enlightenment: An Interpretation* (New York: Alfred A. Knopf, 1969), p. 325.

5. Charles Secondat, baron de Montesquieu, *The Spirit of Laws: a Compendium of the First English Edition*, ed. David Wallace Carrithers (Los Angeles: University of California–Los Angeles Press, 1977), p. 61.

6. Ibid., pp. 118–119.

7. Ibid., Book 3, Chap. 5, Par. 8.

8. Ibid., Book 5, Chaps. 2–4.

9. Quoted in Claire Gaudiani, *The Greater Good* (New York: Henry Holt, 2003), pp. 3–4.

10. Bernard Bailyn, *Voyagers to the West: A Passage in the Peopling of America on the Eve of the Revolution* (New York: Knopf, 1986), p. 200.

11. Edwin J. Perkins, "The Entrepreneurial Spirit in Colonial America: The Foundations of Modern Business History," *Business History Review* 63 (1) (Spring 1989): 165.

12. Ibid., p. 173.

13. See Daniel Walker Howe, *What God Has Wrought* (New York: Oxford University Press, 2007), pp. 45–46.

14. Montesquieu's comment that republics differed from other political systems by the reliance they placed on virtue is explored in Howard Mumford Jones, *O Strange New World* (New York: Viking Press, 1964), p. 431ff.

15. Bret Carroll, *American Masculinities: A Historical Encyclopedia* (New York: Sage Publications, 2003), p. 431.

16. For a more detailed discussion of the Scottish Enlightenment and its impact on our Founders, see Gaudiani, *Generosity Unbound* (New York: Broadway Publications, 2010), Chap. 3.

17. Daniel Walker Howe, "Why the Scottish Enlightenment Was Useful to the Framers of the American Constitution," *Comparative Studies in Society and History* 31 (3) (July 1989): 576.

18. Ryan Patrick Hanley, "Social Science and Human Flourishing: The Scottish Enlightenment and Today," *Journal of Scottish Philosophy* 7 (1) (2009): 29–46. The work of the Rev. Henry Duncan perfectly illustrates this pragmatic integration. Duncan promoted employment opportunities for his worshippers and created a savings bank for their use while writing moral tracts and running a life-insurance cooperative. See George John C. Duncan, *Memoir of the Rev. Henry Duncan, D.D. of Ruthwell* (Edinburgh: William Oliphant and Sons, 1848), pp. 95–96.

19. Adam Smith, *The Wealth of Nations* (New York: Modern Library, 2000), p. 581.

20. Benjamin Franklin, *Autobiography* (New York: W.W. Norton, 1986), p. 39.

21. Benjamin Franklin, "A Proposal for Promoting Useful Knowledge among the British Plantations in America" (1743), available online at numerous sites, including www.books.google.com

22. Lord Kames (Henry Home), *Six Sketches on the History of Man* (abridged version) (Philadelphia, 1776), p. 195.

23. John Witherspoon, "Reflections on Marriage," *Penn. Mag.*, September 1775, pp. 411, 408, later published as "Letters on Marriage," in *The Works of John Witherspoon . . .* , 2nd ed. (Philadelphia, 1802), pp. 161–183.

24. See de Tocqueville, *Democracy in America*, p. 148.

Chapter Two

1. This plan created setbacks for women in some of the states, where existing practice was to apply continental laws that enabled married women to co-own family businesses, to inherit, and so on. See Carol Berkin, *First Generations* (New York: Hill and Wang, 1996), pp. 162–164.

2. See Linda Kerber, "The Republican Mother and the Woman Citizen," in Linda Kerber, ed., *Women's America*, 6th ed. (New York: Oxford University Press, 2004), p. 123.

3. For a clear sense of how seriously these new ideas were considered in society at the time of the Revolutionary War, see Jan Lewis, "The Republican Wife: Virtue and Seduction in the Early Republic," *William and Mary Quarterly* 44 (4), October 1987. pp. 694–696, who cites among other references: "A Father's Advice to His Daughters,"

Christian's Magazine, February–March 1790, p. 697; "On the Choice of Husband," *Columbian Magazine or Monthly Miscellany* (Philadelphia), February 1788, p. 67; "On the Choice of a Wife," *Gent. and Lady's Mag.*, April 1789; "Character of a Good Husband," *Mass. Mag.*, March 1789, p. 177.

4. See Lewis, "The Republican Wife," p. 700. Lewis cites dozens of articles in the contemporary press in which similar quotes appear. Most are concentrated in the period 1789–1800.

5. See, for instance, D. Graham Burnett, *Trying Leviathan* (Princeton: Princeton University Press, 2007), which describes a trial in New York City in 1825, the outcome of which turned on whether whales should be classified as mammals or fish. Citing Genesis, most folks believed firmly that whatever "swims in the sea" should be classified as a "fish."

6. For an extended treatment of these issues, see Carol Karlsen, *The Devil in the Shape of a Woman* (New York: W. W. Norton, 1987), and Berkin, *First Generations*, Chap. 2.

7. Margaret Corbin, who fought alongside her husband in New York City, was recognized with a federal pension following the war. See Edward T. James, *Notable American Women* (Cambridge: Harvard University Press, 1974), Vol. 2, pp. 385–386. Also see Carol Berkin, *Revolutionary Mothers* (New York: Vintage Books, 2006), Chap. 9.

8. The text was republished by the *Pennsylvania Magazine of History and Biography*, Vol. 18, 1894, available online at www.personal.umd.umich.edu/~ppennock/doc. There is some scholarly debate about various contributors to the crafting of the document.

9. Abigail Adams, *My Dearest Friend: Letters of Abigail and John Adams* (Cambridge, MA: Belknap Press, 2007), p. 110.

10. Benjamin Rush, *Essays: Literary, Moral, and Philosophical* (Philadelphia, 1798), pp. 6–7.

11. "By refusing to marry unpatriotic men, by raising their sons to be the next generation of virtuous citizens, women could play a meaningful political role, assuring the future stability of the fragile republic. Political virtue, a revolutionary concept that has troubled writers . . . could be safely domesticated in eighteenth-century America; the mother, not the masses, could be the custodian of civic morality." Linda Kerber, *Toward an Intellectual History of Women* (Chapel Hill: University of North Carolina Press, 1997), p. 16.

12. Bret Carroll, *American Masculinities: A Historical Encyclopedia* (New York: Sage Publications, 2003), p. 411.

13. Linda Kerber, *No Constitutional Right to Be Ladies* (New York: Hill and Wang, 1998), p. 146. Kerber does not view this male perspective as particularly respectful of women's potential contribution to the nation, but more as a matter of convenience.

14. Example offered in Kerber, *Women's America*, p. 122.

15. "On Female Education," *N.Y. Magazine*, September 1794, p. 570, cited by Lewis, "The Republican Wife," p. 701. Similar sentiments are offered in "The Gossip No. XXVII," *Boston Wkly. Mag.*, May 28, 1803, p. 125; "On Female Education," *Royal Am. Mag.*, January 1774, p. 10.

16. Rush, while noted for his support of women's education, wasn't a modern feminist. He thought education would make women better companions for their husbands, but that education should remain a "luxury" item for select members of society. See Abraham Blinderman, *Three Early Champions of Education* (Bloomington: Indiana University Press, 1976), p. 23ff.

17. Quoted in Kerber, *Toward an Intellectual History of Women*, p. 38.

18. *The Gleaner*, Vol. 3 (Boston, 1798), p. 189. Murray is also the author of *On the Equality of the Sexes* (1792).

19. Cited by Kerber, *Toward an Intellectual History of Women*, pp. 38–39.

Chapter Three

1. Perkins, "The Entrepreneurial Spirit in Colonial America," p. 186.

2. See Howe, *What God Hath Wrought*, Chap. 7, for a discussion of this idea, with a focus on John Quincy Adams.

3. See David Pozen, "We Are All Entrepreneurs Now," *Wake Forest Law Review* 43 (2008): 287–288. Pozen's article includes a thoughtful and readable summary of thinking about different kinds of entrepreneurs.

4. Florence Nightingale, the British nurse who invented her profession during the Crimean War, is credited with this powerful visualization tool. See, for instance, "Making Data Dance," in the Technology Quarterly, *Economist*, December 11, 2010, p. 25.

5. "A Big Hairy Audacious Goal," as defined by Jim Collins and Jerry Porras in their 1996 article entitled "Build Your Company's Vision," *Harvard Business Review* 74 (5): 65–77, and elaborated in their book, *Built to Last: Successful Habits of Visionary Companies* (New York: Harper Business, 2002).

6. Paul Light, *The Search for Social Entrepreneurship* (Washington, DC: The Brookings Institution, 2008), p. 148.

7. For instance: "The social entrepreneur should be understood as someone who targets an unfortunate but stable equilibrium that causes the neglect, marginalization, or suffering of a segment of humanity; who brings to bear on this situation his or her inspiration, direct action, creativity, courage, and fortitude; and who aims for and ultimately affects the establishment of a new stable equilibrium that secures permanent benefit for the targeted group and society at large." Roger L. Martin and Sally Osberg, "Social Entrepreneurship: The Case for Definition," *Stanford Social Innovation Review* (Spring 2007): 35.

Chapter Four

1. John 6:11. The history of the Fragment Society is told by Anne Firor Scott in *Natural Allies* (Chicago: University of Illinois Press, 1991), pp. 27–36.

2. Ibid., p. 30.

3. *New York Daily Tribune*, July 20, 1854.

4. Lewis Tappan, "Catharine Ferguson," *American Missionary* 8 (10) (August 1854): 85–86, annotated clipping in Lewis Tappan's journal for July 1, 1853–April 18, 1855, p. 299, in The Papers of Lewis Tappan, 1809–1903, microfilm, reel 2, fr. 238, Manuscript Division, Library of Congress, Washington, DC.

5. For more about Isabella Graham and Ferguson, see David Wills and Albert Raboteau, eds., *African American Religion* (Chicago: University of Chicago Press, 2006). These women's goals were certainly to transmit their religious faith to the poor, but they saw this effort as identical to educating citizens for the new nation.

6. Isabella Graham, *The Power of Faith* (New York: J. Seymour, 1816), p. 60.

7. *Gazetteer of the State of New York*, 1860, ed. John Homer French, p. 425, online at Google Books.

8. It should be noted that some societies envisioned support to missionary work overseas as well as in their local communities. See Scott, *Natural Allies*, Chap. 4.

9. Margaret Morris Haviland, "Beyond Women's Sphere: Young Quaker Women and the Veil of Charity in Philadelphia, 1790–1810," *William and Mary Quarterly* 51 (3) (1994): 439.

10. See Scott, *Natural Allies*, pp. 26–27.

Chapter Five

1. The order is referred to alternately as the Sisters of Charity, but "Daughters" is how the order refers to itself today. See www.thedaughtersofcharity.org.

2. Thomas Spalding, "Elizabeth Ann Bayley Seton," at www.amb.org/articles/08/08–01363.html.

3. See Mark McGarvie, "The Dartmouth College Case and the Legal Design of Civil Society," in Lawrence Friedman and Mark McGarvie, eds., *Charity, Philanthropy and Civility in American History* (New York: Cambridge University Press, 2003) for more detail.

4. See Mary J. Oates, "Faith and Good Works: Catholic Giving and Taking," in ibid., Chap. 13.

5. Maryland was founded as a colony in the 1640s. An area twice the size of today's state was granted by King Charles I of England to Charles Calvert, a Roman Catholic nobleman, who became the first Lord Baltimore. It remained under the direct control of his descendants until the revolution. The colony maintained a position of tolerance for all Christian religions, but Catholic immigrants naturally saw it as a welcoming place. See Jon Butler, Grant Wacker, and Randall Balmer, *Religion in American Life* (New York: Oxford University Press, 2007), Chap. 14.

6. Yes, the same society founded by Isabella Graham.

7. Joseph Dirvan, *Mrs. Seton: Foundress of the American Sisters of Charity* (New York: Farrar, Straus and Cudahy, 1962), p. 148.

8. Ibid., p. 179B.

9. For additional detail on St. Vincent and the original French Daughters of Charity (also referred to as Sisters of Charity), see the Catholic Encyclopedia online at www.newadvent.org/cathen.

10. Dirvan, *Mrs. Seton*, p. 398.

11. Ibid., pp. 398–399.

12. Regina Bechtle, "An American Daughter: Elizabeth Ann Seton and the Birth of the U.S. Church," *America* 199 (5) (September 2008): 5. Others put the number of communities at the time of her death considerably higher. See, for instance, Laura Rupkalvis, "Saint Elizabeth Ann Seton," in Dwight Burlingame, ed., *Philanthropy in America* (Santa Barbara, CA: ABC-CLIO, 2004), p. 437.

13. One cannot help but wonder about Mother Seton's own children both before and after her premature death. Dirvan notes that the boys, Richard and William, received great support, both financial and paternally, from Antonio Filicchi. They apparently did little to show their appreciation, although William eventually joined the U.S. Navy. Of the three girls, only Catherine, the middle daughter, outlived her mother, but she apparently shared none of her mother's social or religious commitments.

14. See Diane Batts Morrow, *Persons of Color and Religious at the Same Time* (Chapel Hill: University of North Carolina Press, 2002), for a complete history of Elizabeth Lange and the Oblate Order.

15. See www.nathanielturner.com/mothermaryelizabethelange.html.

16. Quoted in Diane Batts Morrow, "Embracing the Religious Profession: The Antebellum Mission of the Oblate Sisters of Providence," in Michael Gomez, ed., *Diasporic Africa* (New York: New York University Press, 2006), p. 109.

17. Quoted in Morrow, "Outsiders Within: The Oblate Sisters of Providence in 1830s Church and Society," *U.S. Catholic Historian* 15 (2) (Spring 1997): 52.

18. Among the more famous graduates and contemporary supporters is Camille Cosby, wife of entertainer and activist Bill Cosby.

19. Maureen Fitzgerald, *Habits of Compassion* (Champaign-Urbana: University of Illinois Press, 2006), p. 3.

Chapter Six

1. The definitive source on the Women's Exchange movement is Kathleen W. Sander, *The Business of Charity* (Chicago and Urbana: University of Illinois Press, 1998).

2. Ibid., p. 12.

3. The Philadelphia Ladies' Depository, *Annual Report*, 1834, quoted in Sander, *The Business of Charity*, p. 11.

4. Ibid., Appendix A, Table 1, p. 121.

Chapter Seven

1. Until the Civil War, each state determined laws concerning the ownership of slaves. An accessible source for a complete overview is David Brion Davis, *Inhuman Bondage* (New York: Oxford University Press, 2006).

2. Massachusetts was among the first states to ban the ownership of slaves, as early as 1783. Even then, John Adams noted that the reason was primarily economic. Working-class whites did not want the competition of slave labor. He wrote, "If the gentlemen had been permitted by law to hold slaves, the common people would have put the Negroes to death, and their masters too, perhaps."

3. This quotation was published in the inaugural edition of the *Liberator* on January 1, 1831.

4. Clare Taylor, *Women of the Anti-Slavery Movement: The Weston Sisters* (London: St. Martin's Press, 1995), p. 17.

5. Debra Gold Hansen, "The Boston Female Anti-Slavery Society and the Limits of Gender Politics," in Jean Fagan Yellin and John C. Van Horne, eds., *The Abolitionist Sisterhood: Women's Political Culture in Antebellum America* (Ithaca: Cornell University Press, 1994), p. 47.

6. The text is available online at www.books.google.com and details the many internal struggles of the abolitionist effort in Massachusetts and New York during the 1830s. It demonstrates Maria's stylish writing, her fearless advocacy for Garrison and for the contributions of women, and her absolute command of the multiple political machinations.

7. *Right and Wrong* (1839), p. 12.

8. Taylor, *Women of the Anti-Slavery Movement*, p. 30.

9. Lee Chambers-Schiller, "A Good Work Among the People: The Political Culture of the Boston Antislavery Fair," in Yellin and Van Horne, *The Abolitionist Sisterhood*, p. 250.

10. Beverly Gordon, *Bazaars and Fair Ladies: The History of the American Fundraising Fair* (Knoxville: University of Tennessee Press, 1998), pp. 42–43. Christmas trees were very rare in America before 1850. Only a few German communities decorated a com-

munity tree, and some religious groups, such as the Quakers, forbade this custom. Queen Victoria seems to have introduced the idea to upper-class English society.

11. Chambers-Schiller, "A Good Work Among the People," p. 260.

12. Ibid.

13. *Report of the Twenty-first National Anti-Slavery Bazaar* (Boston: 1855), p. 32.

14. Ronald G. Walters, *The Antislavery Appeal: American Abolitionism After 1830* (New York: Norton, 1978), p. 24.

15. Fairs were also used to raise funds in support of education for blacks and campaigns against alcohol abuse.

16. See Chambers-Schiller, "A Good Work Among the People," pp. 250–251.

17. Ibid., p 259. "Whitty-brown" is presumably the nineteenth-century equivalent of a "plain brown wrapping."

18. Taylor, *Women of the Anti-Slavery Movement*, p. 27. There is more to be found about Maria's sisters, Caroline, Deborah, and Ann, in Taylor as well.

19. Until the Civil War, each state determined laws concerning the ownership of slaves. Massachusetts was among the first states to ban the practice, doing so in 1783. Chapman's fund-raising was thus aimed at a larger cause, the promotion of abolition in other states. "Abolition," however, was difficult to define in many states, as many adopted convoluted rules concerning the gradual liberation of enslaved people according to age, parentage, and so on. Such "gradualism," which in many cases served to extend servitude for decades for certain individuals, led Garrison and others such as Aaron Burr to demand an immediate and complete "abolition" of slavery.

Chapter Eight

1. See Christine Stansell, *The Feminist Promise* (New York: Modern Library, 2010), pp. 108–109, for more detail.

2. Joan Hoff-Wilson notes that changes "ranged from the simple ability of wives to write wills with or without their husbands' consent, to granting *feme sole* status to abandoned women, to allowing women some control over their own wages, to establishing separate estates for women, to protecting land inherited by widows from their husbands' creditors, to allowing widows legal access to their husbands' personal estates." Joan Hoff-Wilson, *Law, Gender, and Injustice: A Legal History of U.S. Women* (New York: New York University Press, 1990), p. 128. For comparisons by state, see http://lcweb2.loc.gov/ammem/awhhtml/awlaw3/notes.html-i31.

3. See Kerber, *Women's America*, p. 217.

4. We are indebted to Kathleen McCarthy, *Women's Culture* (Chicago: University of Chicago Press, 1991) for this particular characterization of women of wealth during the nineteenth and early twentieth centuries.

5. The COS organizations favored organized assistance to those in need, with a focus on work programs. Some see the COS as the predecessor of the United Way. For a more detailed account of the work of the New York City COS, see Joan Waugh, "Give This Man Work!" in *Social Science History* 25 (2) (2001): 217–246.

6. The most recent biography of Livermore is Wendy H. Venet, *A Strong-Minded Woman: The Life of Mary Livermore* (Amherst: University of Massachusetts Press, 2005).

7. Ibid., p. 137.

8. Quoted in "Mary and Daniel Livermore," by Charles A. Howe, at www25.uua.org/duub/articles/livermorefamily.html.

9. Livermore writes about these years in great detail in her autobiography, *The Story of My Life*, reprinted by Kessinger Publications, 2005. Also available online through www.books.google.com.

10. These edifying tales, including *Children's Army* (1844) and *The Story of Two Families: The Twin Sisters* (1848), were apparently quite popular. The latter tale illustrates the salutary liberating effect of exposure to the Universalist faith on the previously somber and troubled twin, while her carefree sister gradually comes to yearn for something substantial in her life. Available online at books.google.co.uk.

11. Judith Ann Geisberg, *Civil War Sisterhood: The U.S. Sanitary Commission and Women's Politics in Transition* (Boston: Northeastern University Press, 2000), provides considerable detail about the structure and dynamics of the commission over its five-year history. Perhaps its most prominent commissioner was Frederick Law Olmsted, the creator of Central Park and Prospect Park in New York City as well as many other urban parks across the eastern United States.

12. This appalling work is chronicled in the first person by volunteer Elizabeth Hobson, in her *Recollections of a Happy Life*, published posthumously in 1916. Available at www. books.google.co.uk, with an introduction by Schuyler.

13. There were, of course, many untrained but well-intentioned women who followed the troops to provide moral and physical support.

14. The idea had been introduced in 1848 by Elizabeth Cady Stanton in her famous "Declaration of Sentiments and Resolutions" at the Seneca Falls (NY) convention. As a measure of how the contemporary press treated women's organizing efforts, the *Chicago Tribune* commented as follows on the existence of factions within the suffrage movement: "The public will now be annoyed for six months by the characteristic ill humor of a lot of old hens trying to hatch out their addled productions."

15. Wendy Venet's *A Strong-Minded Woman* offers a detailed account of Livermore's work in publishing, as well as her involvement in the many permutations of the suffrage movement. See Chaps. 8 and 9.

16. This is Mary's quotation from *The Story of My Life*.

17. *What Shall We Do . . .* is available online through the Schlesinger Library on the History of Women in America, Harvard University. It runs to over 200 pages, which raises the question of how long it took Livermore to deliver these remarks from a podium! Livermore's keen intelligence and common sense shine through on every page. She also offers a passionate endorsement of Candace Wheeler's Society of Decorative Art as an example of high-value "industrial arts" education for women. We discuss Wheeler in the next chapter.

18. Available online at www.ourstory.info, and also highly recommended for its wit and clarity.

19. Lola Montez, whose real name was Eliza Gilbert, was a well-traveled beauty. Following affairs with Franz Liszt, Alexander Dumas, and most prominently the king of Bavaria, Ludwig I, she remade herself into a Spanish dancer and fled to America to avoid legal entanglements from an early marriage (clearly an ideal role model for the young Miriam).

20. These articles have been assembled into a narrative available on the website of the National Parks Service (!). See www.nps.gov/archive/gosp/research/m_f_leslie/html.

21. Lynne Cheney, "Mrs. Frank Leslie's Illustrated Newspaper," *American Heritage Magazine* 26 (6) (October 1975). Available at www.americanheritage.com.

22. Ibid.

23. Presumably a remark designed to shock her audience and shame Willy, as his brother had become a notorious inmate-balladeer of Reading Gaol (jail) for his bisexual and pederast proclivities.

24. Cheney, "Mrs. Frank Leslie's Illustrated Newspaper," p. 8.

25. Catt is a remarkable story in her own right, a newspaper reporter who traveled the world on behalf of women's issues at the turn of the century. She stood down from the presidency of the NAWSA in 1904 to care for her dying husband and was reelected in 1912, having remarried a wealthy and supportive George Catt.

26. Leslie was profiled in A Woman of the Century by Mary Livermore and Frances Willard (New York: William Moulton, 1893). She is included in this compendium of some 400 profiles because of her business leadership. The entry is remarkably bland, given Miriam's outsized persona. It even treats Willy Wilde as a serious "English gentleman," which we suppose he was, in a certain way.

Chapter Nine

1. See www.wctu.org/early history.

2. Ruth Bordin, Frances Willard (Chapel Hill: University of North Carolina Press, 1986), p. 112.

3. Jed Dannenbaum, "The Origins of Temperance Activism and Militancy Among American Women," Journal of Social History 15 (2) (Winter 1981), pp. 235–252.

4. Templar's Magazine, June 1858, p. 191.

5. Wages in factories, depressed by growing numbers of immigrants and freed slaves, did not offer many men the means to support their families. Unemployment and idleness were widespread, and so too was cheap alcohol. See Scott, Natural Allies, p. 95.

6. Frances W. Graham and Georgeanna M. Gardenier, 1874–1894: Two Decades: The History of the first Twenty Years' Work of the Woman's Christian Temperance Union of the State of New York (New York: Woman's Christian Temperance Union, 1894), p. 16.

7. Helen Tyler, Where Prayer and Purpose Meet (Evanston, IL: Signal Press, 1949), at www.wctu.org/crusades.html.

8. Frances Willard, Women and Temperance, or the work and Workers of the Woman's Christian Temperance Union (Hartford: Park Pub. Co., 1883), p. 29.

9. The term "awakenings" is applied by historians to periods when religion, especially Protestant sects, gained considerable influence in American social thought. This period saw the rise of popular Protestant evangelizers such as Dwight Moody and Billy Sunday, as well as the birth of Christian Science and Jehovah's Witnesses sects. See Susan Curtis, A Consuming Faith (Baltimore: Johns Hopkins University Press, 1991).

10. Anna Gordon, The Beautiful Life of Frances E. Willard (New York: Women's Temperance Publishing Committee, 1898), p. 31.

11. Frances Willard, "Extracts from Her Fourth of July Speech," Woman's Journal 24 (January 1880), p. 30.

12. Sections of this tract are excerpted in Let Something Good Be Said: Writings by Frances Willard, ed. Carolyn Gifford and Amy Slagell (Urbana: University of Illinois Press, 2007). This book brings together an excellent selection of Willard's writings and brief, helpful commentary.

13. Willard expanded this favorite strategy to the campaign to globalize the WCTU. She spearheaded the creation of a monumental, multinational, multilingual "petition" with 7 million signatures supporting temperance. The physical petition was displayed at the World's Columbian Exposition in Chicago in 1893.

14. A reflection of the popularity among laymen of the work of Gregor Mendel, who first published his theory of inherited characteristics in 1865.

15. Quoted in Mark Sorensen, "Ahead of Their Time: A Brief History of Woman Suffrage in Illinois," at www.historyillinois.org/links/illinois_history_resource_page /suff.html.

16. Quoted in Scott, *Natural Allies*, p. 103.

17. Stansell, *The Feminist Promise*, p. 113.

18. See Scott, *Natural Allies*, p. 101.

19. Graham and Gardenier, *1874–1894*.

20. Bordin, *Frances Willard*, p. 216.

21. Suzanne M. Marilley, "Frances Willard and the Feminism of Fear," *Feminist Studies* 19 (1) (Spring 1993), pp. 123–146, 142.

22. Ibid., p. 126.

23. Ibid., p. 127.

24. Ibid., p. 136.

25. The story of Candace Lightner and her efforts to criminalize drunk driving through her Mothers Against Drunk Driving (MADD) organization comes to mind.

26. She apprenticed herself for a year or so to Anna Dickinson, an entirely secular speaker/entertainer on the "lyceum circuit" in the 1870s, in a clear effort to develop a more robust stage presence.

27. Candace Wheeler, *Yesterdays in a Busy Life* (New York: Harper and Brothers, 1918), p. 226.

28. Wheeler, quoted in McCarthy, *Women's Culture*, p. 43.

29. The launch is chronicled in the *New York Times* of December 3, 1877, available online at www.nytimes.com.

30. Amelia Peck and Carol Irish, *Candace Wheeler: The Art and Enterprise of American Design* (New Haven: Yale University Press, 2001), p. 30.

31. Sander, *The Business of Charity*, p. 52.

32. Quoted in McCarthy, *Women's Culture*, p. 56.

33. Choate would later found the Rosemary Hall School for Girls, and her husband, the jurist William Choate, would found the Choate School for Boys in Connecticut in 1896.

34. Wheeler, quoted in Sander, *The Business of Charity*, p. 53.

35. F. A. Lincoln, quoted in Sander, p. 60. The guide itself proved an effective tool for expanding the concept to new cities. Wheeler's model was prominently featured.

36. Wheeler, quoted in McCarthy, *Women's Culture*, p. 53.

37. Vassar historian Lucy Salmon penned a robust critique of the exchanges in 1892, arguing that the combination of business and charitable purposes at the heart of the exchange model was untenable. It made the women producers "second-class citizens" and lacked any hope of accumulating growth capital needed to move beyond a "hand-to-mouth existence." See McCarthy, *Women's Culture*, pp. 62–63.

38. Auxiliaries of Wheeler's SDA continued to proliferate throughout the 1880s, even in her absence. The New York chapter sent trained teachers to auxiliaries across the Northeast, and also urged them to send their best products to the New York exhibition/salesrooms, where they could obtain good prices. The society expanded its mission to include public education, creating a lending library function that shipped art and design books on demand across the nation. It also created traveling exhibitions of design objects that could be assembled on-site to instruct and inspire homemakers across the nation.

39. For much more about Wheeler, see Peck and Irish, *Candace Wheeler*. Their volume is the catalogue accompanying the solo exhibit of Wheeler's textiles that they co-curated at the Metropolitan Museum of Art in 2001.

40. Among the female-led businesses, one of the most famous was the Rookwood Pottery Company outside Cincinnati, founded by Maria Nichols.

41. Quoted in Peck and Irish, *Candace Wheeler*, p. 49.

42. Abbie Graham, *Grace Dodge: Merchant of Dreams* (New York: The Woman's Press, 1926). This affectionate portrait of Dodge, while not scholarly in the traditional sense, makes enjoyable and informative reading.

43. Poorhouses run by counties were the frequent ending spot for the impoverished, the destitute, the insane, the debauched, the unemployed, and so on. The committee hoped to avoid this fate for a portion of the poor. See, for instance, www.co.ulster .ny.us./poorhouse for more detail on poorhouses. For a comprehensive treatment, see Michael Katz, *In the Shadow of the Poorhouse: A Social History of Welfare in America* (New York: Basic Books, 1986).

44. Graham, *Grace Dodge*, pp. 64–65.

45. Moody became a world-famous pastor and evangelizer during and after the Civil War. He established the Moody Bible Institute in Chicago to train missionaries as well as the Massachusetts-based schools that today make up the Northfield Mount Herman prep school. See B. J. Evensen, *God's Man for the Gilded Age: D. L. Moody and the Rise of Modern Mass Evangelism* (New York: Oxford University Press, 2003).

46. See Sarah Eisenstein, *Give Us Bread but Give Us Roses* (London: Routledge, 1983), for a sociological examination of the lives of working women during the Victorian period.

47. Dodge ultimately wrote a guidebook on these issues, entitled *A Bundle of Letters to Busy Girls*, published in 1887. It reflects her strong orientation toward preparing the girls for marriage and provides detailed advice on men and marriage, despite the fact that Grace never married.

48. The issue of men in relation to working-girls clubs is a fascinating story too complex to cover here. Dodge gave lots of advice about men but was not sympathetic to the idea of including dances, socials, and other mixed-gender events as part of the clubs' activities. But many clubs did just this, especially when membership waned. The topic of women and popular entertainment is covered in Kathy Lee Peiss, *Cheap Amusements* (Philadelphia: Temple University Press, 1987), esp. Chap. 7.

49. Barbara Welter, "The Cult of True Womanhood, 1820–1869," *American Quarterly* 18 (1966): 151–174, quoted in Joanne Reitano, "Working Girls Unite," *American Quarterly* 36 (1) (Spring 1984): 129.

50. Graham, *Grace Dodge*, p. 86.

51. Reitano, "Working Girls Unite," p. 117.

52. Graham, *Grace Dodge*, p. 88.

53. Contemporary articles detail the New York club's plans to keep its rooms open during the summer months, as well as the curriculum and various cost-management practices. Another covers a choral concert offered by the "choral union" of the Working Girls Clubs, one of many activity groups initiated by the membership. See www .nytimes.com and search for Grace H. Dodge.

54. Reitano, "Working Girls Unite," p. 119.

55. As the organized labor movement got under way at this time, there is little doubt that some working girls were attracted to these proactive reform efforts. These tensions are discussed by Alice Kessler Harris, *Out of Work: The History of Wage Earning Women in America* (New York: Oxford University Press, 1982), p. 94ff.

56. These remarkable data, as well as a selection of the letters she composed, are recorded by Graham, *Grace Dodge*, p. 187ff.

57. Ellen C. Lagemann, *A Generation of Women: Education in the Lives of Progressive Reformers* (Cambridge: Harvard University Press, 1979), p. 28.

58. Dodge, in the introduction to a piece entitled "Wage Earning Women," published in 1907 in the *Association Monthly*, cited by Lagemann, *A Generation of Women*, p. 31.

59. Graham, *Grace Dodge*, p. 329.

Chapter Ten

1. Sophia Smith's will, providing for Smith College, stated that it is "with the design to furnish my sex means and facilities for education equal to those which are afforded now in our Colleges for young men."

2. Charles Darwin, *The Descent of Man*, quoted in Michael S. Kimmel, *The Gendered Society*, 3rd ed. (Oxford: Oxford University Press, 2007), p. 23.

3. Edward H. Clarke, *Sex in Education: or, A fair chance for the girls* (Boston: Rand, Avery and Co., 1873), p. 39.

4. Ibid., p. 48.

5. Ibid., p. 14.

6. Sue Zschoche, "Dr. Clarke Revisited: Science, True Womanhood, and Female Collegiate Education," *History of Education Quarterly* 29 (4) (Winter 1989), p. 546.

7. M. Carey Thomas, "Present Tendencies in Women's College and University Educations," ACA *Publications*, 3rd series (February 1908), p. 20.

8. Zschoche, "Dr. Clarke Revisited," p. 549.

9. An overview of nineteenth-century medical doctrine about women is provided in Charles Rosenberg and Carroll Smith-Rosenberg, "The Female Animal: Medical and Biological Views of Women," in Charles E. Rosenberg, *No Other Gods: On Science and American Social Thought* (Baltimore: Johns Hopkins University Press, 1976; paperback edition, 1978), pp. 54–70. See also Carroll Smith-Rosenberg, "Puberty to Menopause: The Cycle of Femininity in Nineteenth-Century America," *Feminist Studies* 2 (1974).

10. Zschoche, "Dr. Clarke Revisited," p. 557, offers a rich set of primary sources. Louise Newman's *Men's Ideas/Women's Realities* (New York: Pergamon Press, 1985) offers a useful edited collection of articles drawn from PSM in the late nineteenth century. For a discussion that summarizes many of the major scientific themes used against women's rights, see Janice Law Trecker, "Sex, Science, and Education," *American Quarterly* 26 (October 1974): 352–366. See also Jill Conway, "Stereotypes of Femininity in a Theory of Sexual Evolution," in Martha Vicinus, ed., *Suffer and Be Still: Women in the Victorian Age* (Bloomington: Indiana University Press, 1972), pp. 140–152, 557.

11. Kimmel, *The Gendered Society*, p. 24.

12. Subtitle of the Garrett biography by Kathleen Sander, *Mary Elizabeth Garrett: Society and Philanthropy in the Gilded Age* (Baltimore: Johns Hopkins University Press, 2008).

13. Quoted in the archives of the Johns Hopkins School of Medicine. See www.medicalarchives.jhmi.edu/garrett/biography.htm.

14. This project is tracked in great and entertaining detail at the website of the Johns Hopkins Medical School Archive. See www.medicalarchives.jhmi.edu/garrett/biography.htm#enriching.

15. This document is available at www.hopkinsmedecine.org/archive.

16. A profile of Thomas as "the brains behind Garrett" and a tough negotiator in her own right can be found in the article, "The Other Feminist," by Janet F. Worthington, at www.hopkinsmedicine.org/hmn/F98/feminist.html.

17. *Educational Review* 21 (1901).

18. The entire study is available online at www.archives.gov/research/guide-fed-records/groups/012.htm/#12.2.z.

19. Douglas C. Baynton, "Disability and the Justification of Inequality in American History," in Paula S. Rothenberg, ed., *Race, Class and Gender in the United States* (New York: St. Martin's Press, 2007), p. 95.

20. Ibid.

21. Cited in Thomas F. Gossett, *Race: The History of an Idea in America*, new edition (New York and Oxford: Oxford University Press, 1997), p. 263. Van Evrie was the author of *White Supremacy and Negro Subordination* (New York, 1868).

22. Monroe Nathan Work, *The Negro Year Book and Annual Encyclopedia of the Negro* (Tuskegee, AL: Institute Press, 1913).

23. Sibyl E. Moses, "The Influence of Philanthropic Agencies on the Development of Monroe Nathan Work's 'Bibliography of the Negro in Africa and America,'" *Libraries and Culture* 31 (2) (Spring 1996): 326–334.

24. Ibid., p. 329.

25. The Phelps Stokes Fund president, Dr. Frederick Douglass Patterson, created the United Negro College Fund (UNCF), which became an independent organization by 1944. The UNCF now collects and distributes hundreds of millions of dollars in scholarship funds to forty-one of the country's historically black colleges. By 2000, UNCF had amassed contributions totaling $1.6 billion over its fifty-five-year history. See *The UNCF Annual Report*, 1996, pp. 36–37.

26. Ronald A. Wells offers an informative historical essay, "Perspectives on Donor Legacy," which can be found at www.wellsgroup.ws/essays/perspectivves.html. Additional information is also available at www.phelpsstokes.org.

27. Olivia Sage, "Opportunities and Responsibilities of Leisured Women," *North American Review* 181 (1905): 718–719.

28. DeForest was himself a wealthy aristocrat who was active in New York philanthropic circles, including the Charitable Organizations Society. He also created, without Olivia's help, the housing enclave of Forest Hills, New York, now part of Queens, through a public-private partnership in which nonprofit investors received a 5 percent return on their money.

29. Stephen Agoratus, *The Core of Progressivism: Research Institutions and Social Policy, 1907–1940*, Carnegie Mellon University, doctoral thesis, 1994, p. 25.

30. David Hammack, *Social Science in the Making: Essays on the Russell Sage Foundation, 1907–1972* (New York: Russell Sage Foundation, 1994), p. 3. The language used in the acts that created the Carnegie Corporation in 1911 and the Rockefeller Foundation in 1913 was "practically identical," as a Rockefeller attorney emphasized in a successful effort to deflect criticism when the Rockefeller Foundation sought to incorporate in New York.

31. Joan M. Fisher, *A Study of Six Women Philanthropists of the Early Twentieth Century*, Graduate School of the Union Institute of Cincinnati, Ohio, doctoral thesis, 1992, p. 305. There had been specific-purpose funds, devoted to education, for instance, created by Carnegie, Rockefeller, Peabody, and Slater a decade or more earlier.

32. James A. Smith describes the Russell Sage Foundation as "the prototypical think tank" in *The Idea Brokers: Think Tanks and the Rise of the New Policy Elite* (New York: The Free Press, 1991), p. 17, quoted in Hammack, *Social Science in the Making*, p. 29, n. 55.

33. Inspiration for a study of the social service practices of Pittsburgh is credited to another woman, Alice B. Montgomery. She was a juvenile justice activist and chief

probation officer of the Allegheny County Juvenile Court, where Pittsburgh is located. The work was done by a combination of staff from the COS and the foundation. See Randall Miller and William Pencak, *Pennsylvania: A History of the Commonwealth* (State College: Penn State University Press, 2002), pp. 272–274.

34. The complete study is available online at www.openlibrary.org.

35. See Peter H. Boyce, "The Present Position of the Milk Supply Problem from the Public Health Standpoint," *Public Health Pap Rep* 17 (1891): 144–161, available at www.NCBI.hlm.nih.gov.

36. Hammack, *Social Science in the Making*, pp. 46–47.

37. See Ruth Crocker, *Mrs. Russell Sage* (Bloomington: Indiana University Press, 2006), p. 179. Todd eventually became a close associate and personal secretary to Olivia, and perhaps the driving force behind Olivia's creation of Russell Sage College for Women, but their relationship did not end well. Crocker has the details.

38. Ibid., p. 287.

Chapter Eleven

1. Candace Wheeler was not the only observer who had noted the poor quality of American goods on display at the Centennial celebration in 1876, when compared to the European nations. Here was the chance to demonstrate America's remarkable technological progress. See Florence Kelley, *Notes of Sixty Years*, ed. Katharine Sklar (Chicago: Charles Kerr Publishing, 1986), p. 86.

2. The project was "white" in other ways as well, as Frederick Douglass complained bitterly, lamenting the lack of black input in planning, the lack of significant jobs for blacks, and the lack of any significant exhibit featuring the contributions of blacks. See www.jimcrowhistory.org for references.

3. Ellen Fitzpatrick, *Endless Crusade: Women Social Scientists and Progressive Reform* (New York: Oxford University Press, 1990), p. 39. Fitzpatrick traces the careers of four of these women graduate students: Sophonisba Breckinridge, Katharine Davis, Frances Kellor, and Edith Abbott. All had distinguished careers in social profit.

4. The next generation of academics to lead the University of Chicago rejected such activism, arguing that it was not possible to maintain scientific "objectivity" as a social researcher while engaging in social services or social reform efforts. Perhaps the early female social scientists were entrepreneur-scholars, taking what they needed from their new academic toolbox and forging ahead in pursuit of social as well as scholarly, goals. As Peter Drucker notes, this is what entrepreneurs do, and the theorizers come along later.

5. *Our Toiling Children* is available online at http://pds.lib.harvard.edu/pds/view/.

6. This group, created at the WCTU convention in 1879, published the WCTU weekly newspaper, the *Signal*. Frances Willard's mother served as the first editor.

7. Lloyd was best known for his exposé of work practices at Standard Oil and defense of the workers involved in the Haymarket disaster. Toward the end of Kelley's time at Hull House, the children came to live with her and attended the local public school.

8. "Florence Kelley and Women's Activism in the Progressive Era," in Kerber, *Women's America*, p. 330.

9. This organization originated during the Civil War to support the Union Army and its veterans. The ladies formed their own national organization at a convention in Chicago in 1886.

10. Kelley, *Notes of Sixty Years*, pp. 81–82.

11. See Louise Knight, *Citizen: Jane Addams and the Struggle for Democracy* (Chicago: University of Chicago Press, 2005), p. 327.

12. See Skocpol, *Protecting Mothers and Soldiers: The Political Origins of Social Policy in the United States* (Cambridge and London: Belknap Press of Harvard University Press, 1992; paperback edition, 1995), p. 383ff. for additional details.

13. See Ellen Fitzpatrick, *Endless Crusade* (New York: Oxford University Press, 1990), pp. 188–189.

14. For the basic details of Wald's life, see the Jewish Women's Archive at http://jwa.org/exhibits/wov/wald. A contemporary biography is Marjorie N. Feld, *Lillian Wald* (Chapel Hill: University of North Carolina Press, 2008).

15. R. L. Duffus, *Lillian Wald: Neighbor and Crusader* (New York: Macmillan, 1938), is a charmingly written biography.

16. Lillian Wald, *The House on Henry Street* (New York: Henry Holt and Co., 1915).

17. Many of her Jewish colleagues were taken aback by this Christian turn of phrase, but it is typical of Wald, who focused consistently on the unity of the human family rather than on its subdivisions.

18. We have already noted that teaching, another primarily female profession at the time, suffered from a similar lack of professional training, a situation that Grace Dodge worked throughout her life to remedy.

19. The history of nursing is well documented. An excellent introduction, including details of Wald's work, is Karen Buhler-Wilkerson, *No Place Like Home: A History of Nursing and Home Care in the United States* (Baltimore: Johns Hopkins University Press, 2001).

20. Wald, *The House on Henry Street*, p. 38.

21. *Charities* 14 (June 3, 1905): 798–800.

22. Peter Seixas, "Lewis Hine: From Social to Interpretative Photographer," *American Quarterly* 39 (3) (1987): 387.

23. Duffus, *Lillian Wald*, p. 117.

24. The complete set of the Committee's Annual Reports is available online at http://pds.lib.harvard.edu/pds/view/2585661.

25. The irony of this argument was presumably not lost on Kelley and Wald. It must have been less than satisfying to argue that women deserved special treatment because extended physical output risked damage to their well-being, an uncomfortable echo of the anti-female education arguments advanced by Professor Clarke forty years earlier.

26. Seixas, "Lewis Hine," p. 393.

27. Feld, *Lillian Wald*, p. 104.

28. Ibid., pp. 106–107.

Chapter Twelve

1. The role of state and federal governments in "human services" is an enormous topic well beyond the scope of our effort. For a comprehensive analysis of this issue during the period 1865–1940, the ambitious reader should consider Skocpol, *Protecting Soldiers and Mothers*.

2. The Confederate soldiers likewise benefited from the work of many volunteer support groups led by women.

3. The Water Supply Committee of the Woman's Health Protective Association in Philadelphia, for instance, studied filtration systems, conducted site visits to Louisville, KY, hired engineers from Boston, and ultimately won public support for a

bond issue to build the system they recommended to the city fathers—in 1895. See Scott, *Natural Allies*, p. 143.

4. Katz, *In the Shadow of the Poorhouse*, p. 123. Katz's book offers a useful overview of the debates over the division of labor between citizens and government in the social sector.

5. The National Congress of Mothers advocated for increased government support to kindergartens and to working mothers. It eventually morphed into the National Congress of Parents and Teachers, or the Parent Teacher Association (PTA), as it came to be known.

6. Mrs. Helen Gardner quoted in Skocpol, *Protecting Mothers and Soldiers*, p. 335.

7. A number of helpful books describe this idea in more detail: Victoria C. DePaul, *Creating the Intrapreneur: The Search for Leadership Excellence* (Austin, TX: Synergy Publishers, 2008); Walter Baets and Erna Oldenboom, *Rethinking Growth: Social Intrapreneurship for Sustainable Performance* (London and New York: Palgrave Macmillan, 2009); Gifford Pinchot's *Intrapreneuring: Why You Don't Have to Leave the Corporation to Become an Entrepreneur* (New York: Harper and Row, 1985) is the original with the "ten commandments."

8. Cecelia Tichi, *Civic Passions* (Chapel Hill: University of North Carolina Press, 2010), offers a lively portrait of Lathrop, as well as of Florence Kelley.

9. A detailed history of the Children's Bureau is available online through the website of the Social Security Administration: www.ssa.gov/history/childb.html.

10. Addams came to admire Lathrop so greatly that she wrote a biography entitled *My Friend, Julia Lathrop*. The book, with an informative introduction by Anne Firor Scott, was republished by the University of Illinois Press in 2004.

11. See Jane Addams, "A Great Public Servant, Julia C. Lathrop," *Social Service Review* 6 (2) (June 1932): 282.

12. For a detailed history of Julia's work in the creation of the juvenile justice system, see David S. Tanenhaus, *Juvenile Justice in the Making* (New York and Oxford: Oxford University Press, 2004).

13. For a detailed account of this work, see Fitzpatrick, *The Endless Crusade*, Chap. 7. Lathrop's letters to the Foundation seeking funds are reproduced in Anne Scott's edition of Addams, *My Friend, Julia Lathrop*, pp. 107–109.

14. Beers, a victim of mental illness (amnesia? manic depression?) who had spent three years in an asylum, published his autobiography, *A Mind That Found Itself*, in 1908. He founded the NCMH in 1909, recruiting William Welch, dean of public health at Johns Hopkins, as president. The goal was to educate the general public about mental illness, although experts did not agree on its origins. The continuing debate concerning environmental versus genetic causes of "insanity" was only in its formative stages. See Norman Dain, *Clifford Beers: Advocate for the Insane* (Pittsburgh: University of Pittsburgh Press, 1980).

15. Tichi, *Civic Passions*, p. 89.

16. See www.ssa.gov/history/childb.html.

17. History of the Children's Bureau, "Four Decades of Service to Children" by Dorothy Bradbury, p. 11, at www.ssa.gov/history/pdf/child1.pdf.

18. Quoted in Scott's introduction to Addams, *My Friend, Julia Lathrop*, p. xix.

19. Scott, *Natural Allies*, p. 156.

20. Mary Bethune, "Certain Unalienable Rights," reprinted in *Mary McLeod Bethune: Building a Better World*, ed. Audrey T. McCluskey and Elaine Smith (Bloomington: Indiana University Press, 1989), p. 23.

21. We are fortunate that Bethune left writings that enable us to hear her voice directly. The McCluskey and Smith volume offers a wonderful collection of Bethune's writings and speeches helpfully organized with commentary into sections on her life, her educational leadership, her activism on behalf of women, and her government service.

22. See McCluskey and Smith, eds., *Mary McLeod Bethune*, pp. 23–24.

23. The Fourteenth Amendment, 1868, contains the citizenship clause, the due process clause, and the equal protection clause, among others. The Fifteenth, enacted in 1870, prohibits any government from denying a citizen the right to vote based on race, creed, or previous condition of servitude.

24. Mary Bethune's own number cited in her speech "Clarifying our Vision with Facts" from 1938. See McCluskey and Smith, eds., *Mary McLeod Bethune*, p. 215.

25. In fact, while Albertus is listed as a trustee of the school for a period of time, he apparently returned to Georgia sometime during the five years. Mary is listed as a widow in the 1908 census, although Albertus apparently lived well beyond that date.

26. For a detailed account of the political dynamics involving Bethune, the NYA, and the Roosevelt administration, see Joyce Ross, "Mary Bethune and the NYA," in John Hope Franklin and A. Meier, eds., *Black Leaders of the Twentieth Century* (Champaign: University of Illinois Press, 1982), pp. 191–220.

27. McCluskey and Smith, eds., *Mary McLeod Bethune*, p. 200.

28. Mary's second in command at the Council, Robert Weaver, eventually became the first black cabinet member in American history when appointed secretary of housing and urban development by Lyndon Johnson in 1966.

29. The motto of the *American Labor Legislation Review* published by the American Association for Labor Legislation (AALL), quoted in Skocpol, *Protecting Mothers and Soldiers*, p. 185.

30. For a detailed history of the AALL, as well as the relationship of organized labor to "social insurance" legislation, see ibid., Chaps. 3 and 4.

31. Kirstin Downey, *The Woman Behind the New Deal* (New York: Doubleday, 2009). Downey calls Perkins "the moral conscience" of FDR, and we are greatly indebted to her book for many insights into Perkins's life and leadership style.

32. Ibid., p. 36.

33. Ibid., p. 69.

34. For a (very) detailed outline of the work done by nurses employed by the Association, including checklists for childbirth supplies, examination protocols for physicians (to be monitored by the nurses), and postpartum guidelines for new mothers, see Anne Stevens, "The Work of the Maternity Center Association," November 1919, published in the *Transactions of the Tenth Annual Meeting of the Child Hygiene Association*, available at www.womhist.alexanderstreet.com/wccny/doc11.htm. Today the organization is called Childbirth Connection.

35. The Commission was an outgrowth of the Factory Investigating Committee (FIC) established in the wake of the Triangle Factory fire. Perkins had testified before the FIC, led by legislators Al Smith and Robert Wagner. The FIC had championed the passage of several state laws concerning workplace safety practices. There is a brief history at www.dol.gov/history.

36. The drama of policy creation and legislative horse-trading is an acquired taste. Some are guided by the old adage that it is preferable to eat sausage than to watch it being made. Kirstin Downey writes with verve and judicious editing about the unending policy battles that characterized the next forty years of Perkins's life.

37. Mitchell was a legendary labor organizer and former president of the United Mine Workers from 1898–1907. He died in 1919, the same year as the confrontation with Spargo.

38. Downey, *The Woman Behind the New Deal*, p. 233.

39. Ibid., p. 239.

40. Ibid., p. 243.

41. Ibid., p. 244.

42. Ibid.

43. Frances herself managed to negotiate a trust fund for Susanna with her former son-in-law's mother!

Chapter Thirteen

1. Henry R. Luce, *The American Century* (New York: Farrar and Rinehart, Inc., 1941), pp. 32–34.

2. Feld, *Lillian Wald*, p. 106.

3. In 2009, public charities reported $1.4 trillion in total revenue and $2.6 trillion in assets, whereas private foundations reported $181 billion in revenue and $621 billion in assets, and other nonprofits reported $386 billion in revenue and over $1 trillion in assets. See Molly F. Sherlock and Jane G. Gravell, *An Overview of the Nonprofit and Charitable Sector*, Congressional Research Service, 7–5700, www.crs.gov, R40919 (Washington, DC: November 17, 2009).

4. The topic of morality in markets has garnered considerable attention from economists and other disciplinary specialists in recent years. See, for instance, Paul Zak, ed., *Moral Markets: The Critical Role of Values in the Economy* (Princeton: Princeton University Press, 2008).

5. Gary Becker, *The Economics of Life* (New York: McGraw Hill, 1997), p. 300ff.

6. "Spiritual Autobiography" (1946), in McCluskey and Smith, eds., *Mary McLeod Bethune*, p. 54.

7. See "Citizenship Through the Social Sector," in Peter F. Drucker, *The Essential Drucker* (New York: Collins Business Essentials, 2008), pp. 329–336.

BIBLIOGRAPHY

Books

Adams, Abigail. *My Dearest Friend: Letters of Abigail and John Adams*. Cambridge, MA: Belknap Press of Harvard University Press, 2007.

Addams, Jane. *My Friend, Julia Lathrop*. Edited by Anne Firor Scott. Urbana and Chicago: University of Illinois Press, 2004.

Agoratus, Stephen. *The Core of Progressivism: Research Institutions and Social Policy, 1907–1940*. Carnegie Mellon University, doctoral thesis, 1994.

Anonymous. *The UNCF Annual Report*. 1996.

Anonymous. *Report of the Twenty-first National Anti-Slavery Bazaar*. Boston: 1855.

Aristotle. *The Politics*. Translated by B. Jowett. New York: Cosimo Books, 2008.

Baets, Walter, and Erna Oldenboom. *Rethinking Growth: Social Intrapreneurship for Sustainable Performance*. London and New York: Palgrave Macmillan, 2009.

Bailyn, Bernard. *Voyagers to the West: A Passage in the Peopling of America on the Eve of the Revolution*. New York: Knopf, 1986.

Becker, Gary. *The Economics of Life*. New York: McGraw Hill, 1997.

Berkin, Carol. *First Generations: Women in Colonial America*. New York: Hill and Wang, 1996.

———. *Revolutionary Mothers: Women in the Struggle for American Independence*. New York: Random House, 2006.

Blinderman, Abraham. *Three Early Champions of Education*. Bloomington: Indiana University Press, 1976.

Bordin, Ruth. *Frances Willard*. Chapel Hill: University of North Carolina Press, 1986.

Bradbury, Dorothy. *Four Decades of Action for Children: A Short History of the Children's Bureau*. Washington, DC: U.S. Government Printing Office, 1956.

Buhler-Wilkerson, Karen. *No Place Like Home: A History of Nursing and Home Care in the United States*. Baltimore: Johns Hopkins University Press, 2001.

Burlingame, Dwight, ed. *Philanthropy in America*. Santa Barbara, CA: ABC-CLIO, 2004.

Burnett, D. Graham. *Trying Leviathan*. Princeton: Princeton University Press, 2007.

Butler, Jon, Grant Wacker, and Randall Balmer. *Religion in American Life*. New York: Oxford University Press, 2007.

Carroll, Bret. *American Masculinities: A Historical Encyclopedia*. New York: Sage Publications, 2003.

Chapman, Maria. *Right and Wrong*. Boston, 1839.

Chesterton, G. K. *What I Saw in America*. New York: Dodd, Mead and Co., 1923.

Clarke, Edward. *Sex in Education: or, A fair chance for the girls*. Boston: Rand, Avery and Co., 1873; reprint, New York: Arno Press, 1972.

Collins, James, and Jerry Porras. *Built to Last: Successful Habits of Visionary Companies*. New York: Harper Business, 2002.

Cott, Nancy F., ed. *Roots of Bitterness*. New York: Dutton, 1972.

Crocker, Ruth. *Mrs. Russell Sage*. Bloomington: Indiana University Press, 2006.

Curtis, Susan. *A Consuming Faith*. Baltimore: Johns Hopkins University Press, 1991.

Dain, Norman. *Clifford Beers: Advocate for the Insane*. Pittsburgh: University of Pittsburgh Press, 1980.

Darwin, Charles. *The Descent of Man*. Facsimile edition. Digireads Publishing, 2009. Also available online through Project Gutenberg at www.gutenberg.org/ebooks /2300.

———. *The Origin of Species*. New York: Random House, 1979.

Davis, David Brion. *Inhuman Bondage*. New York: Oxford University Press, 2006.

DePaul, Victoria C. *Creating the Intrapreneur: The Search for Leadership Excellence*. Austin, TX: Synergy Publishers, 2008.

de Tocqueville, Alexis. *Democracy in America*. Translated by Francis Bowen. Cambridge, MA: Sever and Francis, 1868.

Dirvan, Joseph. *Mrs. Seton: Foundress of the American Sisters of Charity*. New York: Farrar, Straus and Cudahy, 1962.

Dodge, Grace. *A Bundle of Letters to Busy Girls on Practical Matters*. New York: Funk and Wagnalls, 1887.

Dorr, Rheta Childe. *What Eight Million Women Want* (1910). Facsimile edition. Kessinger Publishers, 2008. Also available online through Project Gutenberg at www.gutenberg.org/ebooks/12226.

Downey, Kirstin. *Frances Perkins:The Woman Behind the New Deal*. New York: Doubleday, 2009.

Drucker, Peter. *Innovation and Entrepreneurship*. New York: Harper, 1985.

———. *The Essential Drucker*. New York: Collins Business Essentials, 2008.

Duffus, R. L. *Lillian Wald: Neighbor and Crusader*. New York: Macmillan, 1938.

Duncan, George John C. *Memoir of the Rev. Henry Duncan, D. D. of Ruthwell*. Edinburgh: William Oliphant and Sons, 1848.

Eisenstein, Sarah. *Give Us Bread but Give Us Roses*. London: Routledge, 1983.

Evensen, B. J. *God's Man for the Gilded Age: D. L. Moody and the Rise of Modern Mass Evangelism*. New York: Oxford University Press, 2003.

Feld, Marjorie N. *Lillian Wald*. Chapel Hill: University of North Carolina Press, 2008.

Fisher, Joan M. *A Study of Six Women Philanthropists of the Early Twentieth Century*. Graduate School of the Union Institute of Cincinnati, Ohio, doctoral thesis, 1992.

Fitzgerald, Maureen. *Habits of Compassion*. Urbana and Chicago: University of Illinois Press, 2006.

Fitzpatrick, Ellen. *Endless Crusade: Women Social Scientists and Progressive Reform*. New York: Oxford University Press, 1990.

Franklin, Benjamin. *Autobiography*. Edited by J. A. Leo LeMay. New York: W. W. Norton, 1986.

———. *A Proposal for Promoting Useful Knowledge among the British Plantations in America*. 1743.

Franklin, John Hope, and A. Meier, eds. *Black Leaders of the Twentieth Century*. Urbana and Chicago: University of Illinois Press, 1982.

French, John Homer, ed. *Gazetteer of the State of New York*. 1860.

Friedman, Lawrence, and Mark McGarvie, eds. *Charity, Philanthropy and Civility in American History*. New York: Cambridge University Press, 2003.

Gaudiani, Claire. *Generosity Unbound*. New York: Broadway Publications, 2010.

———. *The Greater Good*. New York: Henry Holt, 2003.

Gay, Peter. *The Science of Freedom*. Vol. 2 of *The Enlightenment: An Interpretation*. New York: Alfred A. Knopf, 1969.

Geisberg, Judith Ann. *Civil War Sisterhood: The U.S. Sanitary Commission and Women's Politics in Transition*. Boston: Northeastern University Press, 2000.

Gifford, Carolyn, and Amy Slagell. *Let Something Good Be Said: Writings of Frances Willard*. Urbana and Chicago: University of Illinois Press, 2007.

Gomez, Michael, ed. *Diasporic Africa*. New York: New York University Press, 2006.

Gordon, Anna. *The Beautiful Life of Frances E. Willard*. Indianapolis, IN: Woman's Temperance Publishing Association, 1898.

Gordon, Beverly. *Bazaars and Fair Ladies: The History of the American Fundraising Fair*. Knoxville: University of Tennessee Press, 1998.

Gossett, Thomas F. *Race: The History of an Idea in America*. New York: Oxford University Press, 1997.

Graham, Abbie. *Grace Dodge: Merchant of Dreams*. New York: The Woman's Press, 1926.

Graham, Frances W., and Georgeanna M. Gardenier. *1874–1894 Two Decades: The history of the first Twenty Years' Work of the Woman's Christian Temperance Union of the State of New York*. New York: Woman's Christian Temperance Union, 1894, available at Project Gutenberg, www.gutenberg.org/files/20811/20811-h /20811-h.htm.

Graham, Isabella. *The Power of Faith*. New York: J. Seymour, 1816.

Hammack, David. *Social Science in the Making: Essays on the Russell Sage Foundation, 1907–1972*. New York: Russell Sage Foundation, 1994.

Harris, Alice Kessler. *Out of Work: The History of Wage Earning Women in America*. New York: Oxford University Press, 1982.

Hobson, Elizabeth Christophers. *Recollections of a Happy Life* (1916). Facsimile edition. Bibliolife Publishers, 2009.

Hoff-Wilson, Joan. *Law, Gender, and Injustice: A Legal History of U.S. Women*. New York: New York University Press, 1990.

Howe, Daniel Walker. *What God Has Wrought: The Transformation of America 1815– 1848*. New York: Oxford University Press, 2007.

Jones, Howard Mumford. *O Strange New World*. New York: Viking Press, 1964.

Kames, Lord (Henry Home). *Sketches of the History of Man*. Abridged version. Philadelphia, 1776.

Karlsen, Carol. *The Devil in the Shape of a Woman*. New York: W. W. Norton, 1987.

Katz, Michael. *In the Shadow of the Poorhouse: A Social History of Welfare in America*. New York: Basic Books, 1986.

Kelley, Florence. *Notes of Sixty Years*. Edited by Katharine Sklar. Chicago: Charles Kerr Publishing, 1986.

———. *Our Toiling Children*. Chicago: Woman's Temperance Publication Association, 1889. Available online at http://pds.lib.harvard.edu/pds/view/.

Kerber, Linda. *No Constitutional Right to Be Ladies*. New York: Hill and Wang, 1998.

———. *Toward an Intellectual History of Women*. Chapel Hill: University of North Carolina Press, 1997.

———, ed. *Women's America*. 6th ed. New York: Oxford University Press, 2004.

Kimmel, Michael S. *The Gendered Society*. 3rd ed. New York: Oxford University Press, 2007.

Knight, Louise. *Citizen: Jane Addams and the Struggle for Democracy*. Chicago: University of Chicago Press, 2005.

Lagemann, Ellen C. *A Generation of Women: Education in the Lives of Progressive Reformers*. Cambridge: Harvard University Press, 1979.

Leslie, Mrs. Frank. *Are We All Deceivers? The Lovers Blue Book*. New York: Tennyson Neely, 1896.

Light, Paul. *The Search for Social Entrepreneurship*. Washington, DC: The Brookings Institution, 2008.

Livermore, Mary. *My Story of the War* (1887). Facsimile edition, with an introduction by Nina Silber. New York: DaCapo Press, 1995.

———. *The Story of My Life*. Whitefish, MT: Kessinger Publications, 2005.

———. *What Shall We Do with Our Daughters?* New York: Garland Publishing, 1987.

Livermore, Mary, and Frances Willard. *A Woman of the Century*. New York: William Moulton, 1893.

Luce, Henry R. *The American Century*. New York: Farrar and Rinehart, Inc., 1941.

McCarthy, Kathleen D. *Women's Culture*. Chicago: University of Chicago Press, 1991.

McCluskey, Audrey, and Elaine Smith. *Mary McLeod Bethune*. Bloomington: Indiana University Press, 1989.

Miller, Randall, and William Pencak. *Pennsylvania: A History of the Commonwealth*. State College: Pennsylvania State University Press, 2002.

Morrow, Diane Batts. *Persons of Color and Religious at the Same Time*. Chapel Hill: University of North Carolina Press, 2002.

Murray, Judith Sargeant. *The Gleaner*. Vol. 3. Boston, 1798.

Newman, Louise. *Men's Ideas/Women's Realities*. New York: Pergamon Press, 1985.

Peck, Amelia, and Carol Irish. *Candace Wheeler: The Art and Enterprise of American Design*. New Haven: Yale University Press, 2001.

Peiss, Kathy Lee. *Cheap Amusements*. Philadelphia: Temple University Press, 1987.

Pestana, Carla Gardina, and Sharon V. Salinger, eds. *Inequality in Early America*. Hanover and London: Dartmouth/University Press of New England, 1999.

Pinchot, Gilbert. *Intrapreneuring: Why You Don't Have to Leave the Corporation to Become an Entrepreneur*. New York: Harper and Row, 1985.

Reiss, Bob. *Low Risk, High Reward: Practical Prescriptions for Starting and Growing Your Business*. New York: The Free Press, 2000.

Rosenberg, Charles E. *No Other Gods: On Science and American Social Thought*. Baltimore: Johns Hopkins University Press, 1976; paperback edition, 1978.

Rothenberg, Paula S., ed. *Race, Class and Gender in the United States*. New York: St. Martin's Press, 2007.

Rush, Benjamin. *Essays: Literary, Moral, and Philosophical*. Philadelphia, 1798.

Sander, Kathleen W. *The Business of Charity*. Urbana and Chicago: University of Illinois Press, 1998.

———. *Mary Elizabeth Garrett: Society and Philanthropy in the Gilded Age*. Baltimore: Johns Hopkins University Press, 2008.

Schneider, Franz. *A Public Health Survey of Topeka*. Topeka, KS: Topeka Improvement Survey Committee, 1914.

Scott, Anne Firor. *Natural Allies*. Urbana and Chicago: University of Illinois Press, 1991.

Secondat, Charles, baron de Montesquieu. *The Spirit of Laws: a Compendium of the First English Edition*. Edited by David Wallace Carrithers. Los Angeles: University of California–Los Angeles Press, 1977.

Skocpol, Theda. *Protecting Mothers and Soldiers: The Political Origins of Social Policy in the United States*. Cambridge and London: Belknap Press of Harvard University Press, 1992; paperback edition, 1995.

Smith, Adam. *The Theory of Moral Sentiments*. Amherst, NY: Prometheus Books, 2000.
———. *The Wealth of Nations*. New York: Modern Library, 2000.
Smith, James A. *The Idea Brokers: Think Tanks and the Rise of the New Policy Elite*. New York: The Free Press, 1991.
Spain, Daphne. *How Women Saved the City*. Minneapolis: University of Minnesota Press, 2001.
Spargo, John. *The Bitter Cry of the Children*. New York: Macmillan, 1906.
Stansell, Christine. *City of Women: Sex and Class in New York, 1789–1860*. Urbana and Chicago: University of Illinois Press, 1987.
———. *The Feminist Promise*. New York: Modern Library, 2010.
Stern, Madeleine. *Purple Passage: The Life of Mrs. Frank Leslie*. Norman: University of Oklahoma Press, 1953.
Tanenhaus, David S. *Juvenile Justice in the Making*. New York: Oxford University Press, 2004.
Taylor, Clare. *Women of the Anti-Slavery Movement: The Weston Sisters*. London: St. Martin's Press, 1995.
Tichi, Cecelia. *Civic Passions*. Chapel Hill: University of North Carolina Press, 2010.
Tyler, Helen. *Where Prayer and Purpose Meet*. Evanston, IL: Signal Press, 1949.
Van Evrie, John. *White Supremacy and Negro Subordination*. New York, 1868.
Venet, Wendy H. *A Strong-Minded Woman: The Life of Mary Livermore*. Amherst: University of Massachusetts Press, 2005.
Vicinus, Martha, ed. *Suffer and Be Still: Women in the Victorian Age*. Bloomington: Indiana University Press, 1972.
Wald, Lillian. *The House on Henry Street*. New York: Henry Holt and Co., 1915.
Walters, Ronald G. *The Antislavery Appeal: American Abolitionism After 1830*. New York: Norton, 1978.
Wheeler, Candace. *Yesterdays in a Busy Life*. New York: Harper and Brothers, 1918.
Willard, Frances. *Women and Temperance: The Work and workers of the Woman's Christian Temperance Union*. Hartford: Park Publishing Co., 1883.
Wills, David, and Albert Raboteau, eds. *African American Religion*. Chicago: University of Chicago Press, 2006.
Work, Monroe Nathan. *The Negro Year Book and Annual Encyclopedia of the Negro*. Tuskegee, AL: Institute Press, 1913.
Yellin, Jean Fagan, and John C. Van Horne, eds. *The Abolitionist Sisterhood: Women's Political Culture in Antebellum America*. Ithaca: Cornell University Press, 1994.
Zak, Paul, ed. *Moral Markets:The Critical Role of Values in the Economy*. Princeton: Princeton University Press, 2008.

Articles

Addams, Jane. "A Great Public Servant, Julia C Lathrop." *Social Service Review* 6 (2) (June 1932): 280–285.
Anonymous. *Templar's Magazine* (June 1858): 191.
Anonymous. "Making Data Dance." *Economist*, December 11, 2010, 25.
Baynton, Douglas C. "Disability and the Justification of Inequality in American History." In *The New Disability History: American Perspectives*, edited by Paul K. Longmore and Lauri Umansky, 33–57. New York: NYU Press, 2001.
Bechtle, Regina. "An American Daughter: Elizabeth Ann Seton and the Birth of the U.S. Church." *America* 199 (5) (September 1, 2008).

Bethune, Mary. "Americans All, Which Way America?" Reprinted in *Mary McLeod Bethune: Building a Better World,* edited by Audrey T. McCluskey and Elaine Smith, 186–188. Bloomington: Indiana University Press, 1989.

———. "Certain Unalienable Rights." Reprinted in *Mary McLeod Bethune: Building a Better World,* edited by Audrey T. McCluskey and Elaine Smith, 20–27. Bloomington: Indiana University Press, 1989.

———. "Clarifying Our Vision with Facts" (from 1938). Reprinted in *Mary McLeod Bethune: Building a Better World,* edited by Audrey T. McCluskey and Elaine Smith, 212–215. Bloomington: Indiana University Press, 1989.

Boyce, Peter H. "The Present Position of the Milk Supply Problem from the Public Health Standpoint." *Public Health Pap Rep* 17 (1891): 144–161. Available at www.Ncbi.nlm.nih.gov.

Chambers-Schiller, Lee. "A Good Work Among the People: The Political Culture of the Boston Antislavery Fair." In Jean Fagan Yellin and John C. Van Horne, eds., *The Abolitionist Sisterhood: Women's Political Culture in Antebellum America,* 248–274. Ithaca: Cornell University Press, 1994.

Cheney, Lynne. "Mrs. Frank Leslie's Illustrated Newspaper." *American Heritage Magazine* 26 (6) (October 1975).

Collins, Jim, and Jerry Porras. "Build Your Company's Vision." *Harvard Business Review* 74 (5) (1996): 65–77.

Conway, Jill. "Stereotypes of Femininity in a Theory of Sexual Evolution." In Martha Vicinus, ed., *Suffer and Be Still: Women in the Victorian Age,* 140–152. Bloomington: Indiana University Press, 1972.

Dannenbaum, Jed. "The Origins of Temperance Activism and Militancy Among American Women." *Journal of Social History* 15 (2) (Winter 1981): 235–252.

Gaudiani, Claire. "Opinion." *Chronicle of Philanthropy* (July 26, 2007).

Gummere, Richard M. "Some Classical Side Lights on Colonial Education." *Classical Journal* 55 (5) (February 1960): 223–232.

Hanley, Ryan Patrick. "Social Science and Human Flourishing: The Scottish Enlightenment and Today." *Journal of Scottish Philosophy* 7 (1) (2009): 29–46.

Hansen, Debra Gold. "The Boston Female Anti-Slavery Society and the Limits of Gender Politics." In Jean Fagan Yellin and John C. Van Horne, eds., *The Abolitionist Sisterhood: Women's Political Culture in Antebellum America,* 45–66. Ithaca: Cornell University Press, 1994.

Haviland, Margaret Morris. "Beyond Women's Sphere: Young Quaker Women and the Veil of Charity in Philadelphia, 1790–1810." *William and Mary Quarterly* 51 (3) (1994): 419–446.

Howe, Daniel Walker. "Why the Scottish Enlightenment Was Useful to the Framers of the American Constitution." *Comparative Studies in Society and History* 31 (3) (July 1989): 572–587.

Jarrett, William H. II. "Raising the Bar: Mary Elizabeth Garrett, M. Carey Thomas, and the Johns Hopkins Medical School." *Proceedings (Baylor Med Cent)* 24 (1) (2011): 21–26.

Kelley, Florence. "The Needless Destruction of Boys: Night Work in New Jersey Glass Works." *Charities* 14 (June 3, 1905): 798–800.

Kerber, Linda. "The Republican Mother and the Woman Citizen." In Linda Kerber, ed., *Women's America,* 6th ed., 119–127. New York: Oxford University Press, 2004.

Kidd, Colin. "Civil Theology and Church Establishments in Revolutionary America." *Historical Journal* 42 (4) (December 1999): 1007–1026.

Lewis, Jan. "The Republican Wife: Virtue and Seduction in the Early Republic." *William and Mary Quarterly* 44 (4) (October 1987): 689–721.

Marilley, Suzanne M. "Frances Willard and the Feminism of Fear." *Feminist Studies* 19 (1) (Spring 1993): 123–146.

Martin, Roger L., and Sally Osberg. "Social Entrepreneurship: The Case for Definition." *Stanford Social Innovation Review* (Spring 2007): 28–39.

McCarthy, Kathleen. "Women and Political Culture." In Lawrence Friedman and Mark McGarvie, eds., *Charity, Philanthropy and Civility in American History*, 179–198. New York: Cambridge University Press, 2003.

McGarvie, Mark. "The Dartmouth College Case and the Legal Design of Civil Society." In Lawrence Friedman and Mark McGarvie, eds., *Charity, Philanthropy and Civility in American History*, 91–106. New York: Cambridge University Press, 2003.

Morrow, Diane Batts. "Embracing the Religious Profession: The Antebellum Mission of the Oblate Sisters of Providence." In Michael Gomez, ed., *Diasporic Africa*, 105–122. New York: New York University Press, 2006.

———. "Outsiders Within: The Oblate Sisters of Providence in 1830s Church and Society." *U.S. Catholic Historian* 15 (2) (Spring 1997): 35–54.

Moses, Sibyl E. "The Influence of Philanthropic Agencies on the Development of Monroe Nathan Work's 'Bibliography of the Negro in Africa and America,'" *Libraries and Culture* 31 (2) (Spring 1996): 326–334.

Oates, Mary J. "Faith and Good Works: Catholic Giving and Taking." In Lawrence Friedman and Mark McGarvie, eds. *Charity, Philanthropy and Civility in American History*, 281–300. New York: Cambridge University Press, 2003.

Perkins, Edwin J. "The Entrepreneurial Spirit in Colonial America: The Foundations of Modern Business History." *Business History Review* 63 (1) (Spring 1989): 160–186.

Pocock, J. G. A. "Virtues, Rights, and Manners: A Model for Historians of Political Thought." *Political Theory* 9 (3) (August 1981): 353–368.

Porter, Michael. "What Is Strategy?" *Harvard Business Review* 74 (6) (November–December 1996): 61–78.

Pozen, David. "We Are All Entrepreneurs Now." *Wake Forest Law Review* 43 (2008): 283–340.

Reitano, Joanne. "Working Girls Unite." *American Quarterly* 36 (1) (Spring 1984): 112–134.

Rosenberg, Charles, and Carroll Smith-Rosenberg. "The Female Animal: Medical and Biological Views of Women." In Charles E. Rosenberg, *No Other Gods: On Science and American Social Thought*, 54–70. Baltimore: Johns Hopkins University Press, 1976.

Ross, Joyce. "Mary Bethune and the NYA." In John Hope Franklin and A. Meier, eds., *Black Leaders of the Twentieth Century*, 191–220. Urbana and Chicago: University of Illinois Press, 1982.

Rupkalvis, Laura. "Saint Elizabeth Ann Seton." In Dwight Burlingame, ed., *Philanthropy in America*. Santa Barbara, CA: ABC-CLIO, 2004.

Sage, Olivia. "Opportunities and Responsibilities of Leisured Women." *North American Review* 181 (1905): 718–719.

Seixas, Peter. "Lewis Hine: From Social to Interpretative Photographer." *American Quarterly* 39 (3) (1987): 381–409.

Sherlock, Molly F., and Jane G. Gravell. "An Overview of the Nonprofit and Charitable Sector." *Congressional Research Service*, 7–5700, R40919 (Washington, DC, November 17, 2009) at www.crs.gov.

Sklar, Kathryn. "Florence Kelley and Women's Activism in the Progressive Era." In Linda Kerber, *Women's America*, 6th ed., 327–338. New York: Oxford University Press, 2004.

Smith, Elaine. "Introduction." In Audrey McCluskey and Elaine Smith, *Mary McLeod Bethune: Building a Better World*, 199–207. Bloomington: Indiana University Press, 1989.

Smith-Rosenberg, Carroll. "Puberty to Menopause: The Cycle of Femininity in Nineteenth-Century America." *Feminist Studies* 1 (3–4) (Winter–Spring 1973).

Stevens, Anne. "The Work of the Maternity Center Association." In *The Transactions of the Tenth Annual Meeting of the Child Hygiene Association* (November 1919).

Tappan, Lewis. "Catharine Ferguson." *New York Daily Tribune*, July 20, 1854, and *American Missionary* 8 (10) (August 1854): 85–86.

Thomas, M. Carey. "Present Tendencies in Women's College and University Educations." ACA *Publications*, 3rd series (February 1908).

———. "Should the Higher Education of Women Differ from That of Men?" *Educational Review* 21 (1901).

Trecker, Janice Law. "Sex, Science, and Education." *American Quarterly* 26 (October 1974): 352–366.

Waugh, Joan. "Give This Man Work!" *Social Science History* 25 (2) (2001): 217–246.

Welter, Barbara. "The Cult of True Womanhood 1820–1869." *American Quarterly* 18 (1966): 151–174.

Willard, Frances. "Extracts from Her Fourth of July Speech." *Woman's Journal* 24 (January 1880): 30.

Witherspoon, John. "Reflections on Marriage." *Penn. Mag.*, September 1775, pp. 411, 408. Later published as "Letters on Marriage," in *The Works of John Witherspoon . . .* , 2nd ed. (Philadelphia, 1802).

Zschoche, Sue. "Dr. Clarke Revisited: Science, True Womanhood, and Female Collegiate Education." *History of Education Quarterly* 29 (4) (Winter 1989): 545–569.

Websites

All websites consulted are cited in the relevant endnotes.

INDEX

ABOUT THE AUTHORS

Claire Gaudiani, PhD, is an expert on the history and economics of American philanthropy. She served from 1988–2001 as president of Connecticut College, where she was also professor of French. During her tenure at the Yale Law School (2001–2004), she wrote *The Greater Good: How Philanthropy Drives the American Economy and Can Save Capitalism* (Henry Holt/Times Books). From 2004–2009 she served as clinical professor at the Heyman Center for Philanthropy at New York University. Gaudiani has served as director of numerous corporate and social profit enterprises specializing in corporate governance issues. Her current directorships include The Henry Luce Foundation, MBIA Inc., and The Council for Economic Education. Gaudiani is a fellow of the American Academy of Arts and Sciences, and a recipient of the Rosso Medal for Distinguished Service to Philanthropy from Indiana University. She has received ten honorary doctorates and three distinguished teaching awards.

David Graham Burnett, PhD, is Claire's husband of forty-three years as well as her partner in Gaudiani Associates. Burnett is a continuing educator who has held senior administrative positions at Indiana University and the University of Pennsylvania. He joined the research division of Pfizer, Inc. in 1988 as director of human resources. In 1999, he became head of the Pfizer Research University, responsible for the management and dissemination of proprietary scientific knowledge across the research division. He retired in 2004, and serves on the Advisory Board of the Graduate School of New York University. He is a graduate of Princeton and Indiana universities.

Gaudiani and Burnett met in graduate school studying French and Italian Literature in 1966 and now have two married children and four grandchildren.

The authors also published *Generosity Rules!* (2007) and *Generosity Unbound* (2010). For more about the authors and their work, see www.clairegaudiani.com.

PublicAffairs is a publishing house founded in 1997. It is a tribute to the standards, values, and flair of three persons who have served as mentors to countless reporters, writers, editors, and book people of all kinds, including me.

I. F. STONE, proprietor of *I. F. Stone's Weekly*, combined a commitment to the First Amendment with entrepreneurial zeal and reporting skill and became one of the great independent journalists in American history. At the age of eighty, Izzy published *The Trial of Socrates*, which was a national bestseller. He wrote the book after he taught himself ancient Greek.

BENJAMIN C. BRADLEE was for nearly thirty years the charismatic editorial leader of *The Washington Post*. It was Ben who gave the *Post* the range and courage to pursue such historic issues as Watergate. He supported his reporters with a tenacity that made them fearless and it is no accident that so many became authors of influential, best-selling books.

ROBERT L. BERNSTEIN, the chief executive of Random House for more than a quarter century, guided one of the nation's premier publishing houses. Bob was personally responsible for many books of political dissent and argument that challenged tyranny around the globe. He is also the founder and longtime chair of Human Rights Watch, one of the most respected human rights organizations in the world.

·　　·　　·

For fifty years, the banner of Public Affairs Press was carried by its owner Morris B. Schnapper, who published Gandhi, Nasser, Toynbee, Truman, and about 1,500 other authors. In 1983, Schnapper was described by *The Washington Post* as "a redoubtable gadfly." His legacy will endure in the books to come.

Peter Osnos, *Founder and Editor-at-Large*